A Kind and Just Parent

Other Books by William Ayers

To Teach: The Journey of a Teacher

The Good Preschool Teacher: Six Teachers Reflect on Their Lives

To Become a Teacher: Making a Difference in Children's Lives
  EDITED

City Kids/City Teachers
  EDITED WITH PATRICIA FORD

Teacher Lore: Learning from Our Own Experiences
  EDITED WITH WILLIAM SCHUBERT

William Ayers

A Kind and Just Parent

The Children of Juvenile Court

Beacon Press: Boston

Beacon Press
25 Beacon Street
Boston, Massachusetts 02108-2892

Beacon Press books
are published under the auspices of
the Unitarian Universalist Association of Congregations.

03 02 01 00 99 98   8 7 6 5 4 3 2

Text design by Wesley B. Tanner / Passim Editions
Composition by David G. Budmen / Willow Graphics

LIBRARY OF CONGRESS CATALOGING-IN-PUBLICATION DATA

Ayers, William, 1944–
    A kind and just parent : the children of juvenile court / William Ayers.
        p.   cm.
    ISBN 0-8070-4402-4 (cloth)
    ISBN 0-8070-4403-2 (paper)
        1. Juvenile justice, Administration of—Illinois—Chicago.
    2. Juvenile courts—Illinois—Chicago.   I. Title.
HV9106.C4A9   1997
364.3'6'0977311—DC21   96-47832

The law, this Court, this idea of a separate court to administer justice . . . like *a kind and just parent* ought to treat his children . . . has gone beyond the experimental stage and attracted the attention of the entire world. This is a pioneer movement, Illinois being the first State to provide a court for children.

FIRST ANNUAL REPORT, JUVENILE COURT OF
COOK COUNTY, JUNE 1900

Contents

To the memory of HAYWOOD BURNS—beloved brother and friend. As a lawyer Haywood defended the despised and the dispossessed; as a teacher he drew out the dignity and intelligence of each student; as a human being he joyfully walked hand in hand with the downtrodden of the earth.

Acknowledgments

EVERY WORK OF THIS KIND is a collective effort. Whenever I felt lonely along the way, I looked up and realized I was embraced in a wide circle of friends. Thanks to our three children, Zayd, Malik, and Chesa, who show us focus, perseverance, coherence; remind us of the storms, the power, and the beauty of adolescence; and teach us more than we thought there was to know about love, about kindness, about justice. And to my parents, Mary and Tom, who breathed life into me, and went on to model for me the ways of kind, just, and decent parents, thanks always.

Thanks to friends and family who provided models and standards and shared struggles of parenting: B.J. Richards, a co-madre to our three when they were young; Mona Khalidi, sister, friend, and co-parent today; Judi Minter, Yvonne Smith, Denise Prince, Barbara Hernandez, Elaine Myrianthopoulous, Harriett Beinfield, Eleanor Stein, and many more.

I acknowledge my students who were also in important ways my teachers: Betty Banks, Cynthia Beczek, Rodney Boyd, James Butler, Luz Mary Cardenes, Chris Liska Carger, Charles Collins, Stephen Fransen, Gail Grabczynski, Cynthia Hughes, Lourdes Jimenez, Oscar Joseph, Jennifer Klonsky, Michael Klonsky, Vivienne Lund, Leah Mayers, Margy McClain, Yvonne Minor, Steve Mogge, Kate Power, Monica Rodriguez, John Bryce Rumbles, Elaine Smagacz, Hank Tabak, Kimberly Thompson, Yolanda Tillman, Linda Tsao, Audrey Watkins, Dortha Willis, Norman Weston. A special note of thanks to Therese Quinn, who hung in with me for more than a year. Her steady, thoughtful presence led me on; her fervor, passion, and commitment were a model for me.

And I thank my teachers who saw me as I wanted to be seen long before that hope was fully apparent to me: Nancy Balaban, Frithjof Bergman, Harriet Cuffaro, Leah Levinger, Ann Lieberman, Tom Mayer, Ray McDermott, Robert Sklar, Herve Varrenne, Lillian Weber, Leslie Williams, Karen Kepler Zumwalt. A special abrazo to Maxine Greene whose every embrace is also a challenge, whose every challenge is also an invitation. I try to live in her hope.

For feeding me, making the coffee, and allowing me to spread my work across their desks and dining room tables, thanks to Nick Cutforth, Arden Ticzon Cutforth, Jennifer Dohrn, Atariba Dohrn-Melendez, Mara Sapon-Shevin, Meyer Shevin, Dalia Sapon-Shevin, Leora Sapon-Shevin, Therese Pirisi, Leyli Shayegan, Flip Mason, Toddy Mason, Harriett Beinfield, Murray Korngold, Efrem Korngold, Bear Korngold.

Thanks to Andy Hrycyna, my editor at Beacon Press, who believed in this work before it really began, and gave me needed energy and laser-like guidance throughout. None of this could have happened without his extraordinary presence. To Sarah Biondello—for her customary clarity, thoughtfulness, and vision—thank you. Thanks to Zayd Dohrn, again, for a surprise first editing accomplished with power and insight, and to Mona Khalidi and Michelle Oberman for careful critical comments. And thanks to Lorraine Scott for typing every word—and then retyping again and again—with characteristic good humor, patience, and determination.

The good people who toil everyday to lift these children up when it feels the whole world is pushing them down deserve special thanks. None of them, of course, is responsible for the shortcomings or failings here, none endorsed this project, but each has given me insight, knowledge, and the strength to go forward: Judith Adams, Annett Appel, James Bell, Julie Biehl, Bruce Boyer, Frances Carroll, Frank Cervone, Cheryl Cesario, Tony deMarco, Jesse Doyle, Steve Drizin, Cheryl Graves, Tom Geraghty, Sophia Hall, Lisa Kenner, John Lillig, Bart Lubow, Leah Mayers, Donald O'Connell, Meade Polidovsky, David Reid, Bob Schwartz, Marlene Stern, Randolph Stone, Arlemmie (Mack) Thirus, Warren Watkins, William Weber, Barbara Williams.

Acknowledgments

The roots of this book are various. Bernardine Dohrn has stood at the center of my life for thirty years; her wisdom and compassion, her intense sense of justice, her dream of a world that could be but is not yet, guide my steps. She has been an activist and advocate for children and families for many years, first with the Public Guardian, later the Legal Assistance Foundation, the American Civil Liberties Union, and now as director of the Children and Family Justice Center at Northwestern University's School of Law. Her everyday efforts in the Cook County Juvenile Court lie at the dead center of hope and despair; the geography of her struggle provided a powerful map for this project. Whatever insights are here (and most of the poetry) I owe to her.

My friend Frank Tobin, who taught at the detention center school with Mr. B for over twenty years, inspires me with his faith, his courage, and his commitment. Being a teacher myself, I began to write about Tobs; but since teaching is always more surprising, more complex, more intricate, more encompassing than expected, I followed the threads of Frank's story into diverse and far-flung places.

Willie Baldwin—Mr. B—inspires awe in me. He is a rock, and watching him teach renews my faith in humanity.

Jerry Kavinsky and Anthony Ortiz, former residents of the detention center and students of Frank Tobin's, provided perspective, thoughtful commentary, and powerful insights. I hope each will somehow be free someday soon.

Alex Correa, another of Frank's former students, is a friend now, too, and he has shown me again the miracle of human growth and possibility. He is living redemption.

No child or youngster in this account, of course, is identifiable: I invented all the names, scrambled physical descriptions, stretched and compressed time, altered revealing details of their lives. Only their voices are intact—I report their words directly.

Introduction

WHEN I SAT IN A CHICAGO COURTROOM and watched a judge sentence a kid I know to a lifetime locked in prison, I felt suddenly sick. The kid had, in truth, committed a man-sized crime, and there was a certain unsparing logic to the adult judgment that fell upon his head that morning. Neither the chaos of his life nor the circumstances of his one murderous moment counted for much once the kid was caught and in the dock.

The cold facts were these: there was a kid; he had a gun; nearby—a corpse. The terrible rhythm of that reality, I knew, made the outcome a mere formality. Still, it was tough to watch.

I had known the kid for most of a year, tutoring him in reading and writing at the Audy Home school—formally the Nancy B. Jefferson School at the Cook County Juvenile Temporary Detention Center. He had been called a "superpredator" again and again during his trial, creating a powerful image of an armed and amoral monster in sneakers, but the kid I knew was small and scared and mostly way too eager to please. He could, in turn, be charming or obsequious, agreeable or subservient. That he slavishly followed the orders of the gang leader is no surprise in retrospect; that he acted autonomously and willfully is unthinkable.

Still, another child was dead, and whatever else might be said, the victim, too, had claims that day. The dead child's mother took the stand, loss and pain upon her face, and no doubt a heavy price would have to be paid.

The scale of the thing was awesome: there were close to two thousand cases scheduled on that specific day in that particular courthouse in this one American city. The huge spectacle of crime and punishment moved dramatically across the stage, and this kid was, by any measure, a bit player.

That day in court was most difficult for me because by then I had developed a teacher-student relationship with this kid, a kind of intimate bond built on faith. I had begun to see something stir inside him, something beyond the blizzard of labels and stereotypes, tough exteriors and blaring deficiencies—an intelligence, and the singular human capacity to learn and grow and develop. In truth I had known him as a student only; I'd not even heard the charge against him until recently. The kid now looked smaller, more frightened, more servile than I'd ever seen him—an unlucky speck of humanity writhing on the vast, pallid canvas of life. The spark was gone. The victim's mother glared, the kid nodded at me, and I felt awful.

———

My first encounter with Juvenile Court stretches back to a high school field trip organized to observe and study the courts and jails of Chicago. In retrospect, it couldn't have been more grotesque: thirty-five favored white boys, casually prepped-up in ties and jackets, assembled to observe justice dispensed to the mob—hundreds of poor boys, mostly black. We crowded behind the bench and looked appropriately somber as a judge heard about a dozen cases in an hour. The expressions of defiance, anger, and hatred from the boys below were frightening to me; the faces of sadness were heartbreaking. I looked away, but not for long—I was also fascinated and I wanted to see more. I was bursting with questions: What had this kid done? Why? Was he sorry? Was he dangerous? How did the judge know to release one kid and jail another for what sounded like identical offenses? All of those questions stay with me.

I later became a schoolteacher, and for a couple of years taught days and moonlighted nights as resident staff with tough kids in a halfway house, a transition from detention to foster care or back to their own families. Other questions emerged and became more personal: Why was one kid so seemingly insistent on hurting himself and undermining his own best interests? Why couldn't another control his anger in minor disputes? Why did yet another consistently fail to observe what seemed like obvious boundaries of personal space? I learned to love several of those kids, even though they rarely let me sleep through the night, and the main skill I developed seemed to be breaking up fights over Ping-Pong matches or games of hearts. But the questions remain.

Years later Frank Tobin, a teacher I admire enormously, invited me to visit his classroom at Audy Home, and I was caught. I became a devoted caller—for a time I was practically a resident myself. Frank's questions became powerful guides for me: Where is the goodness in this child? What can we do to show him a happier way of life? How can we get him to live beyond the worst thing he ever did? These teacher questions dovetail with a simple, sensible parent question that is a guide for my wife, who founded the Children and Family Justice Center at Northwestern University: What if this were my child? This is, she argues, not a sentimental question, nor a question that begs for a simple or obvious answer. It is, rather, a practical guide to beginning on the right foot and standing on the firmest ground.

Frank's classroom and then the Audy Home school became a window into the twisted and complex world of Juvenile Court for me. Being a teacher myself, there was an easy fit, but it turned out that a teacher's perspective provided other sensible connections. When I learned, for example, that chronic truancy is the most reliable early indicator that a child might end up in Juvenile Court, a light bulb blinked on for me. Most of my energy for years has been focused on challenging the ways city schools fail to educate city kids or even provide enough hope to claim their commitment to attend. I was beginning to see a straight line between failing schools and burgeoning youth jails.

The perspective I had as a teacher had a powerful historical precedent as well: the Juvenile Court in Chicago—the first in the world—was founded in 1899 by Jane Addams and the vigorous women of Hull House. Educators and reformers themselves, they wanted to understand the causes of delinquency: What forces create criminal behavior? What is the role of poverty and social isolation in the life of juvenile delinquents? They struggled to offer children an opportunity to heal, to find for young people a way up and a way out of a life in crime. These same reformers opened the first public playground in a city park, promoted the kindergarten movement, campaigned for child labor laws, and struggled against racism and poverty. They were filled with optimism: the Juvenile Court, they said, would act in every instance exactly as "a kind and just parent" would act.

———

Today, as the Juvenile Court approaches its centennial, it has become by all accounts an unfit parent—unable to see children as full and three-dimensional beings or to solve the problems they bring with them through the doors, incapable of addressing the complicated needs of families. The gap between the crises faced by families and youths in trouble and the capacity of Juvenile Court to address them is vast and growing. The law is a blunt instrument. As a solution to most problems, it is severely limited, and the intervention of the law often causes more harm than good. Len Edwards, a dedicated family court judge in California, calls this phenomenon—like going to the hospital and getting sicker—*jurogenic*.

Reforms typically don't go far enough or deep enough. The structural problems of the system—its massive, unwieldy size, its isolation from the community it serves, its acute lack of resources to do the job it is mandated to do, its descent into narrow and technical legalism—go largely unaddressed, perhaps because of indifference to the plight of these kids and their families, or perhaps because of the difficulty of dismantling, rethinking, and then reinventing the familiar. The larger social issues—the inequities, the historical legacies of oppression and privilege—the root and wellspring of the little horrors at Juvenile Court, are unmentionable. Most reforms simply add a program or a requirement or a procedure to the maze, and the tangle becomes just a twist or a turn more impossible.

The old dictum—"If the only tool you have is a hammer, you tend to regard everything as a nail"—takes a ferocious turn at Juvenile Court. The Court is a whirlwind of writs and claims, accusations and arraignments, impeachments, indictments, warrants, summonses, violations, terminations, continuances, affirmations, and denials. Matters are litigated and contended, negotiated and adjudicated, prosecuted and defended. Contention and dispute hang heavy in the air, they fill up every space through delay after delay, until breathing itself becomes difficult. At the end of an unhappy road: JUDGMENT. Winners and losers. For some, humiliation, pain, loss. For the rest, a kind of hollow victory, thin and costly—it rips, somewhere, the human fabric and leaves the victory feeling false, inadequate. Juvenile Court can feel like a blunt instrument.

Beyond bricks and mortar, steel and glass, all courts are built on the law, and the law posits a world of rational argument and precedent, balance and accountability, facts and judgments. Of course this world of facts and truths is in part illusory. Life is never quite open and shut. The drama of most courtrooms involves a tension: the attempt to somehow capture life as it is lived —ambiguous, idiosyncratic, contrary, filled with fuzzy and messy meanings—and fit it into a frame with straight edges. At its best the law struggles with and accounts for complexity, settles disputes without vengeance, heals more than it hurts. At its caricatured worst, it intensifies the pain. Life is leaky, but too often the law aspires to an interesting, inert standard: airtightness.

While all courtrooms contain some torment, Juvenile Court is a place where, in my wife's memorable indictment and lament, "the walls weep." Children's law was originally conceived in an effort to place the youth, not the offense, at center stage, to see the child as three-dimensional, moving forward, full of promise and possibility, worthy of a second chance. As it is enacted today, the child has all but disappeared. A kind and just parent? That hopeful standard remains on the lips and persists in the hearts and minds of many who toil in Juvenile Court today, but it is a standard obscured by the sheer numbers and anonymity, the tangled maze, the crushing complexity, the seething and unsettling paradoxes of the court.

———

This book chronicles my immersion in the detention center school, my odyssey through Juvenile Court, my encounters with tough kids in tight spots.

It is, as well, an invitation to join me in that immersion in the life-world of the detention center, which, like every other culture, hangs together on shared meanings, on agreed upon expressions, on assigned ways to participate, on accommodation and harmony and assent. I wanted to understand how one acts sensibly in this place, what one needs to know or understand in order to join in fully, what is important or significant for the actors themselves. I was after their meanings, their voices, their intentions, and this book belongs, then, to Alex and Ito and Freddie and Mario and Jeff and the others who are incarcerated in the Cook County Juvenile Detention Center, held, as they say, in "temporary lockdown." It is a tribute as well to Tobs and Mr. B, the boys' teachers and surrogate parents. I try to tell their stories fairly and fully.

Their stories, however, are incomplete without the larger cultural webs that surround their lives—the economic conditions, the historical flow. Mario's story demands some understanding of kids and violence and guns; Jeff's actions beg for some discussion of adolescence as a stage of development; Jesus' life is incomprehensible unless the effects of racism and poverty on young people are considered. In every case I attempt to ground the work in the everyday details of life as it is lived, tacking back and forth when necessary to the overarching contexts that influence and make those lives understandable.

I am neither a lawyer nor a judge, a caseworker nor a cop; I write simply as a parent, a teacher, a citizen. As a parent I have been frightened and pained as I've seen mirror and shadow of my own teenagers here. As a citizen, I've been irritated and outraged, concerned for my own and the public's safety, worried about cost and benefit. But as a teacher I find both a rhythm for the book—chapter one begins on the opening day of school, and the last chapter closes with a graduation ceremony—and a reason to go on.

I meant the phrase "a kind and just parent" to bristle with irony: here was this lofty, sentimental ideal laid low by a dysfunctional system and a society out of control. I was surprised, then, to encounter so many dedicated, hard-working, and good people toiling every day to lift these children up. For me they are everyday heroes in a world desperate for their contributions. We should listen to them closely; we should watch carefully. Kind and just parents to be sure.

Prologue: Jeff

The loss is level.
But our grieving rises
and plunges. It prevails.
We hurt. We hunger.
We elevate to aspects of an anger
with knives to slice us raw.

What is to cherish is the child
who loved us, who loved science and the sunshine,
who
wished the world well.
Keeping those gifts of self, beyond the changes,
we keep the living light of our young dead.

Gwendolyn Brooks
"Of the Young Dead"

O N FEBRUARY 2, adaptation and acclimation notwithstanding, few
people were venturing out of doors into record-breaking Chicago
cold, and those who did, bundled and swaddled, stumbled toward only
the most urgent appointments. My mission fit the criterion: I'd
promised Jeff I would come to his sentencing hearing.

I had known Jeff, a student in the Cook County Juvenile Temporary
Detention Center School, the Audy Home, for most of a year. I tutored
him in reading and writing. He'd been tried as an adult, convicted of a
crime he'd committed when he was two weeks past his fourteenth
birthday. Now sixteen, he was being sentenced today.

For the past couple of weeks Jeff had been even more animated than
usual—jumpy, jittery, sometimes frantic. He hadn't been put on lockup
or punishment up on his living unit, and so he had been able to come
to classes. But he hadn't been able to sit still, either.

Jeff had quick-stepped up and down the halls these past weeks as always, but with a growing urgency. "Can I go see Mrs. Anderson?";
"Gym, Mr. B?"; "I got to see Williams"; "Tobs said come see him. Can
I?" Several requests a day. And as always Mr. B would measure out how
much to hold on, pushing for greater participation in this class, and
how much to let go, responding to Jeff's hyper energy with a bit of un-

I

derstanding and space. "Can I see Dr. Love, Mr. B?" he asks, peering out the door. "She's right there by her office."

"All right, but remember, if you're caught in the hall, I don't know you." This is their agreement: Jeff travels around the school more than any other student, moves unescorted through the halls and offices. It's a specific need, a special dispensation. Jeff is a little kid—wide-eyed, mischievous, quick to smile, immature. Everyone who knows him recognizes Jeff's impulse to stir and jump, and most everyone overlooks his steady transgression of what is, in this case, a minor rule.

But a couple of supervisors will brook no exceptions, and if they see him, they will surely write Jeff up or order him locked in his living unit. "OK, Mr. B," Jeff winks slyly at his co-conspirator, and with a hurried look of authentic gratitude and an audible exhale, he is jetting down the hall.

Jeff is skinny as a knife. He is in one of those preciously awkward moments of adolescent life where he outgrows himself again and again in front of your eyes. He is five-eight, five-ten, six feet in a couple of weeks. Only the sweet face remains unchanged.

"Mr. B," Jeff says, addressing his teacher during a classroom break one morning. "Mr. B, they say they put something in the food at Joliet to kill your sex drive. You know anything about that?" Joliet is the site of the biggest, meanest state penitentiary, and Jeff knows he will be there following a short stay in "Little Joliet"—the juvenile jail.

"Rumor," replies Mr. B matter-of-factly. "Wherever you've got young men together the rumors start—saltpeter, green peppers, mysterious drugs in the food. Don't worry, Jeff," a smile tracks briefly across his face. "You'll be able to get a hard-on."

"I hope so," says Jeff smiling shyly. Then, with emphasis, "I *hope* so," and the manly fervor chases the child-look away.

Jeff focuses on tasks—the more concrete, the happier he is. He likes physical work—cleaning, moving furniture and file cabinets, washing windows. The three days leading up to his sentencing hearing Jeff can be found mopping the offices of Mr. Williams, a friendly counselor, Mrs. Anderson, a popular social worker, or Dr. Love, the sole school psychologist.

Jeff hurt his left leg recently in the gym—wrenched his knee going for a rebound—and he walks now with an exaggerated hitch in his stride. It doesn't slow him down—he still hurries headlong up the hall, now with a bucket of sudsy water sloshing in one hand and a mop as tall and skinny as himself slung over the other shoulder—but it adds a dramatic element to the scene. "Dr. Love? Need any help?" he asks.

I catch up with Jeff on Tuesday, limping manically into Mr. B's classroom from a mop-up job in one of the offices. As he rinses the mop and refills his bucket, I ask him his feelings about Friday, the day he will be sentenced. "Great!" he says quickly. "I can start doing my time on Friday." Jeff is ready to get on with it, ready to hear his fate and then begin dealing with it. Jeff is ready to leave Audy Home.

"Dear Lary," he wrote to a friend about this place when he was first here. "How have your been doing." He continued:

> Fine I hope well that's good. Because you wouldn't want to come in a place like this because it's not fun that you have to ask a stranger can you go to the bath room, can you get some water, can you go in your room, or can you go turn the TV program. Also when you just come in you have to go in intake and that's a nasty place you have to be around them nasty, dirty and stinky people. And you have to watch out for the guys that like to fight over anything. Also you have to worry about [riots] kicking [off] and a lot more. So I advice you not to come her for anything okay Lary. Well keep in touch and god bless you all.

"Intake is so nasty," Jeff tells me. "But I was lucky. I wasn't in intake but three days. See, I'm in for murder and they move you fast when you're in for murder. I might get twenty and get out in ten," Jeff says now about the impending hearing. "Let's go." His face betrays just a hint of doubt, but his words are eager, perhaps a little frenetic, and optimistic. "Let's go!"

"I'm in for murder . . ." Jeff says easily, conversationally, but his words smack me hard in the face. Murder. Of the armies of kids I've known in detention Jeff seems perhaps least capable of such a grim and ghastly act. I've learned by now to take the kids as they are, to work with them exactly as they present themselves to me, to suppress the obvious but unfair and inappropriate question: What are you in for? The ques-

tion is automatic, instinctive at first because of the distinctive circumstances of the place: everyone here is charged with something. . . .
What? But it is unfair because each kid is especially vulnerable here,
and I have the inherent power of the adult, the privilege of freedom.
And it is inappropriate because it is an aspect of their lives that I can
play no productive role in whatever. I can eavesdrop, I can gape, but I
will be at best only a voyeur. I try to remind myself of the presumption
of innocence—they are charged not convicted—and of the tradition of
confidentiality in Juvenile Court. Better to meet each kid as a student,
to resist the urge to know him through his criminal charge, to push all
that to the background. Now, with Jeff at least, it is moving forward,
throwing me off balance. I stumble but resist.

Now it is Friday and I struggle against an arctic onslaught up the
courthouse steps. Inside, the parade of families, defendants, victims,
and court workers through security and toward the courtrooms is diminished slightly by the cold, but the list of cases to be heard is as extravagant as ever—sixty-three computer printed pages, thirty names to
a page. Page two lists Jeff Baron . . . first-degree murder. He will appear
before Judge Porter, Courtroom 205.

Judge Porter's courtroom has a plexiglass rampart separating the
spectators from the working space of the court. The little fence that
usually demarcates these areas is still in place, but it looks quaint, overwhelmed now by the modern floor-to-ceiling barricade.

The plastic barrier creates a series of strange impressions and sensa-
tions. A harsh light in the public gallery plays tricks: every scratch or
nick on my hands is bright purple; across from me a young woman's
afro has turned a glowing blue. A speaker, presumably designed to carry
the proceedings of the court to the public, offers only a thin and narrow twang, punctuated with occasional scratches and shrieking feed-
back. I find myself straining to tune in, only to be rewarded with an
assault on my ears. Even before the judge and the lawyers arrive, as
clerks and sheriffs and bailiffs make their early preparations, there is a
feeling of eavesdropping, of peeping at something forbidden.

Suddenly the door behind me opens and two State's Attorneys
struggle through the public sector toward the protected zone pushing a

lorry loaded with today's files. While I heard the door opening behind me, I saw it open in the mirror of the plastic fence, which is both reflective and transparent. If you don't concentrate, the plexiglass juxtapositions become fantastic: an elderly woman sitting on the judge's desk sobbing silently, a public defender in spike heels standing on a man's shoulders. Here and there: it can be difficult to keep clear.

Judge Porter enters and we are told to all rise. The judge settles quickly into his huge chair and court is underway. His focus is awe-inspiring. Arms moving, head bent to his desk, paper flying, verbal directions hurled at clerks and lawyers, the judge manages his calendar with a frenzy. Cases are called, new dates set, public defenders assigned, bench warrants issued for defendants not in court. Within forty-five minutes he's cut the stack of files on the lorry down to half its original size.

The procession of defendants brought by sheriff's deputies before the judge from behind the bench becomes monotonous. Each is dressed in orange jail coveralls, and each comes forward with his hands clasped behind his back. Each defendant called this morning is black, each is young, and each spends just a moment before the court. "You understand, Mr. Jordan, that if I release you and you fail to appear before this court on the appointed date, you can be tried, and witnesses can be brought against you, and you can be convicted and sentenced whether you are here or not?"

"Yes, Judge."

"Have you got a job?"

"No."

"I'm going to assign you a public defender who will be your lawyer."

A P.D. rises and takes the file, never looking at Jordan. A date is set. Next.

"You understand, Mr. Henderson, that by pleading guilty you are forgoing your right to a trial by jury, and that includes your right to cross-examine witnesses?"

"I do."

Mr. Henderson is given a year of probation for drug possession. His assigned parole officer takes the file without acknowledging Henderson.

"I want you to pay five dollars a month to the court. I don't want you to steal that money, and I don't want you to worry about it, but try to pay that. Understand?"

"Yes."

Possession of a controlled substance. Possession with intent to distribute. Illegal possession of a firearm. Assault with intent to do bodily harm. The parade slogs forward. There are only occasional counterpoints, small disruptions to the forced formality and the steady march. "Your honor, I'm epileptic and I had a seizure on the bus, and that's why I missed court last week. I've got the paperwork."

Well, bring in the paperwork next month and we'll talk.

"Judge, you ask am I satisfied with legal counsel; no I'm not satisfied. This lawyer here said she'd come to see me and talk to me in the County, and she never did."

Do you want to reconsider your guilty plea?

"Naw. I got to get this over with. But she's no kind of lawyer, judge, and I'm a little railroaded here."

The train of justice inches onward.

———

My mind wanders temporarily to yesterday, our middle son's sixteenth birthday. Malik is only a few months younger than Jeff and just as skinny. After breakfast he had opened cards and presents—a couple of videos he'd wanted, gift certificates for clothes and tapes, a basketball hoop for the alley behind our home. And then the true rite of passage: he gathers together all his paperwork and we hurry off to be first in line for a driver's license test.

It's cold, but we stand shivering outside the locked door with two pairs who beat us to it: a young immigrant couple from China just starting the process, and a middle-aged South Side couple who are there so the woman can make a third try for a first-time license. By the time the doors finally open we are thoroughly frozen and relieved to be in the overheated government building. Malik charms his way through forms and fees, and finally he is first for the road test. He appears calm, but entirely focused.

The examiner checks the car's equipment, slides into the passenger seat, and they disappear down the street. I chat with the waiting couples. In a few moments the car reappears, and Malik pulls neatly into a parking space. I walk eagerly to meet them as the examiner steps out and says, "Great kid; great driver. You taught him well."

Malik is ecstatic, trying to stay cool through getting his picture taken.

"How did it go?"

"It was easy except for a three-point turn I messed up a little. He was a nice guy."

When we are finished and ready to go home Malik asks me to drive. "I'm too shook up." He allows himself, uncharacteristically, to be seen as vulnerable: "I was scared, man. I would have hated to go to school and say I flunked it. It was scary." He holds the license in his hands, looks it over and over. "This is a good picture."

He is smiling to himself, shaking his head. He drops me off at work, and heads off alone in the car to find his friends at school. "Thanks, Pops." He shakes my hand like a grown-up guy, and he is off. It is another passage for him, a bittersweet moment in parenting for me.

———

Jeff's rite of passage is altogether different. At 11:30 his case is called and he is brought out with another kid from lockup. I hadn't known there was a codefendant, and they are a contrast: Jeff, wearing his oversized white shirt and tie, a little boy in a man's world; the other guy, muscular, powerful, dressed in the County coveralls. The white shirt covers most of the jailhouse tattoos Jeff carved into himself the last couple of days, but not the raw, red letters on the knuckles of his left hand: H-A-T-E. It's a cliche, of course, but Jeff thought it was original to him.

I exchanged a few words with Jeff's parents earlier: his father, over seventy years old and blind, eager to find my hand and shake it when I told them I tutored Jeff in school and that he was always a good boy with me; his mother tense and incommunicative, her face revealing nothing. Jeff's lawyer—a private attorney whose fee consumed all of the family's savings along with everything they could borrow from more distant relatives—had seen us talking and joined in. When he discovered how I knew Jeff, he asked if I would testify about Jeff's behavior in Audy Home at the hearing. We both know it's just a gesture, possibly a play to prove to Jeff's parents that he's tried everything and earned his fee, but what the hell. Can it hurt? It is my turn.

Jeff is well liked in the school, I tell the Court, a favorite of teachers and staff. He doesn't start fights and he gets along with the other kids. He's agreeable, nervous, a little shy. He is eager to please. He is making progress.

When I finish, the state's attorney starts in on me with a vengeance: "Would you call shooting someone eight times at close range 'eager to please'?"

"Do you consider murder 'agreeable'?"

"Have you ever seen a body with eight bullets in it?"

I tell him I know Jeff only in the context of a classroom, and we've never spoken about the charges or the situation leading to today. I hadn't even known he was charged with murder until last week, and I knew nothing of the circumstances surrounding that charge. I'm thanked by the judge and told to step down.

I am followed to the stand by seven police officers, one after another. Six of them testify about Jeff's codefendant and the different times they have arrested him for dealing drugs, theft, or weapons violations. It's a weighty record, large and intimidating, especially the story of a night this young man beat a woman with a baseball bat and robbed her of her welfare check. Finally one officer tells of an evening two years before when she and her partner chased a group of kids, one of whom was Jeff, and later found cellophane packets of crack cocaine along the path of the chase. No charges were filed.

A picture emerges in the courtroom. Jeff had been a low-level street dealer for a large organization for about a year. He had stopped attending school and was easy pickings for the neighborhood branch of a big Chicago street gang. He was still a shorty when a boss and his lieutenant came around and invited Jeff into the car. As they drove around, the boss told Jeff that there was a guy encroaching on their territory, a guy "disrespecting" them, a guy who had been warned but thought he was tough. "It's time to waste that motherfucker before everyone comes pouring into our territory."

The lieutenant put a heavy .9 millimeter into Jeff's hand. The boss stopped the car, pointed at a young man sitting on a low concrete wall near an alley, and said, "Now fuck him up."

Jeff got out, walked hurriedly toward the guy, and started shooting. Bam! Bam! Bam! Eight times. And then he ran. Two days later, he was arrested, picked out of a lineup by a witness, and charged with the first-degree murder of Joseph Woodford. The gang lieutenant was also picked up; he sits as codefendant.

Joseph Woodford's mother is called by the prosecutor to read her victim impact statement. She looks remarkably like Jeff's mother—same age, same build. The strangest thing is that when she is seated next to the judge, the disorienting and alarming reflecting glass places her next to Jeff's mom. And in the distorted image they are twins, both in their forties, both crushed with anger and sadness, sitting there side by side. Could they tell the same story, one back to front, the other front to back?

Joseph was Mrs. Woodford's oldest child, her favorite. She remembers how he helped with the other children in the family, in the building, and eventually in the neighborhood. He organized games for the kids, and everyone liked him. She can not express the deprivation and bereavement she feels today, nor measure the loss to her family and community for all time. Such a waste. She shows the judge a picture of Joseph. Justice, in her view, demands balance, an eye for an eye. She wishes, she says, that the judge would execute Jeff.

Mrs. Woodford is entirely compelling to me. Her pain is raw, alive. Mrs. Baron is equally inescapable—her son, her son. And there is Jeff: a small boy, a convicted killer. Both things. Two realities.

Jeff's attorney appeals to the judge for leniency. Of course, he concedes, Jeff has been found guilty and he must be punished. But consider his youth—"He is just at the beginning of his life, and he *can* make a contribution if we help him"—and his lack of a criminal record—"This is his first arrest." Furthermore, look at his elderly, blind father and his sickly mother. He has no role models, he says, and no proper parenting. Jeff's first trip to Juvenile Court had been seven years ago, he points out, but in that case he was accompanying his mother, who was cited in a neglect petition. Jeff is slow, perhaps retarded, his lawyer argues, and he begins to paint a pathetic portrait of deprivation piled upon deficit. Of course, his purpose is to help, but I see Jeff's father wince with every word.

The state's attorney recounts the facts evenly, and then builds in volume and intensity. "Joseph Woodford is dead. Gone to us forever. You heard his mother describe the devastation that loss has caused her and her family. Jeffrey Baron, this gang enforcer, this murderer, has shown no common sense and no human decency."

The judge invites Jeff to make a statement before sentencing him. Several months ago I had heard Jeff say, in standard Audy Home parlance, "I caught this case . . .," in the same style and cadence as "I caught the flu," but now he stands awkwardly, head down, hands fidgeting, and tries to take some responsibility as he mumbles a barely audible apology to Joseph Woodford's family: "I'm sorry for what I did." His voice cracks, "It was wrong. I apologize."

"I wish I could believe you are sorry," the judge begins, and it is clear that this will go badly for Jeff. The public gallery has filled with police, those who had testified and others who had not. "But you are a gun waiting to go off." The judge's voice is tired as he speaks of law and order and the destruction wrought by drugs. "Everyone in this scenario is a victim of the drug trade," he says sadly. "Both Mr. Woodford and Mr. Baron were involved in a deadly business, and both have reaped the results of that business. There are no heroes here, only victims." Mrs. Woodford, sitting safely back on the tourist side of the plexiglass, seems stung by these words as she looks daggers at the judge.

Judge Porter turns to address Jeff: "Some day you may be able to rejoin society and make a contribution as your lawyer has said you would. But that day is not now." With that the judge sentences Jeff, not yet seventeen years old, convicted killer of a rival drug dealer, to forty-seven years in prison.

Jeff's father shakes his head and his body heaves, but his mother's face never changes. Jeff looks like a captured bird, eyes blinking, head bobbing. The lawyer quickly establishes that 567 days in custody should count as time served toward the forty-seven years, and then asks that the judge grant a family visit in a side room, since Jeff's parents find regular travel almost impossible and travel to Joliet out of the question. "Denied," says the judge. "I've tried that and had people passing drugs right here in court. I'm not saying you would do that, but the bad apples have spoiled it for everyone."

Jeff is led away by sheriffs' deputies. The state's attorneys leave with Joseph's mother in hand, her eyes moist, her face hard. Jeff's parents sit by themselves for several moments. Finally his mother leans forward with a heavy sigh and rises. She takes her husband's hand and helps him up, guides him carefully down the aisle, and together—her leading, him stumbling slightly behind—they move to the hallway alone.

1. Mr. B

The people I love the best
jump into work head first
without dallying in the shallows
and swim off with sure strokes almost out of sight.
They seem to become natives of that element,
the black sleek heads of seals
bouncing like half-submerged balls.

I love people who harness themselves, an ox to a heavy cart,
who pull like water buffalo, with massive patience,
who strain in the mud and the muck to move things forward,
who do what has to be done, again and again.

I want to be with people who submerge
in the task, who go into the fields to harvest
and work in a row and pass the bags along,
who are not parlor generals and field deserters
but move in a common rhythm
when the food must come in or the fire be put out.

The work of the world is common as mud.
Botched, it smears the hands and crumbles to dust.
But the thing worth doing well done
has a shape that satisfies, clean and evident.
Greek amphoras for wine or oil,
Hopi vases that held corn, are put in museums
but you know they were made to be used.
The pitcher cries for water to carry
and a person for work that is real.

Marge Piercy
"To be of use"

THE DOOR CRASHES OPEN SUDDENLY. "Morning, Mr. B." Rasheed springs into the classroom with a bright greeting.

"Good morning, Rasheed."

"Good morning, Ito."

"Morning, Mr. B," Ito mumbles, shuffling along to his desk. He collapses noisily into his chair, head in arms, and looks to be instantly asleep.

"Good morning, Jeff." Jeff hops in and moves manically around the room.

"Morning, Mr. B."

"Good morning, Freddie."

"Morning, Mr. B."

Eight young men burst or file or stumble into class today, each wearing dark green cotton pants and a white tee-shirt with a simple drawing of an owl or a bluebird or a cardinal printed on the front, the standard-issue uniform for all residents in juvenile lockup. Only their gym shoes are distinctive, with status and style statements run rampant: Ito's shoes are old and beat-up; Rasheed's are red, white, and dazzling; Freddie's are full of gadgets, lights, and pumps; Jeff's are entirely spent.

Alonzo and LeMarque have excused absences today—each has a court date. Merce will be late—it's haircut day on his unit, and he'll come down in an hour. Oscar is on punishment—locked up on the unit for being drunk last week. Where did the liquor come from? No one knows for sure, perhaps his mother or another visitor, an attendant, a teacher. Alcohol and drugs are not prevalent here, but they are always a concern because, as in every other American high school, alcohol and drugs are available.

Today is opening day for the Chicago public schools, and so for the Juvenile Temporary Detention Center School it is also the official start of a new year. School has a predictable rhythm in our common memory: there is the opening in September, the holiday period from Thanksgiving through Christmas and the New Year, then the coming of Spring and graduation. The facts of life at Audy Home can overwhelm the familiar rhythms: court dates, students suddenly leaving, new kids abruptly arriving, transfers to adult prison. This opening, then, is neither as festive nor as promising as it might be: the school meets year round, the students are locked up in living units upstairs, and the break, never particularly restful for the kids, has been only a few days.

Mr. B is a big man with a square head and a chunk of body to match—massive chest, huge arms, rugged shoulders, and thick neck. Horn-rimmed glasses perch on the outcropping of his nose, a full salt and pepper beard provides a forest surround. Dressed in his customary uniform—dark slacks, flannel shirt, brown industrial apron—and settled at his desk in the center of the classroom, Mr. B is a volcano at rest.

Mr. B nods a greeting to me and there is the hint of a welcoming smile, mostly in his eyes. Mr. B wastes no movement, certainly no word. As is customary for him, he has been here since seven this morning and it is now almost nine. He works along silently. I take my place at a corner desk and begin to get organized . . . notebooks, folders, pens.

A slate-topped counter and storage island runs the length of the room and splits the body of the classroom from a smaller work area. Twelve indestructible plastic desks with matching chairs—bright blue, yellow, green—are set in rows; two more are isolated off to themselves in front of the counter. Windows run high along the far wall, but the light is not quite natural; it filters through the metal mesh that muffles every opening.

To the right, one door leads to a toilet and sink, another to a larger anteroom that serves as closet storage area, weight room, and relaxation center. Posters of cities at night (Chicago, New York, Los Angeles, San Francisco), each outlined and set off with an African kente cloth pattern, dominate one wall. A large chalk-board, a classroom clock, student essays and artwork, a neglected American flag in one corner, all the trappings of the imagined typical classroom, share space with an emergency phone system and a heavily secured door—a solid reminder that we are in detention. Temporary lockdown.

Willie Baldwin—Mr. B—has been here since the school opened in 1973. In twenty-two years of teaching he has fashioned an identity and a routine that suit him—solid, genuine, predictable. Participating in a writing exercise with the kids, he lists his last name as "Baldwin" and his first name as "Mr. B." The word among the kids upstairs in the living units is that Mr. B makes you work but that he also lets you play, that he listens carefully to you and that he wants you to learn, that he is firm but fair. A teacher and his classroom can resemble one another, and this space is unmistakably Mr. B's—businesslike, focused, and orderly, with bursts of color and latent possibilities.

The brief school vacation, while not protracted, does mean a few long days of unbroken time on the units. With nothing much to do, everyone watches TV for hour upon hour—almost six hours a day, twice the average for American teenagers. Boredom, depression, purposelessness, gloom covering rage accumulate. Twenty-two young men draped across chairs around the tube is an invitation to a collision, and everyone knows it. "I got in seven fights in ten days," laughs Ito. "Mostly I was locked up, which was OK with me."

"The place is a madhouse," says Mario, fine-featured with long, narrow sideburns and a soft pointy goatee, like a young Ahmad Jamal, "and I'm one of the lunatics." This is no vacation.

There is a palpable sense of relief as the students trickle into Mr. B's class. Coming back to school from their units is a break from the madhouse. There is nothing demonstrative, no lavish displays of affection, but Jeff seems incapable of *not* smiling at Mr. B, a big Cheshire cat grin covering his face, and Andrew, serious, low-keyed, likable, carrying a large look of sadness wherever he goes, has more energy than he's had in months.

"Bathroom, Mr. B," says Jeff, heading toward the toilet.

"Bathroom," responds Mr. B.

"Counter, Mr. B," says Freddie.

"Counter," comes the seemingly automatic response as Freddie slips behind the counter to sharpen his pencil. Rasheed and Mario hover by the door, watching eagerly as the other students come down the hallway to their classes.

Andrew has pulled out a folder at his desk and is leafing through his papers, settling on a piece that he reads thoughtfully. Jesus is applying paint to a plaster mask he made earlier, before break.

"Back room," calls out Mario, aiming himself toward the weights.

"No," says Mr. B in the same quiet register, low-keyed, flat. "No, Mario."

"Yo, Mr. B. Why I can't go lift for a bit?"

"Remember what you told me Friday before the break?"

"What?"

"You said you'd finish your regular work for the day after painting," he says, referring to the ongoing, everyday assignments in math, science, English, and history he designs specifically for each student. "But your work isn't here. I want to see some work. I want you to finish your regular work, then take a break. Do you know what to do?"

"I ain't got my card, Mr. B," says Mario, pouting. "And that was so long ago."

"OK. It was long, long ago, but it's still got to be done. Do you know what to do?"

"Chapter twelve in science, I think. Chapter fourteen in history. Which numbers in history?"

"Do all the Roman numerals at the end. There aren't many in this chapter. Numbers one to three or one to four." Mr. B turns quickly to chapter fourteen. "Here it is. One to four."

"OK, Mr. B. I'll get it. Then can I lift?"

"Of course, Mario," he says, touching his shoulder.

The classroom is calm—peaceful—filled with a sense of quiet expectations. Ito has roused himself and is filling in a simple crossword. Rasheed has moved to a small utility table where he is working on a massive jigsaw puzzle that is only beginning to take shape. Jeff has returned from the bathroom, taken out some colored pencils, and is bent over a large piece of white construction paper creating what looks to be a vivid, flamboyant altar or memorial.

"Mr. B," says Jeff without looking up from his work.

"Yes, Jeff."

"Help, Mr. B." It is neither a question nor a demand, but a quiet declaration delivered in the same tone as "Bathroom," "Counter," "Back room." Mr. B moves over to Jeff's desk and kneels down beside him, his steady hugeness highlighted beside the slight and discombobulated Jeff, their heads bent together over Jeff's work, their voices in quiet conference.

"Should the top of these flowers be red, Mr. B?"

"What do you think?"

"I think yes, but I don't know if it look right."

"Mr. B," says Ito from his desk.

"Just a minute, Ito. I'll be over when I'm finished with Jeff's question." He turns back to Jeff's project. "Well, I like the red set off by this blue, and if you think yes, then I guess I agree with you."

"OK, Mr. B. What about these letters here?" He indicates a row of ballooning graffiti letters: "R.I.P. Lary."

"Now you're making me do most of the work," he smiles. "I thought you had a plan for it." Mr. B. strikes a neat balance between nurturance and challenge.

"OK, Mr. B," Jeff smiles back. "It's cool. They're black."

Mr. B moves on to Ito and again settles on to his knees beside him, one arm around the back of Ito's chair, the other on his desk. He envelopes Ito, leans close and listens.

"What's this mean, Mr. B? A-S-S-E-T-S? I looked in the dictionary and they had 'capital', 'property' and 'possessions'. I want a word that starts with 'M'."

"Did you look in the thesaurus?"

"No."

"Try that and I'll check back with you."

Mr. B gets up and checks in with Mario who is working away. He looks over Rasheed's shoulder at the jigsaw, puts his hand to his chin and furrows his brow in concentration for a moment, picks up a tiny piece and tries unsuccessfully to fit it in, quietly shakes his head, chuckles, and moves back to his desk.

"Gentlemen," he announces in his deepest voice, "ten more minutes of free time, and then we'll be reading *The Piano Lesson*." He pauses. "I will assign parts for today's reading in ten minutes." Rasheed looks up for a moment and then returns to his puzzle; everyone else simply continues.

The Piano Lesson, a play by August Wilson, had been the focus of English class for much of the summer. "I had hoped to have it finished before summer break," says Mr. B, "but one thing or another interfered. We'll finish it this week."

The story is straight and simple enough to begin: Boy Willie and a friend have driven from Sunflower, Mississippi to Pittsburgh to Boy Willie's Uncle Doacker's house with a pickup filled with watermelons that they hope to sell off the back of the truck. Boy Willie wants to get enough money together to buy Sutter's farm back home. He has some money saved up; he should have just enough if he can add to that the money he will make selling watermelons, plus the profit he hopes to realize from his share of the family heirloom—an elegant upright piano with legs intricately carved in the manner of African sculpture, standing in Doacker's parlor.

Here is the conflict: Boy Willie's sister, Berniece, lives with her daughter in Doacker's house. Berniece is proper, staid, and careful while Boy Willie is raucous, wild, and mildly criminal. Berniece distrusts and dislikes Boy Willie, indirectly blaming him for the death of her husband three years earlier; when some men stealing firewood were interrupted by the sheriff, her husband had pulled a pistol. She adamantly refuses to sell the piano, which originally came into the family that owned her ancestors—the Sutter family—when they traded Doacker's grandmother and father for it. Doacker's grandfather, in his grief, carved likenesses of his wife and son on the piano's legs, and then kept carving until he had etched in wood every detail of the family's history—marriages, births, deaths, funerals. Years later, long after formal emancipation, Berniece and Boy Willie's father stole the piano to "free the slaves." After he hid the piano, he was cornered trying to escape town in an empty railway freight car; the boxcar was set ablaze by his captors and he and four hobos were killed.

"Gentlemen," Mr. B breaks in once more just as Merce arrives from upstairs. "Gentlemen, put your things away. We'll be reading from *The Piano Lesson* now. Later this week we'll be viewing the video of the play."

Rasheed and Andrew straighten their desks and pull out their books. Jeff calls out "Bathroom" and heads for the toilet again. Mario detours past the door to the hallway and stretches a look before cruising to his desk. Ito is drooping once more.

"OK," Mr. B pulls the collective attention to himself, "let's sum up what's happened thus far."

"Sutter got drowned in his well," says Mario.

"Yes."

"And Boy Willie don't know who pushed him," he continues. "Could have been the Ghost of the Yellow Dog," a reference to the men burned in the boxcar, "or someone else."

"And now," says Rasheed, "Boy Willie needs to sell that piano to buy Sutter's land. But Berniece wants to keep it."

"Why?"

"Because of the carvings in the legs, and because people died in that piano."

"People died in the piano?"

"Well, they died in the pictures," says Rasheed.

"And her daddy died stealing it," adds Andrew excitedly, "which wasn't really stealing."

"It wasn't?"

"Not the same as *stealing*, since the piano legs was carved by *their* family. In a way it was already theirs."

"And what are Berniece and Boy Willie to each other?" asks Mr. B.

"Brother and sister," says Andrew.

"Uh huh," a chorus of assent.

"Mr. B?"

"Yes, Merce?"

"Mr. B, Berniece been mourning for her husband for three years. Is that too long?"

"Some would think so, and others would think not."

"It's not long," Antoine says quietly but firmly. His face, always tense, draws tight. "Three years is not too long if you love someone. You might mourn that the rest of your life. It could be a good thing. It could be good for her." Perhaps it is the seriousness with which Antoine asserts his position, or the fact that he rarely speaks at all, and now he has spread words across several sentences, or some shared sense of grief or rage, but no one disagrees. Several students nod, some to themselves, others openly in his direction.

"Yo, you right, man," says Jesus. "My little shorty's friend got killed more than three years ago, and I ain't never going to forget. Never. I don't want to forget him. It's a way of respecting him. Woo, woo, woo."

Mr. B points to a line in the play where Avery, the young man courting Berniece, asks her how long she intends to grieve for her dead husband and she responds: "I'll decide." Again a chorus of assent from the students. "Right," says Jesus. "Me, I'm going to grieve. Others can do what they want. Each one's got to decide for theyselves."

"So you agree?" asks Mr. B.

"Sure, Mr. B," says Andrew. "She can decide, and, like Antoine said, it might be good for her to go on being sad for quite a while."

The students have come to like Berniece, to identify with her struggles even as they see parts of themselves more vividly in Boy Willie. Boy Willie is bad, he struts and swaggers, but they no longer object to playing Berniece and reading her lines, in part because her role is substantial and provides major spotlight time, and in part because she is, in her way, vigorous and plucky and tough—qualities they admire and long for. When Freddie had been Berniece he read in his labored way one of her rebukes of Avery:

> You trying to tell me a woman can be nothing without a man. But you alright, huh? You can just walk out of here without me—without a woman—and still be a man. That's alright . . . that's alright for you. But everybody gonna be worried about Berniece. "How Berniece gonna take care of herself? How she gonna raise that child without a man? Wonder what she do with herself. How she gonna live like that?" . . . Everybody telling me I can't be a woman unless I got a man. Well, you tell me, Avery—you know—how much woman I am?

As he finished he broke into a huge smile and exclaimed proudly, "Whom! She zooms it back on him! She's equal, right?"

Today Mr. B says, "Here, Merce," pointing to a piece of dialogue in which Avery pleads with Berniece, and aiming, I think, to complicate matters, "read this."

Merce reads haltingly: "You got to put all of that behind you, Berniece. . . . Everybody got stones in their passway. You got to step over them or walk around them. You picking them up and carrying them with you. All you got to do is set them down by the side of the road. You ain't got to carry them with you."

The passage alludes to the great bluesman Robert Johnson's "Stones in my Passway," a reference these kids will miss. Still, the theme is apparently potent for them, for several voices rise up at once: "He right," "Yeah, but he's forgetting her pain," "Sometimes it's true."

"Merce," Mr. B interrupts again. "Merce, what do you think of what Avery says there?"

"Well," Merce frowns deeply, pulling the book close to his face. "There are some things you need to forget and there are some things you need to remember. It depends on the person, and I say let Berniece decide for her, and let Avery decide for him, and I'll decide for me."

"So which is it, gentlemen?" asks Mr. B. "Should you bring the past along with you or should you leave it behind?"

"You can't really leave it all behind," says Mario. "Because whatever happens, it's part of you. You got to deal with it some way."

"Naw," says Freddie, "you got to get up each day and say, 'Here I am world, a brand new day.'"

"In your dreams, man," Mario responds. "In your dreams it's a brand new day, but you're waking up in jail—the same old thing and what you did sitting right there with you."

"Yo," says Freddie, feigning hurt, "why you got to bring that up? I told you I didn't do it."

"Man," says Jeff quietly, "let's leave the past behind. Let's go on."

"Alright, let's leave it at that for now," says Mr. B. "Let's see what parts we need for today's reading."

Mr. B assigns parts quickly and the reading begins. Mario is Boy Willie today, and he reads with flair and style: "She trying to scare me. Hell, I ain't scared of dying. I look around and see people dying every-day. You got to die to make room for somebody else. . . . See, a nigger that ain't afraid to die is the worse kind of nigger for the white man. He can't hold that power over you."

After the reading I ask the students to write a short poem or poetry fragment focusing on themselves. I give them a structure to help them get started: the first line is your first name; next, write three words to describe yourself; then list in sequence something you love, something you hate, something you are afraid of, and something you hope or wish or long for; the last line is your last name. I give an example: Martin / courageous, nonviolent warrior / I love all people / I hate no one / I am afraid of war and violence / I hope for freedom / King.

This is how Mr. B responds: I am Mr. B / patient, observant, sincere

/ I love fishing / I hate meetings / I fear shortsightedness / I hope for success for all my students / Baldwin.

Merce, whose name is short for "Mercedes," "a sharp car my father hoped to buy one day, but never did," writes: My name is Merce / dark and tall / I love my freedom / I hate being locked up / I'm afraid of going back to the street and do what I was doing to get locked up / I wish I was out in the world and I hope for mercy / Hall.

And Rasheed: Rasheed / handsome, brave, silly / I love my family / I hate people telling me what to do / I fear death / I wish to be rich / Coburn.

Everyone reveals extravagant dreams for a future that is surely shrinking before their eyes: fame, fortune, fantastic moments. And just as uniformly, everyone fears the almost inevitable: conviction, time in prison, death.

Andrew / small, black, nice / I love my family / I hate fish / afraid of getting found guilty / I wish to go home / Johnson.

Ito / I love to girl love and be loved / I love freedom / I hate being down / I don't want to die in jail / I wish to be free / Lopez.

Oscar / I'm real quiet / I love my family / I hate being used / I'm afraid of nothing but guns / I wish to go home soon / Streeter.

The students feel the hold of history over their lives, live with ghosts and debts to be paid. The dream of going home soon is a constant companion, but its extravagance is measured in a simple fact: less than five percent of the scores of students who have passed through Mr. B's class in the past five years have gone directly home. They've mostly gone to "Little Joliet," to Cook County Jail, to Statesville, and to Menard to serve hard time, but not home, at least not right away.

These youngsters are all awaiting transfer to adult court, some petitioned by the state's attorney for transfer to adult court, others as automatic transfer students—or A.T.s—which means they are fifteen or sixteen years old and their charged offenses are felonies that the state of Illinois deems too serious for a juvenile proceeding; they warrant, instead, an automatic transfer to adult court. Until a few years ago such charges were murder, rape, armed robbery; now, with the list seeming to grow longer each year, dealing drugs near public housing projects, carjacking, carrying a gun to school. Going home? They seem at this moment to have a better chance of winning the lottery or being hit by lightning.

Here is Jeff: I am Jeff / Black, scared, nervous / I love my mom / I hate being locked up / I am afraid of being long in prison / I wish for freedom / Baron.

2. Jane Addams: History and Background

i went into my mother as
some souls go into a church,
for the rest only, but there,
even there, from the belly of a
poor woman who could not save herself
i was pushed without my permission
into a tangle of birthdays.
listen, eavesdroppers, there is no such thing
as a bed without affliction;
the bodies all may open wide but
you enter at your own risk.

Lucille Clifton
"to the unborn and waiting children"

JANE ADDAMS AND THE DAUNTLESS WOMEN of Hull House established the first children's court in the world on July 1, 1899 in Chicago. Their goal was straightforward: to create a special, separate place for children in crisis, away from adult courts and the horrors of adult jails and poorhouses. Between 1897 and 1899, 1,705 children had been incarcerated in Cook County Jail; from 1900 to 1902 only 60 children were jailed, the rest diverted to probation and other services by the new Juvenile Court. The founders strove to develop a safe haven, a space to protect, to rehabilitate, and to heal children, a site of nurturance and guidance, understanding and compassion. They envisioned the Juvenile Court functioning in the best interest of children and youth, acting in any circumstance, they said, exactly as "a kind and just parent" would act.

At the turn of the century, Chicago had a population of a million people and was a young and muscular city—hub of commerce and industry, the first skyscraper city, home of the famous world exposition, "hog butcher to the world"—bursting with energy. It was also, like now, reeling from the social dislocations accompanying sudden and frenetic changes in the nature of work, economic boom and bust, widespread poverty, and unprecedented levels of immigration. Chicago was the site of the Haymarket riots, the Pullman strike, the eight-hour day.

Jane Addams moved into Hull House just west of downtown, in the center of the segregated immigrant enclaves—Italian, Greek, Jewish, Irish, Mexican, African American, Polish—that dotted Halsted Street from the stockyards in the south to the shipyards in the north. She was a teacher, an organizer, a social activist, and Hull House functioned as community center, social service agency, organizing headquarters, and focal point for political action. Importantly, the reformers, organizers, and activists who worked at Hull House also lived there, struggling to transcend the patronizing stance of the outside benefactor and to achieve, through their everyday living and working, an authentic partnership, an identity of interests.

Among the vigorous, optimistic social movements that the Hull House settlement championed was the campaign to establish a Juvenile Court that could provide separate hearings and confinement and probation for youngsters in crisis. Delinquent children and youngsters, including those picked up for truancy and pauperism, were routinely tossed into jails with adults who preyed upon and further corrupted them. The Juvenile Court was promoted as a clinic that would "treat" the delinquent and "cure the corruption" of youngsters. The reformers believed that through modern science, they would discover the root causes of juvenile delinquency, and through active intervention, prevent it. Influenced by the efficiency and child-study movements, and the growth of modern sociology and psychology, the watchword was treatment, not retribution.

The movement for a Juvenile Court brought together, besides the reformers of Hull House, society ladies, powerful attorneys of the Chicago Bar Association, and the "child-saving" societies of the Protestant and Catholic Churches. It was in some ways an odd alliance. The "child-saving" societies, for example, strove to take children from "unfit" or destitute homes, places where youngsters were "neglected" or "morally corrupted," and find a foster home (preferably on a farm) or an institution where children could be raised up to be "moral," "fully participating members of society." Large numbers of children, particularly immigrant children from Catholic countries like Italy and Ireland, found themselves literally swept off the streets and ensnared in the legal system, either as delinquents or as paupers, forced from their families and shipped away "for their own good."

What Jane Addams had in mind was more temperate, more family centered: a large, multifaceted settlement house, a living community of solidarity and support, with a tiny children's court settled down somewhere in a corner. Children and families in crisis would find themselves literally encircled in compassion and concern. In a home with chandeliers and without locks, seated around a conference table in comfortable chairs, a caring community would assemble to address a family's or a child's troubles and needs, assess the help available, and assume the duty a society shares with each of its members. The stance would be identical to that taken by the settlement house movement itself: friend and ally and partner rather than benevolent philanthropist. Jane Addams argued that that settlement house "must be grounded in a philosophy whose foundation is on the solidarity of the human race, a philosophy which will not waver when the race happens to be represented by a drunken woman or [a retarded] boy."

What started in Chicago met the hopes and expectations of the country, and by 1925 special courts and legal proceedings for children existed in all but two states. These reforms were built on the idea of child protection and restoration: judges were expected to act flexibly and informally, and to make their decisions in the best interest of the child. Proceedings were not to be legalistic and punitive, but personal and creative.

Jane Addams wanted *no* lawyers at Juvenile Court. She thought lawyers would bring contention and a dangerous narrowing of focus. Until mid-century the Court was lawyer-free, and then the lack of constitutional protections brought with it other abuses: armies of kids were sent to reform schools for years without a proper chance to object or even to defend themselves. In 1967, the U.S. Supreme Court heard the case of Gerald Gault, a fifteen-year-old who had made an obscene phone call and was arrested and sentenced to six years in prison (an adult convicted of a similar crime could be sentenced to thirty days). Gault had no legal representation; his parents were not notified in a timely fashion of his arrest or the charges brought against him; the prosecutor in his case was also the assigned probation officer. The Court threw out Gault's conviction and established that children in our system must have full legal rights, including the right to be notified of charges, the right to confront one's accusers, and protection against self-incrimination—in other words, children are entitled to due process under the law.

There are important differences still between adults and children in court: children do not have the right to bail nor to a trial by jury. The "best interest" standard guides most proceedings in Juvenile Court: petitions in Court are titled "In the interest of John Doe" rather than the familiar "People versus John Doe" of adult criminal proceedings.

The *Gault* case changed practice only marginally in many districts; kids still get little or no legal representation. But in large urban jurisdictions like Chicago, *Gault* brought lawyers into Juvenile Court with a vengeance. Now it is not uncommon to see five lawyers stand up on a single child welfare case: a state's attorney, a public defender, a public guardian, a private attorney for a parent, and an attorney from the Department of Children and Family Services. The place is choked with lawyers.

Today the building itself is a monument to modernism: large, rational, sleek, efficient, impersonal. It is two connected buildings really, one built in the early 1970s, all midnight steel and smoked glass, the other, glistening white, opened in 1994. The new building, eight stories high and sparkling, dwarfs the old, but from the outside they have become one, united by a covering of bright shining paint.

The Court is an impenetrable box set down in the central city, hard to get to on public transportation, easy to miss in the maze of public buildings stretching along the expressway on the near West Side. The tall and spreading white boxes of the Court complex sit, heavy, achromatic.

The entrance at 1100 South Hamilton is a crush of humanity when it opens to the public at 8:30 A.M. While hundreds of county workers, lawyers, and official personnel pass through a special entrance flashing I.D.s to a sheriff's deputy, men and women with business at the Court queue up in separate lines to empty their pockets, pass through metal detectors, and then submit to a search if necessary. It appears necessary to search every child over ten, rigorously.

Security is tight: the doors feed directly to single-file lines patrolled by fifteen young uniformed sheriff's deputies—ten women and five men—each wearing rubber gloves. One deputy, directly in front of the metal detector, calls out repeatedly, "Empty your pockets of everything except dead presidents . . . Empty your pockets." Two supervisors in white dress shirts oversee the enterprise, one taking a walky-talky from his belt and barking sharply: "I need two more men with rubber gloves at the front door, right now!"

The lines are distinctly asymmetrical: the men pass quickly through and into the building, while the women—outnumbering the men decisively to start—have their purses and shoulderbags routinely invaded, slowing the process markedly. The rubber gloves became standard issue a year ago when an unsuspecting deputy thrust her hand into a bag and emerged with a used tampon. AIDS alert!

The regulars in the Court refer to "the old building" and "the new building." The old building is home to eleven courtrooms on the first floor, the Juvenile Justice Division of the Circuit Court, delinquency calendar. The Nancy B. Jefferson School is housed on the second floor, the detention center on the third through fifth floors. Each living unit in the detention center consists of a large locked rectangle behind reinforced plexiglass with the attendants' desk at the entrance and tables and chairs for eating or studying clustered near the center. At one end of the room is the television area, with chairs and a couple of couches; at the other, toilets and showers. Twenty-two small separate sleeping rooms, locked cells, occupy the facing wall.

The new building is the site of the eighteen courtrooms that constitute the Child Protection Division of the Circuit Court, abuse and neglect calendar. It also houses the youth division of the Chicago Police Department (basement and fifth floor), the Citizens' Committee, the Cook County Clerk, the Juvenile Probation Department, the Department of Children and Family Services, the Cook County Guardian Ad Litem, the State's Attorney, Public Defender, assorted projects and services and screening rooms and court files, and the offices of eighteen hearing officers and two chief judges (eighth floor).

At any moment fifteen hundred to two thousand cases are pending on each judge's docket in Juvenile Court compared to two hundred and ten cases in adult criminal court in Cook County. There are fifty thousand active abuse and neglect cases, and twenty-five thousand active delinquency cases in Juvenile Court today. The average time given to any case in Juvenile Court is twelve minutes. On a typical day, each judge makes one hundred decisions. Caseloads for prosecutors and public defenders are twice the national standard.

Part of the problem is that juveniles (unlike adults) overwhelmingly commit crimes in groups—and each child rather than each crime represents a case. Further, the court is clogged with misdemeanors and minor felonies. More than 60% of delinquency cases referred to the Court end in failure to find guilt. The overuse of the Court for minor problems means that serious violent juvenile offenders—who account for only 6% of all juvenile crime—do not receive the attention they need nor is society ensured the vigilance it deserves.

In 1988 the Bureau of Juvenile Statistics estimated that it cost the nation somewhere between $15 and $20 billion a year to arrest, prosecute, and detain juvenile delinquents. Two billion dollars of that was to house youngsters in public facilities. It costs Cook County over $28,000 per child per year to incarcerate delinquent youth. This figure does not include the cost of school, which adds several thousand dollars per year per child. For a crude comparison, Philips Exeter Academy, the most elite prep school in the United States, costs $20,000 per year for a boarding student, and Lake Forest Academy, my alma mater, $18,500. The Juvenile Court's annual budget is over $20 million and it employs over 600 people.

The numbers in the custody of Department of Children and Family Services are also staggering; there were 15,000 children in DCFS custody in Illinois in 1988, 25,000 in 1991, and 50,000 in 1996. The numbers have leaped upward at the rate of 20% a year in the 1990s. The department's budget currently stands at $1.3 billion a year.

In April 1995 the Audy Home held 746 youths, making it the

largest juvenile jail in the world. Compared to the population as a whole, poor kids (95%), African-American (80%) and Latino (15%) kids, and boys (90%) are grossly over-represented. Audy Home is licensed for 498 children. Over 1,000 kids a month—close to 13,000 a year—come through Audy Home, about half for the first time.

Youngsters are brought to Juvenile Court through many channels, but a broad division is made between children who are "victims" (abuse and neglect) and children who are "victimizers," usually charged with an offense that would be a crime for an adult (delinquency). This distinction is small, tactical, and technical. Actually, there is a powerful connection apparent between a child being a victim one day and becoming a victimizer the next.

Typically nondelinquent children come to Court through action by the Department of Children and Family Services. In 1993 there were almost three million reports of child abuse nationwide. It's a staggering number and growing.

When a complaint is received in Illinois, an inquiry is undertaken by the Division of Child Protection (DCP), which has the power to take immediate custody of a child if an investigator finds the child's life or health to be in imminent danger. If DCP takes immediate custody, a formal investigation must begin at once; in other cases an investigation is supposed to begin within twenty-four hours of receiving a complaint. DCP investigations result either in an "undetermined report," meaning that no conclusion could be reached; an "unfounded report," meaning that there was insufficient evidence of abuse or neglect; or an "indicated report," meaning that the complaint was credible. Indicated reports can lead to intervention by various social services outside the legal system, or result in a referral to Juvenile Court, either in an attempt to take custody from the parents or to obtain an "Order for Court Supervision," which alerts parents that they are being tracked and spells out for them concrete responsibilities and actions to be taken.

When a child is removed from his or her parents and the matter is brought into Court, a judge appoints an attorney for the child and a guardian *ad litem* to represent the child's interests before the Court; by statute in Cook County the public guardian serves both functions. This dual appointment can present a real dilemma: a lawyer must represent the client's wishes, while a guardian must argue to the court on behalf of a child's best interest. If the best interest perceived by the guardian is not consistent with the legal path demanded by the client, there is no reasonable exit. The judge also appoints a public defender for the parents (if they do not have the money to hire a lawyer), or, in the case of a dispute between the parents, a public defender for one, and a private attorney paid by the county for the other.

Within ninety days the Court must hold a hearing to determine if there was in fact an instance of abuse or neglect. If there is a finding of abuse or neglect and the child is in custody, there must be a dispositional hearing within thirty days to determine whether the child should return home, and DCFS is required to work with the family toward resolving the problems that led to the child being taken into custody. Within eighteen months, and regularly thereafter, the Court must try to determine a permanent goal for the child: to return home if the family's problems have been resolved, to remain in short-term foster care until the problems are addressed, or to enter long-term foster care. Parents' rights may be terminated for a long list of reasons. Typically, parents lose their rights if two years have passed since a finding of abuse or neglect and they have failed to make reasonable progress in resolving their problems. In Chicago, more than 90% of the children who come before the Court are removed from their parents at the temporary custody hearing. Only 5% are returned home within the first year. This "permanency planning" is perhaps the most perplexing and problematic step in an already arduous, unmanageable path. The child must quickly have some firm ground to stand on, some knowable future. And at the same time parents must be protected from fervent prosecutors and mindless bureaucrats. Matters must move quickly, but decisions must be made carefully and thoughtfully.

Youngsters are brought to the delinquency side of Court primarily by the police, although there are some referrals by schools, parents, or social welfare agencies. When a youth is picked up by the police, the most likely disposition is called a station adjustment. This is a way for the police to alert a youth that a crime was committed, that a record is opened, but that no formal action will be brought on this charge. In some neighborhoods residents suspect that kids are rounded up simply to get their names into the system. Station adjustments are typical for shoplifting, grafitti, petty theft, fighting, or curfew violations, and usually children are released to their parents or guardians. One of our kids was station adjusted for curfew violations in 1993 and 1995. Police keep uneven, spotty records on station adjustments.

If the child is referred to Juvenile Court a police officer for the juvenile division meets with a lawyer from the state's attorney's office and conducts an intake screening. These two determine whether to give the youngster an informal adjustment—supervision for up to six months, then release—or to detain the child and seek either a delinquency petition or a hearing to transfer the case to adult court. In Illinois, transfers to adult court are escalating astronomically: 334 in 1992, 902 in 1993, 2,718 in 1994. The majority of these cases are nonviolent drug and weapons possession cases. Transfer is based on an assumption that the youth is beyond rehabilitation and cannot benefit from youth services. Felony convictions in adult court can mean an "economic death sentence" for many kids. The deck in Juvenile Court is stacked against them: a juvenile cannot appeal a transfer decision until after a conviction, while the state is free to appeal a judge's decision to keep a case in Juvenile Court. It is noteworthy that 98% of transfers in Cook County were African-American and Latino youngsters. Children who are ten or older are detained in Audy Home awaiting trial, or are detained at home under "home confinement." If the child is in custody, a hearing is required within thirty-six hours to determine the probable cause of a delinquent act and whether or not confinement is necessary. With a delinquency petition a Juvenile Court judge assigns the youth a public defender (assuming the family cannot retain private counsel).

The state's attorney may opt for an agreement with the youth and his or her parents for a period of supervision of up to twenty-four months. The Court typically sets conditions—school attendance, a clean record, community service, victim restitution—for such arrangements. Otherwise a trial called an adjudication hearing is held within

120 days or 10 days of a detention hearing. If there is a finding of delinquency—a conviction—a dispositional hearing is held, and the youth
is sentenced to treatment, detention, probation, institutional custody,
or some alternative placement.

———

Near an activity room, a small play area on the abuse and neglect side of
the bifurcated building, Justin is sitting on a chair paging somewhat
aimlessly through a book. His grandmother is talking intently to a social
worker, and he is waiting for their court hearing. His foot is bouncing
methodically and his anxious eyes dart around the room periodically.

"How old are you Justin?" An adult's predictable question.

"Nine."

"How do you feel today?"

"I don't know."

"I mean, being here. How does it feel to be here today?"

"Scary."

"What do you mean 'scary'?"

"You don't know what will happen to you. But if they ask me I
would say I want to live with my grandmother."

"Did your grandmother say you could stay with her?"

His eyes suddenly lock on mine for the first time, emphatically.
"Nobody asked me."

On another morning, Adam, ten years old, sits on a crowded bench
outside an abuse and neglect courtroom, waiting. The sharp clank of
steel meeting steel pulls Adam's attention to the right. His body stiff-
ens and his eyes get even wider as eleven young men, ages twelve to
sixteen, are led by a half dozen uniformed deputies to the delinquency
side of the building from the juvenile jail upstairs. "Clear the hall,"
shouts a deputy, and the crowds moving this way and that are temporarily halted, people pausing to observe the parade. The youngsters
are black; some are tattooed ("Black Gangster Disciples," "The
Family," "Fate"), some scarred, some with elaborate designs cut into
their hair. They are all shackled one to another with leg-irons, and
each has his right hand on the shoulder of the one in front of him. As
they shuffle and stumble past—their eyes intermittently defiant, hol-

low, fearful—Adam turns and asks, "Do they have an electric chair here?"

Ten o'clock. The huge halls have become crushing, crowded, and bustling—a hundred stories of violence and loss. Mothers change diapers and feed hungry children. Public defenders and guardians *ad litem* rush from courtroom to courtroom, meeting clients for the first time, conferencing quickly in the corridors, agreeing to again ask for a continuance. Juvenile Court maintains a strict and important confidentiality requirement. To protect children's best interest, the general public is not allowed to observe proceedings, and inside the Court everyone refers simply to "Mother" and "Minor"—which can over the course of a day or several days lend a deadening sameness to the proceedings. It is ironic, then, to have the buzz and chaos of the waiting rooms and hallways punctuated periodically with a sheriff calling sharply, "Baley . . . the case of Baley in Calendar 4"; "Jimenez . . . David Jimenez in Calendar 13." Troubling, too, to overhear snatches of conversation coming from a semicircle five feet away:

Social worker (loudly, to be heard above the din): "Do you want to continue visits with your dad?"

Seven-year-old girl (with no emotion, mechanically): "Yes."

Two older boys (flat and in unison): "Yes."

Thirteen-year-old girl, examining the floor, wringing her hands, says nothing.

Social worker (looking into the oldest girl's face): "Do you want to continue visits?"

Thirteen-year-old girl (barely audible): "Yes."

People become tired and noticeably irritable. Some look bewildered, others smoldering. The noise and commotion do not let up: families look for their caseworkers, lawyers for their clients, clerks for the files.

"Are you Andrews?" asks a young man with a briefcase and a bulging manila folder in his hand of a woman feeding two babies.

"I'm Parker," she replies flatly.

A gurney with paperwork grinds by. Every few minutes, deputies move through the crowd shouting above the chaos for people to move out of the corridors and into the waiting rooms next to the courtrooms.

Then, a few minutes later, these same deputies enter the waiting rooms and insist that if you need to talk, you must move out to the corridors. It is a grim parade, trudging back and forth continuously, trailing a volcano of resentment.

————

Judge Bloom, following a common Court schedule, sees thirty cases on delinquency calendar this morning without a break. He's nearing retirement and he's seen a lot from the bench, he says: "I lock them up for as long as I can if they carry a gun, but I'm always looking for an angle to help." He tells me that society is going to hell, and that he sees the early warning signs right here every day. "Where are the jobs?" he asks. "No jobs, no future, no family—and then all they have is guns and gangs and drugs to sell. That's fifty percent of what I deal with." He tells me that his work is overwhelming: the number of cases he hears every day, every week, every month is grinding; court support and services are disturbingly inadequate; alternatives to incarceration are dwindling. "But," he adds, "I try to do more good than harm in spite of it all. I didn't ask to be a judge here. Let's face it, Juvenile Court is not a smart career move for anyone, and I didn't become a judge to be a 'Juvenile Court' judge."

Minor. Hispanic. Male. Fifteen years old. Charged with trying to sell less than a quarter gram of cocaine to an undercover cop for ten dollars. Judge Bloom wants to impress the kid: "Don't get into this life, son. For five or ten dollars someone's mother ends up getting killed. You don't want that. You've got a good record, a mother who loves you, a good probation officer. So, I won't lock you up. But if you come back and are convicted, I'll surely lock you up. My order says: Go to school! Obey your parents! Dress nice! But it all boils down to this: You look like a man, which means you got a brain. Use it!"

Minor. African-American. Male. Fourteen years old. Charged with grand theft auto. State's attorney recommends one hundred and fifty dollars restitution payment. Judge Bloom asks, "Where is he supposed to get one hundred and fifty dollars? He's fourteen. He doesn't have a job. Aren't you asking him to commit another crime?" The lawyer explains that the amount was worked out in an agreement with the family. Judge Bloom, reading from the record, "Eight people live in the mother's house and none of them work." He looks up and continues, "This will take food from the family. I don't like it." And then to the young man in a stern, sharp voice, "See what you've done! You're taking food from your family!" The kid starts to cry quietly and covers his embarrassment with his hand. "You're not a team player," the Judge continues. "You make the payment, but slowly. . . . Five dollars a week. And don't steal that five dollars!"

Minor. White. Male. Thirteen years old. He appears alone, slight, dirty, with gray and torn clothing. The Court cannot determine with whom this kid lives. His mother uses two completely different names and addresses, and an uncle and grandmother also have several names. The judge is irritated with all the attorneys and the clerks. The kid explains the situation slowly, but it still baffles the Court. The public defender says, "This child is retarded, Your Honor."

Minor. African-American. Male. Thirteen years old. His older brother has a long record and is a reputed gang leader, and this youngster was arrested standing with him as he sold drugs on public housing property. Case continued.

Minor. African-American. Male. Fifteen years old. This is Freddie from Mr. B's class upstairs. He's facing an automatic transfer case in adult court, charged with dealing drugs in a housing project, but he is here on a juvenile charge of drug possession. Freddie's mother stands with him. The judge leans forward and asks, "When did you last see your father?" "Last summer," Freddie offers tentatively. "Where?" "He was at my aunt's." "When before that?" "I don't know." The judge turns to the recording clerk: "No father."

———

Judge Rotelli—abuse and neglect—is around forty years old, short and sharp-featured. She is businesslike, professional with the lawyers, patient and attentive with every parent or caseworker or child who comes before her. She makes regular eye-contact, deliberate and steady, and she listens closely to every word uttered, occasionally interrupting for clarification or correction. When she reaches a judgment she is careful to explain the consequences to every party involved. She seems trustworthy, firm but fair.

Her constant companions in the courtroom are her clerk and the sheriff's deputy. The clerk is full bodied, friendly, kind-looking. She wears a floor length print dress, big dangly ear-rings, and armfuls of silver bracelets that jingle when she walks from her place at the judge's right hand across the courtroom to deliver a note or to pick up a document. The deputy is young, well over six feet tall, and full of vitality. She stands by the door, holding it open, seeing that it shuts noiselessly, and greets everyone with her embracing smile and her sunny, whispered, "Hello, honey." When the judge calls a case the deputy strides through the door to the waiting area, her booming alto indicating just how much control is represented in her dainty "Hellos": "McGee," she thunders. "All parties on McGee." "Foxx . . . All parties on Foxx please come forward." Together these three women create a courtroom climate that feels particularly caring.

McGee is quick. The public defender asks to be dropped from the case because the father's whereabouts are unknown, and the mother has disappeared and is not complying with the court order that she participate in the service plan. Granted. Permanency planning can go forward for the two McGee children.

The Foxx case, a tangled story, is not new: LaTonya and Rafi Foxx, both in their early twenties, have been before Judge Rotelli four times concerning custody of their three children, ages four, five, and seven. The case came into court when LaTonya's aunt, who sometimes cared for the kids, called DCFS with a complaint of child abuse. The caseworker who investigated found LaTonya and the children living in a basement apartment with inadequate heat and minimal food. LaTonya told the worker that Rafi had left the family two days before after beating her in front of the children, that he regularly disciplined the children by whipping them with his belt or making them hang by their hands from pipes that run along the ceiling of their apartment. The children were placed in foster care, and when Rafi and LaTonya reconciled, a petition to terminate all parental rights was sought. This hearing is on termination, and, while the children are absent, LaTonya and Rafi are both here, each represented by private counsel.

The state's attorney, young and articulate, leads off and presents a powerful rendition of this family's story based on the aunt's account, on LaTonya's original statement, and, most dramatically, on testimony by Sherise, the seven-year-old. The state's attorney describes excessive corporal punishment, an injurious environment, and a pattern of abuse. Sherise's testimony, argues the state's attorney, is powerful, consistent, and credible.

The guardian *ad litem* concurs, arguing that the domestic violence alone puts these youngsters at risk. She attacks LaTonya's recanting of her original testimony as "totally incredible": "Mother claims that she dreamt up the allegations against the common-law husband after seeing something similar on TV, and that she was simply angry at him and trying to punish him. But the aunt heard the same story and saw the bruises, and the mother's recantation came only after she realized she might lose her children. Her contradictions and inconsistencies, lies and presumed lies are ominous and diabolical."

LaTonya and Rafi are slumped in chairs at a table while the lawyers argue. Rafi's eyes are burning and he occasionally shakes his head slowly back and forth. LaTonya sits solid in a dirty red overcoat, head tilted toward her shoulder, thick black horn-rimmed glasses defining her face, resignation covering her.

LaTonya's lawyer begins by urging the judge to allow for a radically different telling of events. LaTonya's aunt, a fundamentalist Christian, has always despised Rafi and disapproved of LaTonya; she had plotted a punishment for a long time. As for Sherise, her testimony was sad, distraught, confused. Yes, that might be seen as the testimony of a victim, but it could as easily be the testimony of a child who had been coached to lie and was now full of remorse and conflict. The basement pipes— "Your honor, the pipes were said to be four inches in diameter. I have here an apple juice bottle that is four inches in diameter. This morning my son, who is an average-sized six-year-old, could not grip this bottle. Indeed, your honor, it is difficult for me to grip this bottle. Hanging from the pipes never happened."

He ends by noting that the judge must, in most cases, err on the side of child protection, but that in this case the facts demand that she find against the state and preserve and protect this family.

Rafi's lawyer begins. "Your Honor, I submit that the only victim in this case today is Rafi Foxx." The judge's eyebrows arch suddenly and there is the sense of heads snapping, the collective breath being held. The lawyer doesn't seem to notice, and so he presses on, with the judge now staring daggers. "We've had witch hunts in this country in Massachusetts, we've had the Red Scare in the '50s, and now we have incendiary and incredible charges of abuse here in Chicago in the '90s. Whenever anyone wants to destroy a perfectly fine person, they just cry out, 'Abuse!' 'Abuse!'"

Finally every lawyer in the room has spoken and the judge has her word. She recounts all the testimony, the contradictory versions, the statements on one side and the other. Whenever the judge quotes LaTonya's testimony, the guardian *ad litem* shakes her head in utter disbelief, and scans the courtroom, beaming. The judge goes on, occasionally running both hands through her long hair as if in real struggle. She is balanced except for once: "I find the argument that Rafi Foxx is a victim here to be entirely repugnant." She supports the findings of DCFS and the state's attorney, and finds the parents abusive and neglectful.

Juvenile Court is where youngsters and families land when all else has failed. It is the bottom of a several-tiered system of justice for children. The privileged and the favored have access to private attorneys, psychiatrists, drug treatment programs, all kinds of services. The unfortunate land here.

I remember a day when my wife, who directs the Children and Family Justice Center, came home shaken from interviewing children in a locked mental facility for a lawsuit she was organizing. She had met a child who was considered violent and incorrigible and who was being maintained on heavy drugs. He was the same age and had a biography frighteningly close to our adopted son's. The difference: our son had a family to fall into with two devoted brothers, an outstanding psychiatrist to see twice a week for several years, a reading tutor, dedicated teachers, a loving biological family, specialists and programs to nurture and challenge him. The other boy was thrown into society's dump.

The Court is pervaded by a feeling of futility and despair. Starved for funds, lacking community programs, appropriate opportunities for children, and the minimal resources to discharge its responsibilities, Juvenile Court has become entangled in self-interested bureaucracies, balkanized by the clash of competing fiefdoms. This arrangement is expensive. It costs money, of course, and, perhaps most important, it saps initiative and courage, human energy and personal responsibility. Hannah Arendt once described bureaucracy as "rule by no one," and Juvenile Court has fit the bill perfectly. Who's in charge here? The chief judge? Presiding judges? The superintendent? The Board of Education? Police and prosecutors? Without anyone particularly intending it to be so, carelessness and thoughtlessness begin to prevail. The most optimistic families and children who come before the Court hope that their situations will at least not deteriorate further; others clearly expect the unraveling and degradation only to become worse. In April 1991 the Illinois Appellate Court noted as an aside in a lengthy opinion that, "There is no doubt that [the Department of Children and Family Services] and our Juvenile Court are abysmal failures. There are reports that almost as many children are harmed as are benefitting by coming under their common aegis."

The Court cannot in a practical sense adequately address the larger contexts within which it operates: poverty, joblessness, and economic distress; racial segregation, class divisions, and the inequitable distribution of resources; a culture of cynicism and despair. But even in its own terms the Court's limitations are apparent. On the delinquency side of Court youngsters receive neither consistently effective legal representation nor powerful alternative care, guidance, or counseling. It is, then, inadequate as a system of social welfare and unsatisfactory as a system of adversarial legal conflict. As the sociologist George Herbert Mead wrote, "The social worker in the court is the sentimentalist, and the legalist in the social settlement, in spite of his learned doctrine, is the ignoramus."

On the abuse and neglect side there is a similar deficiency. The problems of each family are simply huge, and the overwhelming size and scope of the need is entirely unmet. When thousands upon thou-

.sands of families are present, each with a complex tangle of problems, the system closes in on itself. To say Juvenile Court is in crisis is a bit like saying the Titanic is taking on water: it's true, but it doesn't suggest the dimensions of the disaster.

There is a terrible, unmistakable link between poverty, abuse and ne-glect, and juvenile delinquency. According to the Children's Defense Fund, the rate of abuse and neglect is seven times greater for families earning less than $15,000 annually than for families earning more than $15,000. Further, "being abused or neglected as a child increased the likelihood of arrest as a juvenile by 55%, as an adult by 38%, and for a violent crime by 38%." Juveniles who commit the heaviest crimes have almost always suffered a lifetime of abuse and neglect. This is not to say that poor people are criminally inclined, only to point to the powerful impact of poverty on disintegrating the best intentions.

———

The modern Juvenile Court embodies the broken legacy of child-sav-ing, which is to say it is of two minds: one of its goals, to rescue the in-nocent young from their depraved parents and the sewers of their circumstances; the other, to rectify the behavior of bad children through a regimen of strict discipline, inflexible rules and routines, and unsparing punishment. Juvenile Court is a two-headed monster created for both assignments, and fitted for neither.

Young people in Juvenile Court are simultaneously pure *and* rotten, immaculate *and* corrupt, angels *and* brutes. We must love and under-stand the little unformed souls, even as we beat the devil out of the wicked, wayward youth. These seemingly contradictory ideas are unit-ed by a single, severe assumption: *We*—the respectable, the prosperous, the superior, and (especially in modern times) the professional—know what is best for *Them*—the masses, the poor, the outcast, the wretched of the earth—in short, our clients. We know what is best for them at all times and in all circumstances and without a doubt. Of course, this stance leads to a kind of self-justifying, insistent piousness, which in turn leads to disaster after disaster in both policy and practice. Other people are made into the objects of our interest and experimentation. They are rendered voiceless and faceless.

That this arrogance lands heavily upon the poor is no surprise. For centuries the prevailing view has been that poverty is somehow earned. It is God's will, genetic bad luck, moral failing, or a collection of scientifically discovered behaviors that make people poor. No one in officialdom believes that poverty can be understood as the lack of necessary resources. To put that thought into the popular language of social science: a new study has found that an overwhelming number of the poor lack the resources to live in decent homes or avoid impoverished neighborhoods, send their children to the best schools, access the greatest health care, or participate fully in the social or cultural life of our great cities. Poor people don't have enough money.

Child-saving, the mission of late-nineteenth-century reformers, has always been a movement against the poor. Proclaiming lofty ideals, the child-saving societies initially targeted poor and immigrant children crowded into the rapidly growing cities for its interventions and ministrations. The London Philanthropic society, for example, was founded "for the Prevention of Crimes, and for a Reform Among the Poor, by training up to Virtue and Industry the Children of Vagrants and Criminals, and such who are in the Paths of Vice and Infamy." Steven Schlossman points out that the distinction between "vagrant" and "criminal" was blithely blurred, and that "the term 'delinquency' was used rather elastically to legitimate the incarceration of any youngsters who, in the judgment of a court or of a reform school's managing directors, might benefit from a highly structured regime of discipline and instruction." The notion of "juvenile delinquency," then and now, focused on children of the urban poor—from Charles Dickens's "street urchins" to today's "superpredators."

Jane Addams noted that "four fifths of the children brought into the Juvenile Court in Chicago are the children of foreigners. The Germans are the greatest offenders, Polish next." It sounds quaint, but what Addams was pointing to was the crushing power of poverty and social isolation to push youth toward petty thieving and then worse. Recently the National Academy of Sciences drew a similar conclusion: "Data from the Centers for Disease Control indicate that personal and neighborhood income are the strongest predictors of violent crime." Poverty and street crime go hand in hand, and underlying so much of the work and activity of Juvenile Court is the growing emiseration of children. Jane Addams believed, of course, that no outcome was inevitable. With intervention and support, she demonstrated, young people could find firm footing out of disaster.

Over ninety years ago she wrote this: "We may either smother the divine fire of youth or we may feed it. We may either stand stupidly staring as it sinks into a murky fire of crime and flares into the inter-mittent blaze of folly or we may tend it into a lambent flame with power to make clean and bright our dingy city streets."

The legal justification for child-saving—including juvenile courts, detention centers, and reform schools—is a doctrine that emerged from English common law. *Parens patriae* asserts the right of the Crown to intervene in family matters when a child is in jeopardy. The doctrine rests on one reasonable assumption: children are members of society, and society as a whole benefits from the contributions and suffers from the difficulties of each child. But it opens, as well, the possibility of all kinds of abuse, beginning with the Crown exercising power in an abu-sive or arbitrary manner. In the nineteenth century the Pennsylvania Supreme Court created the modern foundation of *parens patriae* writing:

> May not the natural parents, when unequal to the tasks of educa-tion, or unworthy of it, be superseded by the *parens patriae*, or com-mon guardian of the community? It is to be remembered that the public has a paramount interest in the virtue and knowledge of its members, and that, of strict right, the business of education belongs to it. That parents are ordinarily entrusted with it, is because it can seldom be put into better hands; but where they are incompetent and corrupt, what is there to prevent the public from withdrawing their faculties, held as they obviously are, as its sufferance?

For a hundred and thirty years *parens partiae* stood solidly as the law of the land. In 1967 the landmark *Gault* decision established that chil-dren are entitled to full legal rights as persons, a decision that chal-lenged a fundamental pillar of *parens patriae*, offering a different leg to stand on. Still the deep impact of that nineteenth-century decision lives on, side by side with *Gault*, and so we consider children full moral and legal beings one moment, objects of our paternal ownership and concerns the next. In juvenile courts throughout the land that duality, that often unhappy marriage, shapes our actions and our debates today.

———

When Jane Addams asked, "How shall we respond to the dreams of youth?" she gave voice to the big ideas and larger purposes that powered her efforts. The condition of children was appalling and the popular attitude toward children ambivalent. Childhood itself was contested territory, a combat zone between a Puritan view of children as born with original sin, ignorant and evil, requiring adults to beat the devil out of them, and an Enlightenment view that children are born innocent and respond best to love and nurturance. Jane Addams and her colleagues imagined a bolder and brighter future for children, a world that could be, but was not yet. The movement that they built was, of course, time-bound, flawed, and incomplete. And it has been in many ways undone. But the accomplishment was awesome: Through massive effort, thought, and study, through intense organizing and agitating, Jane Addams notably improved the world for children and youth. That is her legacy, and that is the challenge she offers us across a century.

3. Tobs

Is not this what I require of you as a fast:
to loose the fetters of injustice,
to untie the knots of the yoke,
to snap every yoke
and set free those who have been crushed?
Then shall your light break forth like the dawn
and soon you will grow healthy like a wound newly healed . . .
If you cease to pervert justice,
to point the accusing finger and lay false charges,
if you feed the hungry from your own plenty
and satisfy the needs of the wretched,
then your light will rise like dawn out of darkness
and your dusk be like noonday . . .
The ancient ruins will be restored by your own kindred
and you will build once more on ancestral foundations;
you shall be called Rebuilder of broken walls,
Restorer of houses in ruin.

Isaiah 58

THE BLACK-AND-WHITE CLASS PHOTOGRAPHS are tossed into a couple of old shoeboxes now. They are jumbled together, their edges curling. There are scores of them, hundreds of them, different in detail but identical in frame: at the center, Frank Tobin, the teacher whose classroom is just around the corner from Mr. B's, a little grayer, a little thicker as the years pass, but the same unmistakable expression of bemused kindness in each photo; and then crowded around him, smiling, scowling, flexing, giving horns, mugging for the camera in a thousand predictable postures, a group of adolescent boys. The students' faces change, but after a dozen pictures, they begin to take on a sameness too—the adolescent swagger, the tough-guy pose.

I am reminded of an occasion two decades ago, when I was robbed at gunpoint. I was paralyzed—the gun loomed larger than the kid who held it; his hand shook violently as he croaked his terrified commands. The next day I was taken to the Twentieth Precinct, where I searched for the assailant in files marked "Black, 16-24, Armed Robbery, Manhattan." It took hours—there was a pageant of outlaws on display.

After a while, the faces began to blur and look the same. I was stunned by the scale and spectacle of the thing, and, of course, I never did find the perpetrator there.

I mention this to Frank—the blurring together, the collapsing of individual identities—but he objects: "Every one of these guys is distinct," he says. "Each has a name, a face, a unique story, and a mother and a father." Every one of these guys is worthy of our respect and care, he argues, simply because he is human. Each is, Frank says, "a child of God."

———

"How many guys in this class are Hispanic?" Frank is at his desk and Jamie is sitting beside him being tutored on fractions.

"Two."

Frank draws two red circles on a blank page.

"OK. How many are black?"

"Eight."

Frank draws eight blue circles.

"And how many white?"

"None."

"None?" says Frank surprised. "None?" He looks around dramatically. "How about . . . ?" He sticks his thumb into his own chest.

Jamie smiles. "Oh, man, you don't count."

"OK. I don't count. You really know how to hurt a guy."

For beginning fractions, ten is a convenient number, and Frank moves along, not counting himself.

———

"When visitors come through the Audy Home, what do they see?" Frank asks, beginning the morning discussion.

"Kids locked up."

"Bad boys."

"Thugs."

"Gang-bangers."

"The next Michael Jordan."

"Crazy attendants."

"OK," he continues, "and let's say these visitors are from the suburbs and they look in our classroom here, and they see all these black kids, and no white kids. What will they think? Eighty percent of the students are black kids. And they go next door—80%. They might think: Blacks are more violent than whites. Blacks are more criminally inclined."

"They'd be right, Tobs," says Jefferson. "Because it's true. I was over to County to see my uncle last year—all black."

"Yes, but that's racism," says Jamie.

"You mean people were framed?" asks Frank. "They never committed the crime?"

"Everyone breaks the law," Jamie responds. "Only white people get away with it more."

The discussion runs on. Frank doesn't simply provoke: he tells stories of the civil rights movement, draws diagrams linking history, poverty, inferior education, and crime. Through it all he wants to challenge the image of prison as a place designed for black people. "It is simply awful," he says later. "These kids drink in that image, breathe it in, see it enacted in every single moment."

"Hey, Tobs," says Fredo. "Now Choco, he's black, so OK. But how come I got to be here?" Everyone laughs.

Over several days the morning discussion stays on the themes of crime and punishment. "I don't ask about the specific cases," Frank tells me. "I don't ask a kid if he's sorry. I tell them to keep their own counsel; they're going to trial and they need to be controlled. But a lot of times they can't help it, they need to talk about it, and they need to say how sorry they are. Sometimes cases are in the papers, and sometimes coming back from court, they're just exploding to talk, dying to understand what's happening to them. Among themselves, it's irresistible."

Frank preaches forgiveness, free will, moral choice. He teaches out of his faith and activism, out of his belief in God's infinite love for all people and humanity's huge capacity to do better. "God loves this kid," he reminds himself, especially when faced with a particularly challenging child. "God lives in this kid and is revealed in this kid in a unique, singular way. No other person can reveal this specific dimension of God."

I think of our own three boys—Zayd, Malik, Chesa. Each is precious; Frank would say each is sacred. I remember my anxiety and occasionally my anger when I saw them treated as things: a learning disability, a threatening teenager, a behavior problem. Pinned to the board like a butterfly. I imagine them here—lined up, controlled, pushed around, and mostly not allowed their little-boyness. Of course, I remind myself, our three are not charged with crimes; they experience a relatively safe passage; they are unlikely ever to set foot in this place. But I can't help thinking: What if? And, perhaps because I know these kids through Frank, or because I know them beyond their criminal records, I can't entirely resist the obvious and powerful similarities between them and ours: the adolescent bravado, the sense of invulnerability, the natural narcissism, the precariousness, the frightening lapses in judgment. They are kids, after all, and nothing that they did can possibly change them into adults. The fourteen-year-old who pulled a gun is a kid with a gun; the sixteen-year-old in the gang war is a kid in a gang. And I want to will the Court—and then all of us—to set the highest possible standard when determining judgments: "If this were my child. . . ." Nothing in that standard frees kids of consequences, nothing in it predetermines outcomes. It does, however set a tone that is at once caring and complex.

"What hinders your free will?" Frank asks, and the students' minds lock on the particulars of detention: "lights out," "wake up," "the attendants." Frank acknowledges the limits here, the ways the institution takes away your ability to choose, but moves the conversation to *before* here, and *after* here. He offers imagined scenarios, but they are close to home and students add details and vignettes to elaborate:

- A kid is hanging with his group, and it's his turn to get some money. He's going to steal a wallet, and a friend gives him a gun just to scare the guy. The guy reaches into his pocket, and the kid shoots him.

- Another kid goes into a gas station and demands cash. He's not planning to hurt anyone or get killed himself. The guy has a gun. Bam!

- One day some guys beat up a kid. Driving around with his crew, they spot the guys and the kid grabs a baseball bat. A friend warns him that they may be armed so he puts a pistol in his pocket, just in case.

"Under certain circumstances every one of us will do the wrong thing," Frank says. "The point is to keep your head clear, to make good choices so you don't find yourself trapped by a string of stupid choices." Writing about the horrors of war and humanity's gaudy tendencies toward cruelty, Clive James notes that, while it is tempting to construct a political or psychological theory, "finally you are faced with the possibility that, however deeply buried, such nefarious capacities are within all of us." And so, Frank continues, "I know I'm capable. With the wrong influences, without love and support, with rage and frustration and drugs and guns . . . So I'm in no position to judge. That's up to God. All I can do is create an environment to bring out their goodness, to display it for them and for me. I want them to experience being loved, being good, and to feel a more peaceful, happier way of living."

For Frank Tobin the criminal act, the violence, is one thing. The circumstances are a second thing. And the person still another. "People say you're criminals," Frank tells the students one morning. "And if you believe that, you're doomed. Oh, you may have committed a crime, you may have done something terrible. And you need to account for that, and sometimes that accounting is heavy. But everything you do is not criminal. You are more than a single act, and you have a life ahead of you that is more than that one bad act. Your job is to find a way to live beyond the worst thing you ever did."

Frank shows them how they might move to control the circumstances that surround them: how to avoid certain scenes, how to think through to the possible end of a chain of choices. "Don't let yourself be a thing," he says. "Even here. Take every chance you can to make a choice for yourself, to do something because you want to do it, not because you're told to." This is not soft-hearted moralizing from Frank: kids listen to him and begin to follow the advice. His credentials are hard-won in the toughest of circumstances.

Frank Tobin began teaching at the Audy Home in 1973, the same year as Mr. B. Frank had just left the priesthood. "I was not exactly enthused with the church hierarchy," he says with characteristic understatement, referring to a series of bitter struggles over most of a decade. But leaving the priesthood had a more intensely personal dimension: "I realized that my relationships with women were of growing importance, and I finally understood that celibacy was not for me."

In the rough South Side Irish ward of his youth, Frank's parents followed the path of other hard-working second-generation Americans: Mom raised the four kids and kept the home, Dad was a mechanic and then a truck driver. He had been a teamster during the days of rugged territorial struggles and violent wildcat strikes; the geography of his life was mapped around hard work and solidarity, family and faith. It was a legacy to Frank.

Frank, the second child and the first boy, attended the neighborhood Catholic school with the other Irish kids, and then went to high school at prestigious St. Ignatius Prep on Roosevelt Road—only about a mile east of the Audy Home. His family couldn't afford the University of Illinois, so Frank spent two years at the old Navy Pier and then went to night school at the Illinois Institute of Technology, where he studied civil engineering. Frank worked days for the Cook County Highway Department building roads and bridges.

After a year Frank answered what had been a persistent calling to the priesthood and entered a program at an archdiocesan minor seminary. There he learned Latin, the language of instruction in the major seminaries, including Mundelein, where he studied for seven more years. "Seminary was beautiful," he says now, with a hint of irony. "We studied Thomistic philosophy and Thomistic theology. Nothing eclectic, very rigid. Everything in St. Thomas' thinking is orderly and absolute and known—fantastic. There is a lot of peace in that, of course, a lot of calm in being absolutely certain, and so it is terribly tempting. The whole messy world worked out in strict logic, black and white: thesis, arguments, proofs. Well, that was seminary, and I did love it, although by the end I was eager to get out and get to work."

The banal, traditional conservatism of the Church was a constant thorn for Frank: "I was assigned to a racially changing neighborhood, and I wanted to embrace the change and become a model for the Church. I supported the goals of the black struggle, and I thought I could help people reach deep into their faith to overcome their fears. Of course, that was never easy." The biggest obstacle and enemy was "the real estate interests who ripped neighborhoods apart, setting people against one another to make a quick buck." The pattern was predictable: "FOR SALE" signs would suddenly appear in a white working-class neighborhood; residents would begin getting phone calls asking if they'd be interested in selling their homes; and then African-Americans ("always very large, very dark black men") were hired by realtors to canvass the whole area, knocking on every door and telling every homeowner the same lie: "I'm interested in buying a house in the neighborhood." If one or two residents sold, the stampede would create its own momentum, and the neighborhood would be gobbled up in short order at bargain-basement prices by realtors who would then sell the homes to rising middle-class black families. "Don't make it sound un-American," one realtor told Father Frank at the time. "We're doing what everyone else does—buy cheap, sell dear, clear a little profit in the middle."

"I organized meetings where we talked about how the pressure would come," Frank says, "and how we could resist it. But it was tough." When Frank went to Our Lady Gate of Heaven there were two real estate agencies in the neighborhood; two years later there were twenty-eight. "I organized one large meeting and invited all the realtors to come and have a community dialogue. I put twenty-eight chairs on the stage, one for each realtor. A couple hundred people from the parish came, but only one realtor. And he was bold as brass: 'I love green,' he said. 'But it's still a free country. I can't buy your house if you don't want to sell it.' He really laid it out."

The old neighborhood was gone within months. "We'd invited black people into the church," says Frank, "and we welcomed them. No matter what we said after that, some parishioners said, 'You're driving me out.' When people lost money in the real estate crash, priests like me were scapegoated."

Frank and another associate priest were working with Sister Joan Stucker, the principal of the parish school ("Mother Stucker" was the irresistible nickname to some students), and a group of other nuns from the Sisters of St. Joseph to realize a new idea called team ministry; it was a challenge to the whole parish pastor tradition and indirectly to the larger church hierarchy. One Sunday, while Frank was giving a talk about team ministry to an enthusiastic group at the cathedral, Cardinal Cody, the Church leader in Chicago, entered. Seeing five nuns sitting in the back of the sanctuary, Cody barked at an aide, "Get those women out of here."

Frank was opposed at every turn by the pastor, "a weak and timid fellow who played his little part in the hierarchy" and who resisted opening the parish to black people. "I went to the cardinal about reassigning the pastor so that we could get on with building something worthwhile there. Cody always considered me a rabble-rouser. We sat in his big stately mansion on State Parkway, and he put a set of papers in front of me. He was offering me my own parish, elevating me to pastor, and, of course, trying to break up our little effort at change. I said I'd take it after he got rid of the awful pastor at Our Lady Gate of Heaven. He gave me a long, cold look, reached over and pulled the papers back."

When the whites left, the parish took a terrible financial hit. Only ten percent of the black community is Catholic, and the numbers were bleeding red. The pastor left but the team struggled on. Frank did the janitorial repair work—"I considered it appropriate work, very priestly work, but, of course, the hierarchy frowned"—and Joan and Frank separated the school from the church, creating an independent school board to see to its finances. The school was racially integrated for only a short while. The night of the school's first integrated dance, Frank's car was stolen from in front of the church. When he found it, the old Chevy had been beaten shapeless with sledgehammers. This was no joy ride, but rather a punishment and a threat. Too soon the school became a segregated black school.

Frank went back to school himself, this time to Loyola University, where he got a master's degree in teaching. Joan also left the parish, got a degree at the Jane Addams College of Social Work at the University of Illinois at Chicago, and moved to Calumet City, where she worked with teenage girls.

Frank began teaching part-time at Quigly, where there was a male-female integrated staff. "That was a blessing," says Frank, "because I was learning a lot about life from women, and it was opening up new worlds for me." In his work at Quigly and at Our Lady Gate of Heaven he was discovering something that would become central to his developing theology and his life: "God lives within human relationships, and God is revealed in relationships. What women can reveal about life and about God became important in my life." Not surprisingly, the woman Frank loved shared his work—Joan Stucker.

"One Sunday," he says, "I told the parishioners that I loved my work and that I wanted to be a priest, but that I also wanted to marry." Frank walked up and down the aisles explaining his dilemma and his decision. He never preached from the pulpit—"it was another wall, another barrier"—but this time there was an even more intense connection. "It was almost a kind of instant reception."

The cardinal's reaction was not supportive. "This is scandalous to your class," Cody scowled, referring to the priests who graduated together from Mundelein. "You were the oldest and looked to for leadership. And now," he spit the words at Frank, "you are giving up the love of God for the lesser love of man."

"Of course the cardinal was in a politically tough place," Frank says now. "Priests were leaving in droves and he probably felt like the boy with his finger in the dike. But still," he shakes his head in disbelief, looking suddenly twenty years younger, the rebuke fresh, the wound immediate, "listen to his words and think of the implications for ordinary people. Cody was a real disaster."

Frank and Joan married, and Frank took a teaching job at the Evelyn Edwards Emergency Child Care Center. The Center had just been opened by the Department of Children and Family Services in an effort to create a residential school for "minors in need of supervision"—DCFS-dependent kids, mainly runaways—separate from the delinquent kids housed at Audy Home. "I liked the teaching a lot," Frank says. "I saw the power of it. These kids were mixed up, angry, incredibly needy. They'd bounced from group home to foster home and back. They needed love so badly, and when I reached out to them, they responded. It was just awesome."

But the place quickly went up in well-publicized flames. Weak administration, lack of funds, and poorly paid, badly trained child-care workers led to the predictable scandal—drug use and sex in the living units—and the place was closed. Frank transferred to Audy Home and established himself as a teacher with the automatic transfer students: "Teaching has always been for me a kind of ministry."

———

"I got this thing beat, Tobs," says Fredo, smiling. He has talked with his mother, who has hired a private attorney to defend him and he's referring to the first-degree murder charge he is facing. "All they got on me is my statement, that's it. Once I get my statement thrown out, there's nothing. My lawyer told my mom that I had a good chance."

Frank nods and responds, "That's good, Fredo. When's your hearing?" He glances at the three-by-five cards on his desk and quickly finds the answer for himself. They respond simultaneously: "The seventeenth." "Well," repeats Frank, "that's good."

Scared, isolated, ignorant of the law, kids typically tell a story that they imagine will help them out, but that, in fact, entangles them. "I snatched her purse, but I didn't have the gun," says Fredo. When Fredo's adult friend—one year his senior—shot the boyfriend who pursued them, Fredo was booked for felony murder. His statement is the noose around his neck.

Fredo wants to think he has a second chance, a possible way to do it right, to start over. Frank wants him to have some hope, too, to seek redemption, to try again. But Frank has seen a lot in twenty-five years. "Every guy here imagines he can get his statement quashed," says Frank. "It might happen. But I've only seen it rarely. They convict themselves time after time. One kid I had here thought that when he waived his rights that meant they'd let him out. They really have no idea that they have any rights whatsoever, and if anyone read Fredo his Miranda [the statement police putatively make to all criminal suspects regarding their right to remain silent and to engage legal counsel] he had no idea what it meant."

James Clifton, an officer from the Youth Division, gives a different spin: "These guys are caught up in a life that dead-ends here. They're guilty as hell, and everyone, including them, is better off when we lock them up. We read them their rights, sure, but it's a fine point."

———

"Who would you rather be?" Frank asks the class one afternoon, pointing with his chalk to two circles he has drawn on the board. One circle encloses the word *Ignored*, the other *Abused*; the word *Self* floats alone and beside. "Would you rather be ignored," he asks, gesturing to the first circle. "Or, would you rather, you know, not be ignored, but kicked around a lot? Maybe put down a lot, maybe physically abused? Which do you think is better?"

The chorus of responses splits evenly: "I been hit a lot, I'd rather be left alone"; "Well, when you abused, at least they showing me *something*."

The comments charge and retreat across the room with Frank probing, questioning, challenging, occasionally leading an onslaught himself. "How can you say getting hurt beats not getting hurt?"; "OK, but if you're getting kicked in the butt, at least you're being noticed"; "Which one lets you know you're a person, that you're worth something?"

"Neither one," responds Jefferson. "Neither one lets you know you're a worthy person. One, it's like you're hateful; two, it's like you're invisible. Neither one lets you know what good you are."

"Next person on the outside puts a hand on me," says Ty, "will die." There is complete silence as the easy conversation ends abruptly.

Jefferson, Fredo, and Jamie are working on word games. Each work sheet has a large grid of letters. One sheet asks students to identify notable African-Americans who, "like vibrant threads in African Kente cloth have enlivened the tapestry of human history," and then reading up, down, forward, backward, or diagonally, to circle those names. Cornel West, Colin Powell, Muhammad Ali, Arthur Ashe. Another sheet challenges the student to find sixty hairstyles and cuts (Afro, extensions, crewcut, Cleopatra). And a third focuses on geography: mountains, valleys, glaciers.

"Tobs," says Jamie, "look at this pencil." He holds up a little useless stub of a thing.

"Is that your way of asking for a new one?"

"I guess so," Jamie smiles sheepishly.

"Here you are Jamie. You can have as many pencils as you need. You can have an abundance of pencils my friend."

"Who's that nigger that invented peanuts?" asks Jamie.

"You can't invent peanuts, nigger," says Fredo.

Jefferson correctly identifies the astronaut Mae Jemison on a sheet and exclaims, "I saw her once in a school assembly when I was a shorty. She say, 'Be all you can be.'" He raises his eyebrows and offers a sweeping gesture indicating the fate that has befallen him. "She must be old, old now, man."

"Old?" says Tobs amused. "She's half my age."

"You're old as dirt, Tobs. You're old beyond old."

Later, when Jefferson comes up to get his work checked, Tobs says, "Your answers are correct, Jefferson, even though you called me old."

"Come on, Tobs," Jefferson pleads, laughing. "That's all in the past."

"Yes," agrees Tobs. "But not too far in the past."

———

Jefferson was absent yesterday—court date. He comes into class this morning agitated. "Morning, Jefferson," says Frank.

"Tobs," Jefferson says urgently, "I heard from guys in court that Harold was killed last week."

"No!" Frank is stunned, thrown. Harold was a quiet kid, kept mainly to himself, did his work. He was in for a gangland shooting, transferred to Cook County Jail on his seventeenth birthday, just three weeks ago. Frank and his classmates gave him a little party, ate pizza, wished him well. Now he is dead.

The way Jefferson heard it, when Harold went to County he figured to protect himself by "claiming rank"—telling other inmates that he was higher up in the organizational hierarchy than was in fact true. When word came back that he had lied, an order was given to other gang members to "violate him"—a ritual beating, standard punishment for all kinds of infractions. Because Harold had broken the rules, he was supposed to submit passively to being violated. "He refused to take it," Jefferson says, "so they got him ten times worse." He died in Cook County Hospital of a brain hemorrhage two days later.

———

"Harold was a good guy," Frank says to the class, "and his killing is a senseless waste. I'm just sick about it."

Everyone looks sad and uneasy. Finally Ty says, "I ain't never claiming rank, boy. I'll just go on about my own business."

"Claiming rank! Claiming rank!" Frank is agitated and you can hear it in his high voice as it turns and takes on a sudden sharp edge. Just as suddenly it drops back to normal. "What you're right about, Tyrone, is that you've got to each figure out a way to do your own time. *Do your own time!* It's not as easy as knowing now not to claim rank. It's about having the determination to make something positive out of yourself no matter what's put in your path."

Frank passes around several snapshots he had taken secretly when he last visited alumns at Little Joliet, the youth prison, and at Joliet State Prison. "It's one of the sad but essential tasks," Frank tells me later, "getting them ready to do time. Over the years almost all my students end up doing time, and even those who don't can use some disciplined self-reflection."

"Look at these arms," says Choco flexing toward me. Choco does push-ups all day long, pumps iron whenever possible. He's got a hard, buff body, and in his mind that will prepare him for prison.

"Choco," says Frank, "that won't get you ready for the joint. It's all about attitude, my friend, about mental toughness."

Frank stresses education. "You might want to get an associate degree. Here's one in food services, and they have them in law, and horticulture." He tells them the names of teachers to look for. "Don't wait for someone to come to you. Take charge of yourself. Ask, 'What classes are available?' 'Where's the library?' 'How many books can I take out?' 'What jobs or job training is there?' 'Sign me up or put me on the waiting lists.' 'I want my G.E.D.' 'I want to read, read, read!'"

"Knowledge is power," he says, "and I'm giving you a little knowledge about what to expect."

Frank says "knowledge is power" several times a day, and the students pick it up as a kind of class mantra. Ty reads a passage successfully, smiles and says, "Knowledge is power." Jefferson finishes a math assignment, and closing his book sighs, "Knowledge is power." Choco is putting his books away and he holds up his hand in mock salute: "Yeah, Tobs, I know knowledge is power." And Jamie, examining the diagram of a naked woman in a class on human sexuality, gives it a lustful, lascivious turn, purring, "Knowledge is power."

"Nobody's going to give a damn what you do once you leave this class," Frank says. "Nobody's going to care. If you hang with this group, you'll go down with them. If you hang with this other group, you'll go down with them. The gang won't help you, they don't care, but neither will the system, because they don't care either. You're being warehoused, thrown on the garbage heap. If you die and rot there, that's fine. If you get stupid and get hurt, that's OK, too. No one cares." He pauses for a long moment.

"But if *you* care," he says dramatically, "well, it's suddenly a different story with a different ending. If *you* care, everything changes. Then you start to make smart choices. Then you start to fashion a way out, and, once out, a way to survive. So the real question is, do *you* care enough about *you* to do your own time, to take charge of your time for *you?*"

4. Alex

I crawl from under
childhood's
dark table,
black tree
bleeding
spiraling to apogee,
broke doll yawning:
ma ma ma ma
childhood consumed.
black moon
rising,
eating up
the sky,
a survivor—
heading home,
to my own house.

Sapphire
"In My Father's House"

ALEX CORREA'S FIRST GLIMPSE of Frank Tobin was inauspicious. "Tobs was wearing rumpled clothes," Alex recalls—a short-sleeved, button-down shirt open at the collar, belt buckled way too high on his waist. "He had on bifocals and a pocket-protector. He looked like a complete wuss. I was all of fourteen, half a lifetime ago."

To Frank, Alex looked much like the long line of boys who had entered his classroom. Filled with grievance and rage, he had hurt someone and was, no doubt, capable of inflicting even greater injury. But he had surely been hurt as well, and, as with the others, Frank was determined to "find his goodness, to see God working through him."

Frank is short and shapeless—maybe five-nine—with a shock of white hair topping a reddish, round Irish mug. He was the only white guy in the room (Alex remembers), the only Anglo, the only adult. His eyes twinkled and he smiled easily, but still, Alex thought, considering this leprechaun chatting easily with a circle of goliaths, "If we're the toughest kids in Chicago, how come they gave us this pussy?"

"Nice to meet you, Alex. I'm Frank Tobin," Frank said, in his nasal, slightly squeaky voice, and extended his hand. "I'm sorry I can't talk to you just now, but have a seat over there, and I'll be with you in a couple of minutes."

Alex settled into a large red plastic chair, affected a look that he hoped was detached but hard, dispassionate but unyielding, and scrutinized the scene. The desks and chairs were sturdy and brightly colored—fire-engine red, electric blue, school-bus yellow. They looked cheerful and unbreakable, like furniture from a day-care center that had undergone a weird metamorphosis, inflated into equipment for giants. And the room was filled with giants—eleven of them, each one stronger, harder, more buff than the next. If he had been able to read their eyes he might have noticed the pain and the anger, the confusion mixed in with the fear, the abiding apprehension of chronically insecure adolescent boys. But mostly what he saw on that first day was man-sized arms and chests, taut and rippling. In the back of the room, next to a metal storage closet, sat a nice looking set of barbells and weights—toys for titans. While he felt squishy inside, he desperately projected the image of a coldblooded roughneck.

When Frank Tobin finished his conversation and turned toward Alex, he announced without fanfare, "We have a new student with us. This is Alex Correa, and I want you to welcome him." Alex nodded self-consciously as Frank turned with a gentle command: "OK, guys. Let's get some work done. I want everyone to finish up the math pages due this week. Some of you are done, I know. You can settle in and read your book. Whenever you finish your particular math pages, settle in with your books and if you get stuck in the next little while, check with Scott—Is that OK, Scott?—so I can have a little talk with Alex here."

Frank took Alex's arm and gently steered him to a corner near the back of the room, grabbing a chair along the way. He placed his chair directly in front of Alex's, and, as the busy sounds of the other students faded, Frank put his hand on Alex's arm and looked into his face for a long moment. "I heard you were coming, Alex, and I'm glad you're here." He paused, and Alex gave him as cold and bad a look as he could muster under the circumstances.

"I expect a lot of you here, Alex," Frank continued after a moment of silence. "This is a pretty relaxed space, and you can do things at your own speed. I won't try to force you to learn, but at the same time we might as well face the fact that we're locked in here together for six hours a day. If you don't bother anyone else, you can decide to just hang out quietly. But you can also decide to work hard, use this time to better yourself, get your education. That's what I would do. It's your choice, Alex. But whether you work or don't work, I want you here."

Another long silence. "OK, Mr. Tobin, whatever," Alex finally mumbled noncommittally.

"All the guys call me Tobs."

"OK, Tobs."

———

"This is Alex Correa," Frank says. "He was a student in this class not long ago, and I asked him to come and talk with you about his experiences and answer any questions you might have about doing time, Joliet, whatever." It's 9:15 and—miracle—everyone is present. Frank has smuggled Alex into class. It is against policy for ex-inmates to visit, so he has signed him in as a friend.

Today Alex is wired—broad face tensed, short, firm body flexed, bulging arms crossed over his extra large chest. Stiff as the Oscar statuette—metallic, golden, V-shaped—dressed in a sleeveless tee-shirt, gym shoes, and sweatpants, Alex is at attention, speaking to Tobs' class as a successful alumnus. In sharp contrast to his hard body, Alex's delivery is soft, gentle, and sweetly sad. The tension is all physical, while the voice is vulnerable, confessional. The students arch slightly toward him to catch his words. They are eager to hear him, and a little surprised at their eagerness. Alex is like them, but different—his story is also their story, but with a twist. He got out.

"The other kids in the joint called me 'Rocky,'" he says, "because I was up and running at daybreak. I did push-ups and crunchies every chance I got. I was in the gym with weights every free moment. I'd set a goal: I was going to get out of that hell I'd put myself in. Building myself up was a step, a step to being back on the outside." Alex did seven hard years in juvenile detention and adult prison. The goal-setting came somewhere mid-stream, after he'd established himself first in Little Joliet and then in adult prison as a tough guy. "I was a badass and nobody fucked with me. It took me a while, but slowly it dawned on me: I'm at the top of the heap, going nowhere."

Alex grew up in pain and trouble, and he spares no detail. His stepfather would be startled today to be told he was cruel or abusive or mean—those categories didn't exist for him. He was just a man doing what men do, controlling what men control, occupying a man's corner and possessing a man's inheritance, nothing but his own holdings. To Alex the old man was terror itself, a source of hurt and humiliation, arbitrary and unpredictable eruptions of fury. To remember the Alberto of Alex's youth is to summon up bedlam, wreckage, and whirlpools of rage. And remember he does, every item, the entire bill of particulars.

"We were new in Chicago, illegal immigrants, speaking no English," Alex recalls. "I went with my new stepfather to get groceries, and when we returned he told me to watch the car while he took some bags into our apartment. I was five or six, and I stood shivering by the car, frightened out of my mind, waiting for him to return. He was gone for a long long time, and I had a growing sense of lostness and of terror. What would I do if someone touched the car? Spoke to me? What about the cops? When he finally appeared on the street, I was overcome with relief, and I shouted and raced toward him. When I reached him he slapped me as hard as he could in the face and knocked me down. He growled, 'No me hizo caso. You disobeyed me!' He dragged me into the house and beat me with a belt until I bled."

Alex's thick eyebrows vault over his melancholy eyes. "I was happy to see him, and for that I was beaten senseless. And there was my mother in the next room," as always, somewhere in the background, weeping quietly, helpless, usually bleeding herself.

By eleven Alex was a hard-core alcoholic. The slide toward harder drugs—cocaine, crack, smack—was greased with speedballs and acid and reds. "I was looking for some anesthetics," Alex says matter of factly. Several students in Tobs's class nod unself-consciously, mesmerized. "I was in a torture chamber, and I needed some painkiller just to get up and get going."

Alex did get going. By twelve he was out of the house and living in the streets. Farewell to all that, he thought. Goodbye to the monster. New demons would welcome him, of course, but he didn't know that yet. For now he would be free, and he would kill the past. He would kill Alberto, too, he thought, when he was bigger. The Avenging Angel returning.

Freedom came with a price tag—major payments demanded with fierce regularity. "The hallways, the abandoned cars, the crawl spaces under the highways—these are mostly a blur now," Alex says. "The pain remains vivid. I had to survive and I did everything—snatching purses, knocking people in the head, breaking into newspaper boxes, selling my body to older men."

But it was never enough. Invariably another payment came due. And so the pulse and heartbeat of his existence became the steady rhythm of the urban hunter/gatherer: hustle and rob, eat, take your painkiller, crash, hustle and rob again. The rhythm was broken by illness, by occasional overnights to rest and dry out and clean up at his grandparents' apartment, and by increasingly frequent encounters with the police.

There were lots of kids like Alex on the streets, and they found each other. Once a petty thief, Alex was now part of a gang of thieves, unaffiliated with the powerful street gangs who run the drug trade, prostitution, and protection rackets, off the radar screen of the police gang unit, just a group of disorganized street thugs going nowhere, motivated by hunger and fueled by alcohol and drugs. They were a blundering band of refugees, screwy, absurd, but capable of lavish outbursts of violence. Alex had by now become a toxic mixture of narcissism, narcotics, and nihilism.

"I was young and I was small. I needed a reputation to get by, and I built one, crime by crime, deed by deed. Before long I became known as one crazy dude, a guy who would try anything, take any risk, go on any ride."

Older men began to employ Alex on a pay-per-job basis for home invasions, stickups, robberies. He was a perfect journeyman: fearless, eager to please, expendable. The jobs became more frequent and more intense, and Alex grew into them. For two years he developed his criminal crafts, honing his talents, growing more proficient. Each encounter with the law led to a stretch in the Audy Home, where he met more experienced felons, and a short stay in a group home, perhaps a foster home; then he went back to the streets until the next bust landed him at the Audy Home. And always there was the little gang. It was a life he knew, a cadence he could follow.

When he was fourteen he did a couple of stickups for a neighborhood tough named Jack Ireland. Jack was in his mid-twenties, a hardened criminal, a mean man to be feared. But he liked Alex, bought him dinner at a steakhouse once, and carried himself with a lot of swagger. Jack had bullets, blueprints, and brains. Alex provided the body. Oliver Twist and Fagin. It was a perfect marriage.

Alex and his Artful Dodger, an older kid named Dion, did a couple of jobs for Jack, and then Dion had an idea of his own. He had worked briefly for a guy who owned a restaurant. The guy followed a routine every night, returning home loaded with cash. When he came to Alex with a scheme to rob the guy, there was no reason to say no.

The guy would have a huge load of cash in a canvas bag, and he would leave his car at precisely 2:15 A.M., enter an empty hallway, and head up a flight of stairs—a perfect place for an ambush. The limit of their imaginative horizons was severe: the guy lived one block from Alex's parents and two blocks from Dion's. In any case, Dion had checked it out. Dion couldn't be seen, of course, but he had a gun that Jack had given him. Alex could use it to scare the guy. The pace quickened.

All day Alex felt sick. It was a cold, gray Chicago day and Alex was listless. He started popping pills around noon. By midnight he looked half-dead crouched behind the appointed stairs, twitching and shivering and flying high in his head. He waited. No one came. The sound of cars became more sporadic, the street noises began to dissipate. He nodded off, then snapped back, took another pill. He saw his stepfather in a blur round a corner down the block and he shivered. Suddenly the sound of a car purring to the curb. A car door opening and closing. Footsteps outside and then the hallway door opening. Alex is poised. The guy starts up the stairs. Alex comes from below, points the gun, and commands, a little too excitedly, "Freeze!" The guy turns and, never hesitating, leaps through the air at Alex, spread-eagle, skydiving. He looks like Batman. Boom! Boom! Boom! The guy hits Alex with a fierce, enormous thud, and then crumples, lifeless. Alex, shocked, terrified, scrambles out from the sickening weight, covered with blood, and careens out the door, flailing. The cold air slaps him to consciousness and he is sobbing, gasping, running. Around the first corner—bam— into the arms of two cops who'd been cruising and heard the shots. "Move and you're dead," came the orders. Alex stopped cold, realized he still had the gun, dropped it fast, and stood shaking.

Alex is carried calmly along in the steady flow of stormy words, vignettes, anecdotes leading to other stories. He is opening himself up, cutting back the skin, showing raw nerves and beneath that a roiling sea of emotion, unthinkable childhood experiences, seemingly unavoidable crises and confrontations. And still the voice is steady, calm. The tough kids, the students, are riveted. Last month a professional basketball player gave a motivational talk to these same kids, and they concentrated for about ten minutes and then drifted away. Alex, forty-five minutes and rolling, and no one has moved, no one has taken his eyes off him. Alex is so brutally honest, so authentic, so matter of fact in his talk that each kid feels personally pulled in. "You can get everything inside you can get outside—drugs, alcohol, sex, weapons. It's set up for you to go on living the same life you've been living. I sat in my cell and masturbated myself into a coma many days, took a pill, masturbated some more." Not a smile from the boys.

"Tobs told me not to sum up my life by one act," says Alex now. "'You're not a killer, Alex,' Frank would say. 'You're a human being. You've got a mind and you've got a heart. You've got a soul. Now you've got to make something of yourself. You've got to do something worthy of a human being.'" Alex is focused on the young toughs—people—before him, and his story is about being a kid, about hardship and struggle and redemption.

Alex ends with something Frank taught him, "I know you've got it tough. You can whine and say that it's all so cruel and unfair. You'd be right, but that won't take you anywhere. Or you can choose to get ahold of your life. Frank gave me a book once that moved me. The guy seemed to speak to me when he said, 'To live is to suffer; to survive is to find a meaning for that suffering.'" Alex chokes back a sob suddenly, without warning, and the kids catch their breaths. "Your opportunity is in the way you bear your burden. How you do it. Make a change in your life now." And he is done.

Jamie and Jefferson are wiping their eyes discreetly. Tyrone offers wearily, "You caught a break, man. Because my cousin's doing fifty years for just what you did, murder one."

"That's right," Alex responds evenly. "I caught a break. And your cousin didn't. There but for the grace of God go you and me. What about you? What are you going to do? Are you going to catch a break? That's what I worry about."

"Do you think Audy Home weakens you?" asks Choco.

"What do you mean?" Alex furrows his brow.

"I mean like telling you what to do and when to do it, and sort of protecting you, watching your back. On the bricks, who's going to watch your back?"

"In a way you're right," Alex responds. "Not so much for watching your back as for taking responsibility for yourself. Like you can get used to someone saying, 'Eat now,' 'Shower now,' 'Brush your teeth now,' 'Shit now.'" Everyone laughs. "You can turn a little passive, kind of mushy. Then if no one says, 'Eat,' you'll starve. So it's important, as I said, to set goals, to practice a discipline of some kind. For me it was running, working-out, staying focused, reading, getting my degrees, weight-training. I got kind of obsessed to where the guards thought I must be planning an escape. Run, run, run. Lift, lift, lift. They thought I was crazy, but who's crazy now?"

The weights have an amplified importance to a lot of students. Tobs's class is desirable in part because he has weights; his decision to let the kids work out describes part of his wisdom as a teacher. Ironically, new teachers are told by the school administration not to use weights. It will scare the constant visitors to see the boys getting stronger, as if physical well-being, strength, is the deciding factor in their criminal behavior. Their bodies play a bombastic part in their lives at this age;

working-out gives them visible proof of their control over some aspects of their lives and selves and of changes they can effect over time. For Alex it was literally a way out: he now runs his own small business as a personal trainer and fitness teacher.

"Did you ever get locked up on punishment?" asks Jamie, who spends an inordinate amount of time on punishment.

"I learned to control myself, but it took a lot of time. That was part of my self-training, my discipline. But before I figured it out I fought constantly. I smoked, I drank, I even had Tobs send me up once."

"That's right," remembers Frank. "It's rare for me to send anyone upstairs, but I did send you up."

Alex recalls smoking a smuggled joint in the back room during break, with fans blowing and a classmate standing sentry. No good. It stunk up the class and Frank exploded. "You were bright red, Tobs," Alex laughs. "I thought you might bust an artery right there."

"I was plenty angry," Frank replies. "You're right about that. Because I felt I wanted a relationship of trust with you, and you were violating that trust. I felt hurt."

"That's what you said. I remember you saying, 'I'm hurt,' and that surprised me. I didn't realize until then that I could hurt you in that way. It made a big impression."

The students watch the easy exchange. There is laughter, glee, admiration.

"I'm sure I said to Alex what I always tell you. I want you here, but if you're telling me you don't want to be here, well OK. I'm not forcing you to do anything, and when you want to be here, come on back. I'd love to have you back."

Teachers here sometimes send students up on punishment for not working. In light of Frank's speech it seems even sillier and more contradictory.

"Luck and chance and breaks are all part of it," says Alex. "But bad breaks or good, there are always choices to make, always goals to reach for. I got a little knowledge and that made me a more powerful person. That led to me getting more knowledge and more power. I just want to keep on growing."

In unison the class chants: "Knowledge is power."

5. Mediated Images: Media, Crime, and Kids

IN EARLY 1996 the *Chicago Tribune* told a story of monstrous propor-
tions. "Father charged in 'hellish' abuse," bellowed the banner front-
page headline. "Child abuse reports come these days with a numbing
frequency; always sad, frequently sick and often depraved," the story
began. "But what authorities claim happened for more than four years
in one South Side family still has the power to shock." A stunned community felt its moorings shift; the rock of its most cherished assumptions about parental bonds and family responsibility and elemental
human decency began to heave and shake. And not for the first time.

What had happened?

"Four children beaten, sexually assaulted, injected with drugs and
fed rats and roaches, over and over again."

The story details a 1,238 count indictment brought by the office of
State's Attorney Jack O'Malley against the father of two of the children, a man who had been arrested and held for over two months, and
the mother, who had been in custody for several days: "The children,
prosecutors said, were fed, 'as a regular diet,' skinned and boiled rats,

rolled in flour and deep-fried. They also allegedly were fed cockroaches boiled and served with hot sauce."

Further, "all four children had evidence of hypodermic needle tracks," and one child had a burn on her leg, the "result of an attempt by her mother to cover up needle marks by lighting a piece of paper and burning the child's skin."

I read the story early, before even a cup of coffee, and it blew my mind: A predictable reaction I think. So when my wife came into the kitchen a few minutes later, and I read her the highlights, I was surprised that she looked neither shocked nor alarmed. In fact she looked bored and irritated. With one hand on her hip, her head cocked skeptically to the left and her eyes frowning sleepily, she offered a matter-of-fact one-word response: "Lies."

Bernardine Dohrn has worked in and around Juvenile Court for many years, written a series of law review articles and popular pieces on issues of family law and juvenile justice, and, most important for me, is my steady and perceptive guide into the murky world of the Court. Still, I needed some elaboration from her.

"This is a fantasy case that exists somewhere in the space between Jack O'Malley's political ambition and the *Tribune* writers' lurid imaginations," she went on. "What's happening out there is bad enough, but it's overwhelmingly about poverty and related problems—drugs, violence, mental breakdown. Deal with poverty in a serious and sustained way and Juvenile Court could be closed. Deep-fried rats? Roaches with hot sauce? A thousand count indictment? That's about headlines. It's off the deep end. Lies."

But while it may not be the typical case, I argued, it certainly is possible.

"Let's start with the facts and move toward the headline," she responds. "A little more than a third of the investigations of abuse and neglect result in substantiated findings. In those cases that can be substantiated, a large majority are neglect cases, and most of those are linked to poverty and drugs: Mom leaves the young kids alone, goes to the store, and a fire starts. Mom gets sick for several days and the baby hasn't got proper food. Mean lives, mean circumstances, less than perfect outcomes." This is a start.

"Terrible, yes," she goes on, "but not a headline-grabber like the distraught girl who throws her newborn out the window, or the family so whacked out on drugs that they're completely dysfunctional, except at dinnertime when they can catch a rat, skin and clean it, roll it in flour, deep-fry it, and serve it up as the main course. Roaches and hot sauce as a side dish. It's an apocalyptic tale, and it's going to turn out to be garbage."

I'm not so sure. But the front-page headline the very next day reads, "Abuse reports a lie, 3 kids insist." A lie, just as Bernardine had said. But not so fast. The following day, same prominent place, "Doctors not backing down." The examiners at Mount Sinai Medical Center defend their investigation and their conclusions. And so it goes, back and forth, day after day.

Patrick Murphy, a politically connected Cook County public guardian who ran for O'Malley's job and lost, is well known in child advocacy circles for his attack-dog style and his artful public statements; he weighs in regularly with opinions and commentary. When the children recant the abuse stories, and one is quoted as saying, "We didn't eat no rats. That's crazy," Murphy responds, "I trust the Mt. Sinai reports. . . . They are the Gospel as far as I'm concerned. . . . Kids recanting is not unusual, especially when relatives have a shot at them."

Finally, more than two weeks after the initial story surfaced, the *Tribune* reports that the couple has been released from jail and that "prosecutors were acknowledging that their case is in jeopardy of collapse." It turns out there is no medical evidence of sexual abuse and no mention in the Mt. Sinai reports of either needle tracks or rats—big items in the state's attorney's press release. The children lived in poverty, yes, and they were apparently abandoned two years before, prompting the Illinois Department of Children and Family Services (DCFS) to place them with their oldest brother. Now, because of O'Malley and Murphy's rigorous pursuit, the children have been moved again, this time into foster care. In an editorial entitled, "The incredible shrinking abuse case," the *Tribune* concluded, "Child sex abuse is an abominable crime, deserving of the most aggressive prosecution and the stiffest punishment. But more than a few judicial abominations have been committed by cowboy prosecutors pursuing child abusers who weren't. We can't say that [the parents] really aren't abusers. Unfortunately, neither can we say that Jack O'Malley isn't a cowboy."

As a "true-life" mini-series or a media "docudrama" the case is closed. The criminal abuse charges fell apart, as Bernardine said they would, and there was almost certainly child neglect, as she had also predicted. Now as a news consumer I suppose I'm expected to turn the page and wait for the next entertaining offering. But it feels suddenly wrong. The caricature of mistreatment and cruelty eclipsed, in a sense, the serious problem of the real abuse and neglect that occurs daily in our society by turning my attention from the reality to myth. The whole spectacle must have played havoc in the lives of this family as the entire city peered in at them day after day. Everyone must feel a bit ripped off: first horrified but not informed, then perhaps relieved but not enlightened. Bitter, not engaged. I know I do.

At roughly the same time another chilling story involving children and justice was competing for front-page space as it lurched unhappily toward a kind of conclusion. This story, too, had stretched the limits of believability, raised questions of culpability, vulnerability, and responsibility, and had played in garish headlines across the country for two years. It is the story of Eric Morse, five years old, dropped to his death from a public housing apartment by a ten and an eleven-year-old who had demanded that he steal for them. Now it is ending: in this instance the state's attorney had proven his case in court and the judge had found the two boys "delinquent," the euphemism for guilty. Having convicted the youngsters, the problem narrowed: what to do with the now twelve and thirteen-year-olds who had become celebrity killers. This became a popular question and a public concern shaped by the media.

The *Tribune's* front-page headline posed the question this way: "Is there any real hope for young killers?" Although focused on a particular case, the headline is ambiguous; it could be a cynic's rhetorical question about all of juvenile justice or a philosopher's dilemma. The second head reads, "Kids who dropped boy to death face treatment or youth prison." A Juvenile Court judge has been holding an extraordinary sentencing hearing for several days, listening to testimony from prison officials, social workers, teachers, psychiatrists. The judge is under intense scrutiny, nationally and locally, and a lot of political pressure—whatever she decides will be criticized and second-guessed. She pushes all sides to respond to the complexity of the thing: How will the youngsters "work through" this? Where will they get treatment? What programs will allow them to explore remorse and accountability?

The DCFS lawyer was reported in the article to have recommended prison, arguing that regardless of the age of the perpetrators, "there are situations where rehabilitation has to take a back seat to punishment. These two individuals are so violent, aggressive, and out of control that the only viable alternative is the Department of Corrections." A lawyer for one of the boys responded, "The whole purpose of Juvenile Court is rehabilitation. These kids are not unreconstructable. If we give up on kids who are eleven, twelve, and thirteen years old, then we may as well shut down this building." The debate, in the words of the *Tribune* story, is "whether to treat Morse's victimizers as children or as predators."

I saw both boys in detention several times. The older boy tried hard in school, seemed protective of the younger one, fit in to the routine. The younger boy seemed scared out of his mind—he interpreted every gesture as an attack or provocation, every glance as an unwanted intrusion—and he affected the stance the world seemed to demand of him: tough, out of control, menacing. That he was a little shorty—small, vulnerable, considerably younger than most residents—didn't help matters.

I also witnessed an intense early morning encounter between some staff and the superintendent of the facility when the two were first residents. The staff wanted the two boys isolated, locked down, kept out of school, and fed in isolation, because, as one put it, "These two are simply evil." The superintendent listened patiently to each complaint, took notes, and then calmly reminded them of Audy Home's larger purpose: "I hear your concerns, but please remember two facts. First, this is a temporary detention center, and each child held here is presumed innocent. There has been no determination in this case. We cannot make that determination—that is the job of the Court. We have no right to judge them because of something we read in the newspapers. Second, we work here to take care of children who cannot at this point take care of themselves. We will—each of us—give these two the very best we have to give." Case closed.

Predictably, both youths have half-a-dozen prior arrests: shoplifting, burglary, theft, weapons violations, drug possession. Both are achingly poor, desperately neglected, throwaway kids. The father of the youngest boy, just out of prison for a drug conviction himself, attended the hearing and said outside the courtroom: "A twelve-year-old doesn't belong in prison. It wouldn't help him. What kind of future will he have? He won't have a future."

In the end the judge sentences the boys to juvenile prison—an historic decision that is the first use of an Illinois law allowing children as young as ten to be imprisoned, lowering the age from fourteen. "They got Docked,"—removed to D.O.C., the Department of Corrections—in the vernacular of Audy Home, and it was no surprise to anyone. The new law allowing them to be jailed was passed in reaction to Eric Morse's death and the case of Robert "Yummy" Sandifer, an eleven-year-old who allegedly aimed at a rival gang member and accidentally shot and killed Shavon Dean, a fourteen-year-old girl, in 1994. He in turn was shot and killed by two young boys (said to be fellow gang members dispatched to silence him) a few days later while on the run. The *Tribune* applauded the sentence, saying, "With offenders as remorseless and predatory as these, a judge's first concern must be to protect the rest of society from them." Noting that these boys will be on the street when they turn twenty-one, the *Tribune* pushes toward something tougher: "the theoretical basis for our different ways of handling adult criminals and juvenile delinquents is being challenged by the harrowing reality of young superpredators like Eric's killers. The violence of their crimes and the apparent hardness of their hearts mock our notions of 'treatment' and 'rehabilitation.' Increasingly, we wonder not whether they can be saved, but whether we can save ourselves from them."

Once again a caricature discourages careful consideration and serious thought. The horror of this particularly grotesque act completely fills our collective consciousness, becomes emblematic of all juvenile crime, and leaves virtually no space to understand and combat the reality of juvenile delinquency. It distorts the public discussion, confuses and enervates people, leaves us shaken but resigned.

————

Common sense tells us that teen crime is a runaway train—reckless and out of control, unpredictably dangerous, picking up speed as it careens down the tracks toward our town or neighborhood. We read in *Newsweek* about teenagers being "wild in the streets" and in *U.S. News and World Report* of "a ticking demographic time bomb" involving "scary kids around the corner." *Time* headlines "A Teenage Time Bomb" and reports: "They are just four, five, and six years old right now, but already they are making criminologists nervous. . . . By the year 2005 they will be teenagers—a group that tends to be . . . 'temporary sociopaths—impulsive and immature.'" "This is the calm before the storm," *Time* quotes one criminologist predicting as he ponders the recent downturn in crime nationwide. "So long as we fool ourselves into thinking that we're winning the war against crime, we may be blindsided by this bloodbath of teenage violence that is lurking in the future."

With repetition these opinions take on the luster of Truth. In a front-page *Sun-Times* story headlined "Shootings in City Drop," the big news is not the decline in violence, but rather the prediction that this is "the lull before the storm" (again), and that "a population bubble [is] coming our way in which the violence-prone 15-to-29 age group" may well bring with them a "40% increase in murder nationwide." This kind of hyperbolic, fevered reporting has a measurable impact: according to a 1994 Gallup Poll, the average American adult thought that teenagers under 18 committed 43% of violent crime; the true figure is 13%.

Of course nothing is harder to disprove than received "wisdom." In spite of that, this dire prediction, based on the common belief that demographics is destiny, is incorrect.

Mike Males, from the University of California, Irvine, argues that poverty, not age, correlates most decisively with crime: "Adjusted for poverty, 13-to-19-year-olds have almost the same crime rate as people in their 40s, and have a crime rate well below that of those in their 20s and 30s." Similarly, adjusting "the crime rate for the number of individuals living in extreme poverty, non-whites have a crime rate similar to that of whites at every age level." Males points out that murder rates in the United States are always higher when poverty is more widespread: "during the Great Depression murder spiraled upward—peaking in 1933 with a rate of 9.7 murders per 100,000, higher than 1993's 9.5 per 100,000 rate." Even the scary *Time* article nods an aside in Males's direction: "Though crime and unemployment don't rise and fall perfectly in tandem, policy makers recognize that people without jobs are a crime wave waiting to happen." Males points out that "the U.S. raises three to eight times more children in poverty than any other Western nation," and "has the largest and fastest-growing gap in income between its richest 5% and poorest 5% of any industrial country." Furthermore, the story of scary kids preying on hapless adults has put reality on its head. Most murder victims under eighteen are killed by adults: 70% of the murderers of children in 1994 were adults. Moreover, "parents are six times more likely to murder their teenage children than the other way around." Males estimates that seven million American children a year are "subjected to at least one 'severe violent act'"—punched, scalded, burned, threatened with a knife or a gun—at the hands of their parents. In one year, 1993, when "350,000 juveniles were arrested for violent felonies and misdemeanors" in the United States, "370,000 children and youth were confirmed victims of violent and sexual offenses perpetrated by their parents or caretakers." The link is obvious: violence against children generates violent children; child abuse "increases the number of violent criminals by 38%, and raises the national crime volume by over 60%."

Superpredators have entered our lives through our language—the word precedes the reality, the image tends to shape the facts. As defined by Bob Greene, the popular columnist for the *Chicago Tribune* syndicated in over two hundred newspapers and read daily by millions of people, superpredators are "increasingly more violent young people who not only commit crimes and acts of violence in dismaying numbers, but who do it with no apparent sense of remorse." He cites the grim projections: "the superpredators will multiply not because they have rejected right and chosen wrong—but because they recognize no difference between right and wrong." Greene is echoing James Q. Wilson, a public policy professor at UCLA who writes of young offenders who "show us the blank, unremorseful stare of a feral, presocial being," and, most insistently, John J. DiIulio, Jr., a criminologist at Princeton who writes of a national "wolf pack" of "fatherless, godless, and jobless" youth. DiIulio's distorted representations of youth undoubtedly have reductive power. We are left with an archetype, a pernicious image of violent youth (overwhelmingly black), of the Other, of a child unlike any we have ever known.

John DiIulio projects 270,000 more superpredators by the year 2010 and argues for massive juvenile prison expansion to be ready for them. Frank Zimring, the only criminologist who seems to have examined DiIulio's numbers, points out that DiIulio simply takes the projected increase in the number of boys in the US under eighteen from about 32 million to 36.5 million in the next fourteen years. Noting that 6% of all boys account for half of all police contacts, DiIulio multiplies 4.5 million additional male children by 0.06 and gets 270,000. Zimring observes, "if six percent of all males under 18 are superpredators, that means we currently have over 1.9 million juvenile superpredators in our streets (32 million boys x 0.06 = 1,920,000). We would hardly notice another 270,000 by 2010. But the total estimate of current superpredators we obtain by this method is about twice as many as the total number of kids referred to juvenile court last year for anything at all."

Zimring demonstrates that a larger percentage of DiIulio's superpredators will be under six than over thirteen in 2010, and as many will be under three as over fifteen. Zimring calls these imaginary superpredators "desperadoes in diapers."

Of course the power of DiIulio's campaign is that it requires no correspondence with fact, no link to reality. If crime rates increase, DiIulio was right. If crimes rates decrease, DiIulio's warning was heeded, and he was right again.

New York's Bernard Goetz, the reclusive and pale electrical consultant, had locked onto the superpredator image when, confronted by four young black men demanding $5 in 1984, he pulled an unregistered pistol and coolly shot each one, including one in the back as he scrambled for the door, and became known as the subway vigilante.

Goetz was acquitted of criminal charges in 1987 by an all-white jury that apparently bought the depiction of Goetz as a law-abiding, embattled citizen, and the four youngsters as dangerous street criminals and superpredators. Twelve years later, in a civil suit, Goetz was asked by the lawyer representing one of the shooting victims—a man paralyzed in the incident and seeking $50 million in damages—"You made the decision to kill when you saw the shine in [his] eyes?." Goetz replied, "And the smile on his face. . . . It was that shine and that smile that set me off."

According to the *New York Times*, Goetz stated that the shootings could be seen as a kind of public service. Asked if he had indeed said that the mothers of the four should have had abortions, he said, "It would have been better off than the situation we have now."

Goetz had pulled his gun on others before he shot the four. He described confronting a man he thought was threatening him, and his pleasure as the man "turned a shade of gray . . . his knees . . . buckling." He pulled a gun on a youth who, he said, was verbally threatening him, and, when asked if he thought the youth should die, replied, "Well, maybe that would make the world a better place." By the time of the subway shooting Goetz was a hate-filled, frightened, aggressive man, stoking his paranoia with drugs. In his testimony, he even compared the shooting to a drug trip: "I've never experienced anything quite like it. . . . Everything—a flood of emotions. One's perception of reality changes."

———

The *Tribune* editorials in both the rat-eating and the superpredator cases cast blame this way and that—abominations on both your houses—while deftly avoiding any deep reflection or self-criticism in the matter. There are rotten parents out there, it asserts, and overly zealous prosecutors; there are superpredators and a frightened public. We in the concerned but sensible and objective middle are watching the spectacle disapprovingly. At a safe distance we can remain indifferent much of the time, horrified, outraged, and full of sentimentality at select moments. It's a stance editorial writers and readers alike can embrace.

What is missing here, of course, is any serious analysis of the violent conditions in which children find themselves, of juvenile crime or child abuse itself—their scope and scale and history, causes and effects, and meaning in a larger social context. The relation between juvenile crime and a life of abuse and neglect is unexamined. Robert Sandifer, for example, was found guilty of armed robbery at nine, arson and auto theft at ten, and was charged with a felony a month during the last year of his life. Superpredator? But he also had a long history of being abused and neglected, and first came to the attention of DCFS caseworkers when he was three. Victim? There is something obscene about winking at the unspeakable conditions of children's lives, and then being shocked and horrified at the death of a child victim—Robert Sandifer, Eric Morse, or Joseph Wallace—and grieving for him once he's dead.

The personal, singular, sense-making subject is also silent in the editorials. We all disapprove of the actions of politically motivated prosecutors, and we all deplore the behavior of *those* parents and children and families, but we conveniently erase ourselves from the picture. The story we tell ourselves about others is fascinating, and that story, if looked at from a different angle, might reveal us in new ways to ourselves.

As a teacher I've been aware of the stories we tell about teaching and how those stories tell us. A typical story is the hero-teacher, the lone individual who fights the backward parents, the hopeless colleagues, and the sewer of society to redeem the good juvenile delinquent. Popular films, from *Blackboard Jungle* to *Stand and Deliver*, repeat this tired tale. While it's a cliché, its impact is potent: like people of a certain age and background describing a childhood lived in a *Leave It to Beaver* family—editing out the alcoholic neighbor, the tormented gay uncle, the teen suicide just across the street—teachers themselves, whose lives are a kaleidoscope of nuanced and particular stories, refer to James Olmos and Michelle Pfeiffer and Sidney Poitier as if they were colleagues. The mediated image elbows aside actual experience, animates and transcends who we know we are—in spite of ourselves.

Recently I spent some time with my active ninety-two-year-old father-in-law in a retirement community. One of his daily routines is watching the five-o'clock news, and so we watched and commented together, day after day. There was, of course, sports (a gamble), stocks (speculation), and weather (out of control). But mostly what we saw was that the five o'clock news tells a single story over and over on what seems like a continuous feed. The story is this: you have a chance of falling victim to a random act of violence, wreckage, or mayhem, or, conversely, (and this is a much smaller story) you might win the lottery. We counted up the stories: one evening a murder, a huge warehouse fire, a bank robbery with hostages; the next evening, two murders, a gas explosion, and a rape. And on and on. Nothing that we saw on the news was the result of human effort or agency or sustained hard work or commitment or thoughtful analysis or efficacy; everything was accident, fate, fortune.

The message conveyed by all this speaks to something deep in the modern predicament: the sensation of incapacity and alienation, the awful feeling of impotence, the suspicion that a desolate, frightening landscape lies just outside, the impression that nothing you do matters or means anything or could possibly make a palpable difference. In any case our stories echo our anxieties and our fears, take root in our lives, perform particular roles in a larger social play.

The myths surrounding Juvenile Court provide standards of reassurance for the rest of us. Mostly the myths are constructed through a steady drumbeat of B-section, page three fillers: two youths shot on the South Side, three children found living in filth are taken into custody, a baby is beaten to death. But sometimes a combination of factors—"slow news day," gruesome pictures, fantastic details—conspire to create a big, big story, and then we find a tale to give a kind of counterfeit coherence to drive the everyday stories. Amanda Wallace, for example, mother of three-year-old Joseph Wallace, became a national symbol when she hung her son with an extension cord in 1993. Joseph was the sixteenth child murdered in the Chicago area that year, the fifth murdered by a parent. Amanda Wallace—who herself had been a ward of DCFS, sexually abused, locked in a basement as routine punishment, beaten with a hammer as a child—had a long history of mental illness. One week before the murder she set her apartment on fire. State psychiatrists reported that she was severely disturbed, ate batteries and lightbulbs, drank Drano, inserted soda cans into her vagina at least once while pregnant, and on and on.

Wallace stood trial after other psychiatrists convinced a judge that she was a "malingerer" who was "manipulating the system." She took the stand and described wrapping a cord around Joseph's neck five times, standing him on a chair, and attaching the cord to a transom over a door: "I told him, 'Bye.' . . . He waved at me . . . and told me, 'Bye.'" She was convicted of murder, and the state's attorney asked for the death penalty.

The famous "Keystone 19" case in 1994 was another Chicago media event that fed the national news for several days: drug officers entered a West Side building and discovered nineteen children in an apartment without a working stove or refrigerator sleeping several to a mattress on the floor. It turned out that the crowded conditions were the result of the tenant's generosity: she had allowed one sister and her family to move in when they were evicted from a nearby apartment, and two other sisters and their children to move in after a fire destroyed their building. So it might have been a story of tenaciousness, resourcefulness, and family bonds, but the storytellers set the scene on the first day— filth, neglect, drugs, promiscuity. In an echo of Louie in *Casablanca* closing down Rick's with the memorable line, "I'm shocked, shocked to find that there's gambling going on" as he collects his winnings, President Clinton expressed amazement and horror that anyone in America lived in those conditions. I felt like screaming, "Look out your window. Walk four blocks from the White House." Most important, nineteen people were brought forth from obscurity, held up to public, lip-smacking scrutiny, and the short-lived entertainment value of their circumstances played against the complexity of their lived reality.

The problem here is in part paralysis. The monstrousness of Wallace, the extravagance of Keystone, leave us horrified, disgusted, and powerless. It is either too big or too outlandish or both. As consumers of mediated images we need to be mindful that there is always something more, something beneath the headline, beyond the spectacle. We should remember that the mediated image is voyeuristic and full of the thrill of danger, and wonder why there is no comparable, sustained story focused on the suffering of children. The designated monster—the rat-chef, the superpredator—the manifestation of evil, of sickness, of depravity, may signal back to us that we are healthy and good and well, but the symbolic brute sings a siren song of normalcy for the rest of us.

"Goodbye guys," I call to our three sleepy-looking sons gathered around bagels, juice, and the morning sports pages. "I love you. See you tonight."

I'm out the door, on my bike, off to Juvenile Court—about an eight-mile ride. We live in Hyde Park-Kenwood south of the Loop on the lake. In a tree across the street I see two green parrots, mutant urban birds descended from escaped pets decades ago, now perfectly happy winter or summer. It's said that many Hyde Parkers have a bit of the mutant parrot in them.

Once a summer colony, Hyde Park is today dominated by the University of Chicago. It is home to the famous Museum of Science and Industry (the coal mine, the chickens hatching constantly), the Oriental Institute, and the DuSable Museum of African-American History. Other important institutions include Jesse Jackson's Operation Push, Doc Films, 57th Street Books, and the Hyde Park-Kenwood Little League, which brings a joyful crowd of children and families to the park across from our house every summer evening. Hyde Park boasts the world's thickest concentration of Nobel Laureates and thinnest selection of good restaurants. Mike Nichols once described Hyde Park as "the only racially integrated neighborhood in Chicago," and then added caustically, "it's black and white shoulder to shoulder against the poor." There's painful truth in that description as the powerful university and its allied neighborhood association have worked to manipulate boundaries and borders to assure "stability" and separation. Our neighbors include Muhammad Ali, former mayor Eugene Sawyer, poets Gwendolyn Brooks and Elizabeth Alexander, and writer Barack Obama. Minister Louis Farrakhan lives a block from our home and adds, we think, a unique dimension to the idea of "safe neighborhood watch": the Fruit of Islam, his security force, has an eye on things twenty-four-hours a day. I pass Farrakhan's mansion, offer a cheery wave to the Fruit, get a formal nod in response, and turn north two blocks across 47th Street, into the lap of urban blight.

To my right the lake, a shining sea of blues and greens, Navy Pier, all glitter and silver light jutting a half mile into the lake, museums, planetarium, giant ferris wheel way up in the middle of the air, a fairy-land skyline. To my left, vacant lot, vacant lot, vacant lot, abandoned building, vacant lot. Here a knot of young men stand around a stoop talking and passing a bottle. A little further on, a makeshift tire repair business operates from behind a ragged fence. Another large empty space—once a substantial community church, then headquarters and Mosque #1 to Jeff Fort's powerful El Rukn Nation street gang—the result of a police seizure and subsequent demolition. I pass the building where Eric Morse lived, the exact spot where he was dropped to his death. I hang a left and shoot past a legendary blues club, toward Comisky Park, home of the White Sox.

Just south I see the Robert Taylor Homes, named for the first head of the Chicago Housing Authority whose daughter, a neighbor and friend, is president of the Erikson Institute. Freddie was arrested at Robert Taylor; so was Andrew.

Wendell Phillips High School.

Pilgrim Missionary Baptist Church.

Harvest Memorial Church.

Dave's Liquors.

Here is a spot where two plainclothes cops stopped me while I was picking up a friend at her apartment and checked my I.D. at gunpoint two years ago. One of the cops asked, "What are you doing in a neighborhood like this?"

And here is the vacant lot where last summer two groups of kids clashed with baseball bats just as I was pedaling past at ten at night. I saw and flagged a squad car only seconds later, and, miracle!, the cops prevented what might have been a blood bath.

I head north on Martin Luther King, Jr. Boulevard, and remember the old caveat that when they name a street or a school after you, you're either safe or dead. For the first time I have the benefit of a little bike lane designated on the right side of the road. Small consolation amidst the aggressive buses and careening auto traffic, the lane disappears fifty feet before each intersection, making it less than useless.

I am in Richard Wright's Chicago, Nikki Giovanni's Chicago, the Chicago of Dreiser and Sandburg and Terkel. It is a city of contrasts, a site of contradiction and contention. It soars and plunges, builds you up and tears you down, offers opportunities and slaps you as it slams the door. It can be liberating or constraining, pulsing with positive energy or vibrating with danger. It asks you to choose between engagement and alienation, hope and paranoia, solidarity and solipsism. Nelson Algren in his love song to the city wrote:

> Not that there's been any lack of honest men and women sweating out Jane Addams' hopes here—but they get only two outs to the inning while the hustlers are taking four. When Big Bill Thompson put in the fix for Capone he tied the town to the rackets for keeps . . .

> Yet the Do-Gooders still go doggedly forward, making the hustlers struggle for their gold week in and week out, year after year, once or twice a decade tossing an unholy fright into the boys. And since it's a ninth-inning town, the ball game never being over till the last man is out, it remains Jane Addams' town as well as Big Bill's. The ball game isn't over yet.

A hard left. Abandoned building, boarded-up storefront, vacant lot, storefront church, bar. Suddenly a small house with beautifully tended rose bushes and wisteria. I pass the clubhouse of the Windy City Motorcycle Club—old guys on Harleys. Just north is the spot where Mario was arrested and charged with attempted carjacking. A little north and west and I am on the street where Jesus was arrested.

Left on Roosevelt Road, over the Illinois Central tracks. I love this bridge—beautiful *beaux-arts* streetlights and little bronze globes covered with porpoises, dinosaurs, and exotic animals, a bike lane that narrows as I ride until it disappears to a point midspan. Incredible.

I pass Jane Addams's Hull House, now a museum, the fire department training academy (built on the exact spot where the great Chicago fire began over a century ago), the old Maxwell Street Market, St. Ignatius Prep School, then pull up in front of Juvenile Court. Thirty-five minutes.

All my life people have told me not to ride in the city—too dangerous, too hostile. That's not my experience. From the air Chicago looks like a grid of light, and from a car it can become a series of freeze-frames, a blur. At ground level it is more vivid, more various, more colorful, more human. I choose to live in a city where riding my bike is a possibility—where seeing and listening and touching helps build a sense of community—and so I do it. I don't want to rely on more distant images to tell me about a place minutes from my home.

6. Ito

Sit down. Inhale. Exhale.
The gun will wait. The lake will wait.
The tall gall in the small seductive vial
will wait will wait:
will wait a week: will wait through April.
You do not have to die this certain day.
Death will abide, will pamper your postponement.
I assure you death will wait. Death has
a lot of time. Death can
attend to you tomorrow. Or next week. Death is
just down the street; is most obliging neighbor;
can meet you any moment.

You need not die today.
Stay here—through pout or pain or peskyness.
Stay here. See what the news is going to be tomorrow.

Graves grow no green that you can use.
Remember, green's your color. You are Spring.

Gwendolyn Brooks
"To the Young Who Want to Die"

M ERCE'S HAIRCUT IS SHARP—shaved clean along the sides, a radical fade tapering out to a wide-angled, abundant flat top, two
stripes chiseled into the foreground, just left of center. He's walking
tall. "Morning, Mr. B," he smiles.

"Morning, Merce," replies Mr. B, and then, without a pause and with
a spreading smile, "Say, that haircut really suits you. Looks good on you."

Merce straightens up, even taller and sharper. "Yeah. I finally got
Scissorhands to do it right. Last time he was trippin', so I was careful to
keep him calm before my turn." Mr. Glen, Scissorhands, is a regular
feature of the landscape here, like lining up, showering on schedule,
walking the line in the halls. He has a reputation for sculpting his feelings into the heads of his conscripted clients.

Merce—in this, his third encounter with Scissorhands—has figured
out how to play it for results, and not simply the last word. His first
time to the barber resulted in a ragged mess, after Merce told Mr. Glen
that if he were a real hair stylist, he'd have himself a business and be

85

making real money, and not traveling the units. That comment was not only counter-productive, but wrong. Mr. Glen owns a lot of real estate and runs two barbershops. Like a lot of people here Mr. Glen comes out of a desire to give back.

Merce goes to County on his seventeenth birthday in a few weeks. "I'll just take it as it comes," he sighs. "Lots of people telling me, 'Do this,' 'Do that!' to where I don't know what to expect. I don't want to go, but I got to go. What I can do? So I'll take it as it comes. I'll figure it out when I get there."

He is quiet, resigned. While life here is boring, depressing, gloomy in many ways, it is also predictable and safe. There are even some bright spots, occasional friends, relationships with a couple of caring adults like Mr. B or Mr. Williams or Mrs. Anderson. It's a protected harbor between what was—gangs, guns, drugs, imminent death—and what may be again. For Merce it's time to leave, and behind his smile he blinks back tears, a reminder that he is suspended between childhood and adulthood, a passage tough enough to negotiate with a thick safety net firmly in place. For Merce there is no safe support, and yet there are bridges that must be crossed, and soon.

———

Today Mr. B's class begins reading a short story called "The Kind of Light that Shines on Texas," by Reginald McKnight. The class is conducted round-robin style with everyone reading silently along at his desk as one and then another student is called upon by Mr. B to read aloud. The range of reading ability is vast, and yet everyone is patient and accepting. Mario, possibly the most fluent reader and certainly the most mature and articulate student in this class, corrects mispronunciations and missed words routinely and without flair or apparent judgment. He attends to the text, rarely looking up, and his intervention is never a show, never a putdown. He simply inserts corrections seamlessly where needed.

Zo begins reading word by word in monotone: "I never liked Marvin Pruitt. Never liked him, never knew him, even though there were only three of us in the class. Three black kids. In our school there were fourteen classrooms of thirty-odd white kids (in '66 they considered Chicanos pro . . ." [he halts and stumbles a bit, and Mario adds, "provisionally"] "provisionally white) and three or four black kids. Primary school in primary colors. Neat division." Pause.

"Alphabetized," says Mario. "Alphabetized. They didn't stick us in the back, or arrange us by degrees of hue, apartheid-like. This was real integration, a ten-to-one ratio as tidy as upper-class landscaping. If it all worked out you could have ten white kids all to yourself. They could talk to you, get the feel of you, scrutinize you bone deep if they wanted to. They seldom wanted to, and that was fine with me for two reasons. The first was that their scrutinizing was irritating. How do you comb your hair—why do you comb your hair—may I please touch your hair—were the kinds of questions they asked. This is no way to feel at home. The second reason was Marvin. He embarrassed me. He smelled bad, was at least two grades behind, was hostile, dark skinned, homely, close-mouthed. I feared him for his size, pitied him for his dress, watched him all the time. Marveled at him, mystified, astonished, uneasy."

"All right, Zo," Mr. B cuts in, "what is happening here?"

"Dude don't like Marvin Pruitt. He smells."

"Who is 'Dude'?" asks Mr. B.

"The one telling the story. What do you call it?"

"The narrator," says Mr. B.

"Right. The narrator."

"Mr. B," says Oscar. "Mr. B, I don't think he doesn't like Marvin. I think he's unsure what to think, because, like he says, he never knew him. And he surely doesn't like the white kids."

"Where it says that?" Merce challenges. "I don't see that."

"Well, he says the white kids never talked to him, which was fine."

"But he doesn't say he doesn't like them."

Mario enters the fray. "All we know really is that the narrator telling this is 'uneasy'. He's uneasy being with so many whites, and he's uneasy being with Marvin. Let's go on."

"Mr. B," says Ito, "this part about 'scrutinize you bone deep' makes him uneasy too. It makes me think about what we talked about last week with people coming through here scrutinizing us." Ito smiles, satisfied at his laserlike connection to an earlier conversation about the parade of visitors cycling regularly through the jail and the school—

sometimes up to three tour groups a day. Ito had complained that it made him feel like a monkey in the zoo, and Mr. B had agreed.

Ito is no whiner, but he pays close attention to what happens to him, and he shares his critique with Mr. B, with his mom, with me, and in a steady stream of letters to friends. Early in his stay he wrote this:

Dear Pablo,

Okay my friends today I want to write about how it is in the Audy Home! First when you come in you go to a section in this building called intake, you stay there for about a week with the same clothes you got picked up with! Then if you're lucky you get 1 shower through that whole week, yes just one shower! Second, you have a t.v. room enough to hold about 28 people and while you stay in intake you have to sit there all day long, 7 days a week, and if you or any of the other people talk with out permission not that group but the whole section have to suffer. Like stand on the wall facing bricks for about 5 hours! Or if not you get just enough food on your plate to fill you up for about half the night! And then after that week is over and you get put on a regular section it starts to get a little more excited because not only do you get to go to gym but if you are in a gang you have to watch out for other gangs, because if your gang starts a fight they are going to pick up chairs and start throwing them at you. Then we have the people who are not in gangs and come to places like this! They get picked on even more because they don't have no one to have there back! So people who are in gangs start to take stuff from them! Or start to pick fights with them! And let me tell you about the food! This food they give here is nasty because it makes bumps come out on your back and on your face! For me it makes me bust out on my back and my face! Then about the visits they are only on Saturdays, Sundays, and Wednesdays, and no person can come see you but your father or your mother! Any other person has to go through courts order! And if your lucky the judge will say yes but only once! Then we have the staff, you will bump into a staff who does not like you so you will fight with him. I my self had fights with 2 staff and lost both of them! And you will do about 10 days in confinement, that's when you have to stay in a room for about 10 days, the only time you come out is for shower! 5 minutes! Well this is all. I know it ain't all what goes on but this should give you the idea!

Love,
Ito

"What do you think might happen?" asks Mr. B pointedly, returning to the text.

Mario laughs: "I already told you that, Mr. B. We don't know, but let's see."

Oscar reads next, stumbling through a few paragraphs. Then, in turn, Jeff, Merce, and Antoine with his shy, whispery voice. The story is an account of childhood in the newly integrating South. Clint, the narrator, remembers the intense conflicts he experienced in those days—conflicts of identity and loyalty, courage and compromise. Wanting to distinguish himself, he created a big distance from Marvin and the only black girl in the class. When another student asks Clint if Marvin embarrasses him, he responds, "Can you believe that guy? . . . He's like a pig or something. Makes me sick." He thinks, "I was ashamed. Ashamed for not defending Marvin and ashamed that Marvin even existed."

When the class bully, Oakley, provokes Clint to fight, Clint reacts: "And then unconsciously, as if scratching, as if breathing, I walked toward Marvin, who stood a few feet from Oakley. . . . 'Why not him?' I said. 'How come you're after *me* and not *him?'* The room froze. Froze for a moment that was both evanescent and eternal, somewhere between an eye blink and a week in hell."

Clint escapes to the bus after school but worries all night about the impending fight. More than this, he is tortured by what he has done and he rehearses an explanation: "*See, Marvin, what I meant was that he wants to fight a colored guy, but is afraid to fight you cause you could beat him.*"

The next morning Oakley confronts Clint in the schoolyard. Oakley slaps him twice and Clint shouts, "Call me a nigger": "I have no idea what made me say this. All I know is it kept me from crying." Oakley tells him to shut up and slaps him again. At that moment Marvin Pruitt steps up, pushes Clint aside, and knocks Oakley down. Marvin stands calmly and stares at Clint "with cool eyes."

Reading the story aloud, allowing for occasional discussion, brief interpretive remarks, and clarifications or corrections, took the group almost forty minutes—a protracted period of concentration and attention for this class. No one called out "Bathroom" or "Counter," no one put his book away, lost his place, or started doodling. The story seemed to capture them, to invite their steady collective regard and absorb their thoughtfulness.

Jeff, hyper and in high gear, had been the last reader and he becomes the first commentator: "Marvin stared with cool eyes—he was showing Clint to never back down, to be ready to fight always. Sometimes you've got to fight."

"I think he's waiting for a 'thank you'," says Ito. "I mean Marvin went down for him. He's expecting some gratitude."

Mario is next: "Marvin's cool because he's showing Clint that he was wrong about him. See Clint thought Marvin was just an ugly, embarrassing pig. And in a way he *was* nasty. But still he stood by Clint in his time of need, and he showed he had heart. So he's proud of himself."

"So it's a proud look?" asks Mr. B.

"Yeah. Proud and brave. He's like the champ being carried out the ring."

"But he's not being carried by his fans. He's in trouble,"

"Right. And he don't care. He was right and he's looking at Clint, saying, like, 'What do you think of me now, homey?'"

Everyone laughs. Jeff returns vigorously to his point. "But he's showing the guy that he can't ever back down. If you back down, you're a punk. And you'll be wasted for sure. You got to fight."

"Possibly," Mr. B concedes. "Of course the cool eyes could mean more than one thing, and I've heard good arguments on all sides. Later I'll want you to write up your interpretations. But before we do that, what did you think of Clint trying to show the teacher that he was different from Marvin?"

Merce: "That was sickening. Just doing his Tom-thing to show he's like white."

Zo: "It's part why he was so uncomfortable all the time. Trying to be neat all the time put him on edge."

Antoine: "See, showing he's different is bad and good. Because it's bad to pretend you're better or to set someone up or to always be kissing up to a teacher or something, but it's good to show people that we're not all a bunch of monkeys."

Mr. B: "So *some* of you *are* monkeys?"

"Not that we're monkeys, Mr. B," says Antoine smiling softly. "But, you know, just we are not all the same."

Ito jumps in with his earlier connection: "See, Mr. B, like I said, you get to *feeling* like people think you're a monkey. That's what he means."

Mr. B keeps the conversation here: "What about that? Is Clint's attempt to be different good or bad?"

His question provokes a vigorous exchange about race and color, surface and depth. Several students see Clint as "kissing up," "Toming," betraying himself and his race. Antoine connects Clint's goody-goody classroom behavior with shouting at Oakley to "call me a nigger": "See, he's trying to be not-black, so he needs something to make him snap if he's going to fight the big dude. I mean, we call each other 'nigger' and don't snap, but Clint would snap. He'd be ready to fight."

Other students see the inevitability of Clint's internal conflict, a black speck in a sea of whiteness. He wants to differentiate himself, to avoid being labeled and dismissed, but also to fit in, to belong.

"See, Clint wants to show he's the same as the white kids in some ways, the same as Marvin in other ways, and still just himself," says Mario. He points to a sentence from the text: "I wondered what kind of light I could shine for Marvin, Oakley, and me that would reveal us as the same." Mario continues, "He's saying, I'm me, Clint, special. One and only. And still I'm a person like you."

Ito won't let his earlier idea die: "Like when all these visitors come by here staring at us. They think we're all the same—killers, gang-bangers, monsters. We're like monkeys in the zoo. But I ain't a monkey. I ain't a monster." His face is pulled in tight, constricted, his eyes burn. "They should skip bringing in those tourists. Is this the zoo? Am I a monkey? No! No more visitors! Leave us alone!"

Jeff makes a lively monkey face, cheeks puffed up, eyes wide open, and calls out sharply, "Ito, you are a killer and a gang-banger."

Ito smiles self-consciously and simultaneously says, "Fuck you, Jeff." There is no rancor, just an automatic reaction.

"On the wall," says Mr. B matter-of-factly. Ito gets up smiling to himself and goes to stand against the wall for five minutes, the standard punishment for cursing. He cuts his eyes sharply to Jeff who laughs quietly.

You can see Ito straining to define himself, intensely aware of his own growth and development, his being and becoming. He has been a mid-level gang leader and feels some loyalty and the pull of the group, but he also wants to forge his own way. He misses his family, a baby brother and sister, his dad, and especially his mom, who comes to see him every visiting day and cries through the entire hour. Ito has recently fallen in love, which gives him a mix of hope and focus and energy and aching misery. Tina had been working in the school as a volunteer staffer on a gang intervention program, and their love affair was barely underway when it was uncovered, causing a minor scandal. An attendant, shaking down Ito's room, had discovered a stack of graphic, fervent letters from Tina. When she showed up for work with "ITO" tattooed on her arm she was fired. They continue to write letters.

The reading and discussion have now reached toward an astonishing hour. Mr. B, sensing that he has engaged the class to its limit and wanting to end on a positive note, announces that it's time for a break. "Bathroom," says Mario. "Back room," "back room," "back room." The radio is clicked on and rap music drifts from the ante room, punctuated by the sounds of heavy weights being pumped to the rhythm.

For close to twenty minutes the guys lift, joke, take turns looking out the door and using the bathroom. Ito comes off the wall, and he and Andrew finish a few fine details on their paintings. Mario reads a book. Mr. B pulls out three giant bags of tortilla chips—bringing food to class is another of the school rules Mr. B breaks routinely—and everyone finds time for a paper plate piled with chips and spiced with his choice of hot sauce.

When Mr. B begins again the students refocus quickly. "Look at this sentence here, after Clint suggests that Oakley beat Marvin instead of himself," he says, and then reads: "The room froze. Froze for a moment that was both evanescent and eternal, somewhere between an eye blink and a week in hell." Mr. B continues, "I like that image—an eye blink, something fleeting and swift, and a week in hell, something unending, unendurably long. The first thing I want you to do, before you answer the questions on the work sheet, is to write a paragraph on a time in your life when it felt like it was between an eye blink and a week in hell."

LeMarque gets up to sharpen his pencil, while Freddie decides it's time for another bathroom break. The others take paper from folders and bend to the task. Mario is coiled concentration: "I should have stayed in school because I could have been playing ball, have freedom and would be happy at the same time. Most of all I wouldn't be here where I'm at now!"

Andrew takes a more literal approach, describing an incident here earlier in the year: "Well one day while in school at gym I got into an fight. It was worth it but then I regretted it because I had to suffer the consequences. I went in confinement for five days behind a steel door and it wasn't nice and that's a eye blink and a week in hell."

Merce remembers an incident not so long ago on the bricks: "I can remember one day my friends and I was playing this card game that involved liquor and every time we played I lost. I was so drunk I was stuck, I couldn't move. I hated that day."

For others the assignment becomes an occasion to once again worry about the direction of their lives. Zo writes: "Well to start this little essay I would like to tell you that I've had lot's of problems during my childhood. Ever since I was 9 or 10 years old I was a menace. I've made all kinds of mistake but the biggest mistake of all was coming here to the Audy Home. And this is a place where I never thought I would be so I just wish that I could go back in time and change my life the way it really should be and this is hell for real."

And Rasheed: "I wish I never start smoking or hanging with the wrong crowd because I wouldn't be in here right now. If I was going to school I probably would of had mostly everything I wanted, but now I'm stuck in this place. I wish I could go back to the past and change everything but now it's too late."

Antoine fingers his neck while he writes: "I wish for a lot of things like the crap I'm up in here for I wish it would never have happened. But I'm locked up for a while. One day I went to a party and I got shot in the neck with a .38. I wish I had never went to that party."

And Ito, thinking of Tina, writes: "When we kissed it was freedom and hope. When she left it was eternal suffering until we meet again."

Ito has a lot on his mind: he is torn up by his mother's grief and her constant crying. When he talks about her his eyes fill up with tears too; his history and his rank as the top Latin King at Audy divide him from his growing personal desire to stop active gang-banging; he worries about how to prepare to do serious time. As if those struggles are not enough, his mind is filled with Tina, and it shows.

"You're lovesick, Ito," says Mr. B without a trace of condescension or teasing. "It's the best and the worst thing you'll ever feel. Why don't you write to her?"

Over the next several days Ito spends every moment of free time bent over paper at his desk, head down. Finally he shows me the fruit of his labor, love poems for Tina:

Wondering

I'm sitting here thinking about you just wondering what can I do to make you feel about me the way I feel about you! If it was with in my power I'd give you the moon and stars but I'm afraid that I can't do that so instead I'll give you my heart!

Forever

Sometimes I think of you and tears fill my eyes to think of the memory you gave my life. You touch me in a place no one ever reached, you gave me reasons and cause to believe. You are my rainbow you color my life, and you are my sunshine. I'm warm in your light. You are my fountain that never runs dry, you are my inspiration, my reasons to try. I'll love you till green grass turns lavender blue, and all the stars from the heavens vanish like dew, when horses and chariots fly like the wind! That's when I'll leave you, I'll love you till then!

In Love

My love is unconditional, I told you from the start. You can see it in my eyes, you can feel it in my heart, from here on ever after, we'll stay the way we are now, and share the love and laughter that a lifetime will allow. You always be the miracle that makes my life complete, as long as there's a breath in me I'll make yours just as sweet. As we look into the future, just as far as we can see, let us make every tomorrow be the best that it can be. As we live our lives together, comes a day when it should storm, you have the promise of my love to protect, and keep you warm. You may search the whole world over and I'm sure you'll never find, any one who'll love you with a love as true as mine. I cross my heart and promise to give you everything I have to give, to make all your dreams come true, in all the world you'll never find a love as true as mine.

Ito wonders and worries about his actions and responsibilities, his new dreams now in stark contrast with his heavy situation. He struggles to understand what is happening to him and is willing to be generous, critical, self-reflective. In another poem to Tina, he credits her with "drawing out into the light my beauty":

I Love You

I love you not only for what you are but for what I am when I am with you. I love you not only for what you have made of yourself, but for what you are making of me. I love you for the part of me that you bring out. I love you for passing over all my foolishness and traits that you can't help but to see. I love you for drawing out into the light my beauty, that no one had looked quite hard enough to find.

Ito is locked up on punishment for five days. He had sent "I Love You" to Tina on Wednesday morning; that afternoon a letter arrived from her saying she wanted "to just be friends." When an attendant told him before dinner that night to straighten a table he went off like a bomb.

7. Jesus

When I
die
I'm sure
I will have a
Big Funeral . . .
Curiosity
seekers . . .
coming to see
if I
am really
Dead . . .
or just
trying to make
Trouble . . .

Mari Evans
"The Rebel"

MR. B ASKS ME to tutor Jesus in reading. A soft, round-faced kid with a little goatee and a ready smile, Jesus is assigned to Mr. Petersen's class, but he and Petersen don't get along much, so he often comes here after checking in there. "Me and Petersen straight," Jesus tells me. "But he's boring—no weights, no art, no doughnuts on Friday." Petersen's students mostly sit and shut up and peck away at work sheets. There are many trips to the gym, but little engaged teaching. The place feels depressed.

"Besides, Mr. B wants me to learn to read, and that's what I want, too. Everybody telling my mother, 'If Jesus learns to read and write he'll make something of himself because he's a smart kid.'"

I have watched him day after day bent to whatever task Mr. B assigns, working diligently, often asking for assistance from Mr. B. Now it is my turn.

Mr. B hands me a small pile of flashcards with words Jesus has been working on and we move to the side of the room. I start through the words: "he," "she," "they," "then," "hook," "took." He can't read most of these, whether trying for the whole word or attending consistently to first consonant sounds; dealing with vowels or second consonants is even worse. I put the cards aside and ask him why he wants to read anyway. His response is quick and direct: "I hate reading and writing really, man." He smiles self-consciously. "But I got a lot of letters to write. My room is filling up with letters to answer." He gets a friend upstairs to read his letters from home to him, but now he has the hard job of writing back.

I suggest that Jesus dictate a letter to me, that I write what he tells me to, and that then he copy it over and send it. He likes the idea. "I'll bring my letters down later, but I remember one from my cousin I got to answer."

He dictates:

Dear Ana,

How you doing? I received your letter. Thanks for writing. How are things going for the family? About the "Midnight Hours," Northside Kings came and hit a brother with a bottle and a fight broke out. But everything is straight because they had a nationwide meeting and everyone got violated. Tell Tate I say hi. I want you to come for a special visit before I go to the County. Call my mom and get your name on the list for a special visit. I go to the County March 11. Tell your friends to write me and send me pictures. Try to hook me up so I don't be lonely. Well, I'll see you.

Love, Jesus.

I read it back to him, and Jesus likes it. He smiles at the part about getting hooked up. "Yes, man. Ana's hooked me up with some good-looking friends of hers. I got to write Priscilla, too, because she wrote me and maybe she'll come for a visit. I'd like her to be my girl."

I make Jesus five personalized flashcards based on his letter: "lonely," "hook me up," "brother," "love," and "Northside Kings." I tell him to keep these word cards and we'll add to them after every letter we write.

"OK, man," says Jesus agreeably. "I'm going to bring down those letters. Plus I got to write a letter to my chief and explain that my ex-girlfriend don't know what went down and that I didn't kill that guy, even though she's set to testify against me." And he wants to write his mom before she goes to meet the lawyer who might represent him for free.

I sign in this morning at the office just as Jim Williams is unlocking the door to go into school. He holds the door for me and I hurry through. As we walk the thirty or so steps together down the wide corridor to the second locked door, Jim shows me a computer printout he's been reading. "The count is an all-time high," he says with a mixture of sadness and disgust. "Eight hundred and fifty four."

He's referring to the number of juveniles being held upstairs. Over forty were brought in last night.

"That's the record?"

"Everyday is a record now. The trend is up, up and away. Nothing will surprise me anymore. Nine hundred. A thousand. Not long ago no one believed we would ever break the magic barrier of five hundred. Now it's cold outside, and we've got these numbers. Watch out this summer. Terrible."

In a facility that was built in 1973 for an extravagant projection of five hundred, the "overflow" spend their days in a large group around a TV, and their nights in hallways or the common rooms of each unit on folding cots. The kids describe intake: "nasty—everybody packed together, everybody stinking" (Rasheed); "dangerous because you're jammed in there with your enemies and you're tense, and fights be jumping off, bang, bang" (Jeff); "harsh—no showers, no activity, no space, no way to know what's happening to you" (Antoine).

"There's politics driving the numbers of course," Jim says: "'Get tough on hoodlums'; 'Don't coddle criminals.' Especially when they're talking about poor black city kids. It gets the cowboys elected." Judges, then, feel the pressure to cover their backs. "When in doubt, lock them up." Audy Home simply reflects the larger crisis; it is the bottom of the avalanche.

"What's needed is jobs," he adds. "Stable, worthwhile work for a start, and then a lot of social programs to work with these kids before this." Without work, what? Grinding poverty. Racial segregation and isolation. The easy availability of drugs and guns. My friend Pat Ford, who grew up in Cabrini-Green and works with young people in Lawndale today, tells me, "I can go to any corner here and get a gun and a little bit of drugs. Yet there's not a single corner I know of where I can secure a job or get a meaningful education. Figure it out." In North Lawndale, where sixty-six thousand people live, there is one bank, one supermarket, forty state-run lottery agents, fifty currency exchanges, and over one hundred licensed liquor stores and bars.

"We locked up forty last night, right?" Jim says finally. "Assume each of them was dealing drugs. OK, that means that this morning there are a hundred and sixty guys with their resumes in hand standing in line for jobs." His reference to resumes in the traditional sense is, of course, facetious. But his larger point highlights the free market in action.

———

After regular work I bring out a large bag of fortune cookies and everyone takes a couple. A few students actually like to eat them; almost everyone is eager to read his fortune:

"Answer just what your heart prompts you."

"Many receive advice, only the wise profit from it."

Several fortunes require a trip to the dictionary. For example, when Andrew reads, "Your winsome smile will take you far," it takes a few minutes to figure out what it means. "Yeah," says Mario as the light-bulb goes on. "You always giving me that innocent, childlike smile and getting some of my chips." Everyone cracks up.

Merce gets, "You will be forgiven this time." Mario laughs and whoops, and then gives a dramatic reading of his: "The current year will bring you great happiness." He throws up his hands and looks heavenward. "Yes, Lord. I'm getting out of here."

Antoine follows. "Me, too. Check this out: 'Your everlasting patience will be rewarded sooner or later.'"

"Naw," says Mario quickly, "that's sooner *or* later. Could be you'll be patient for twenty years, then get out." Everyone rocks and roars again.

Mario tells about the last time he had a fortune cookie. He went with friends to a Chinese restaurant, and when each person read a fortune, the group would respond in unison, ". . . while in bed." This prompts a new, more hilarious round of reading.

"You will meet new friends . . . while in bed." And so on.

When things settle a bit, I pass out strips of paper for each student to write his own fortune. The mood turns serious. The students write fortunes for family members and friends:

"J.J., your attitude will cost you."

"Success will lead you on."

"Mom—To have what you want in life."

"Bug, I wish you stop gang-banging."

"You will live a long life of happiness and wealthiness."

"You in the family, I want to see you grow stronger together."

And for themselves, as always, the fortunes are lavish, profuse, and, to me at least, sweetly sad:

"I will live a happy life with a lot of money."

"To be rich and famous."

"To stop gang-banging."

"A decision soon will be the best one of your life."

"Lead myself in confidence to go home."

"Your lucky day is April 3."

What happens April 3, Zo?

"I'm in court April 3 and my mother fired that lawyer who was trippin' and messin' with us. So I got a new lawyer for April 3."

———

Jesus carries a fat sheaf of letters bound by a thick red ribbon into class today. "Yo, Bill," he smiles, "here's my stash." He holds the package aloft proudly, turning it slightly this way and that. I half expect him to twist his hands and say, "Oh, gosh," but instead he says, "I got to get to work, man, or I'm going to lose some ladies."

Dear Jesus,

Hey Sweetie. How you feeling? Me OK. I was a little sad cause how you say about killing yourself is on your mind. I hope your dream come true. I got a good feeling you are going to get out. Hopefully soon you could be kissing my lips and making love to me.

I thought you dropped me when you didn't write. So when I got your letter and I was all happy. I'm going to send you two pictures. One of me and Myrna, and one of me in my daisy dukes. I don't like how I came out but I promised. Your ass better have my other pictures or I'm going to have to kick your ass when you get out. Na! Just kidding.

Good luck in court Mijo. And when you do come home we can do what you want. Well I gotta go now. Be good. Try to stay out of trouble. I love you.

Love always and 4 ever be your lady

Priscilla

Priscilla
-N-
Jesus por vida

Dear Priscilla,

I received your letter and some words you said, I felt bad, because I had told you I was going to kill myself. Well, I ain't going to kill myself, all I'm saying is I'm mad because I've been locked up so long and I'm getting tired of looking at the same walls over and over.

About what you said that you thought that I had left you, how can I betray you if you haven't did nothing wrong to me? I want you to feel good, and pray and pray and pray to God that I be next to you soon. And I get to make all your dreams come true—and my dreams too.

Love
Jesus

P.S. Thank you for the picture you sent me. I go to court on the 18th, and I go to County on the 11th.

———

Jesus has a collection of photos accompanying his letters: Priscilla, Myrna, Linda, Ronnie. He has three pictures of his kid brother, Mookie, twelve years old. "I was just like my shorty here when I came in," says Jesus. "But I ate and worked with weights and I guess I just grew." In the snapshots Mookie is kneeling, then standing, flexing, posing. He is wearing khakis, a crisp white tee-shirt deeply creased, and the black and gold colors of the Latin Kings. He stares at the camera, hands throwing the L.K. signs, affecting what must seem to him the expression of a hard-ass, but if I didn't know better, he would look to me like a kid heading for the dress-up corner to play superheroes. He is posed in front of a brick wall that has been tagged by the Latin Kings: an upside down bear face, with the words "Lil Bear, Burn in Hell" elaborately arching above the painted head, refers to the murder of a rival gang member by the Kings.

Dear Noel,

Whats up brother? How have you been doing lately?

I hope you're trying your best to stay out of trouble and don't get into fights or nothing.

I know how it is in the joint. You got to run on the law. That's how it is. Well, Noel, I got to ask you a question: I heard rumors about you, that you had flipped. To me, that's only rumors. Because you know that I know you wouldn't do nothing stupid like that—to flip Folks. Locked up in the Audy Home, nothing's changed. All that has changed only is that the brothers have been kicking it off with the Latino Folks. All Crazy T does is fight with the Latino Folks. He and a couple other brothers beat up Sharkey in the gym.

Well, brother, I ain't got nothing else to say. All I'm saying is God bless you. And I hope one day you'll be out in the world and I'll get to see you again. More always. Your boy,

Jesus

Jesus loves to talk and talk, so during break he tells me his story:

I was at my uncle's because there'd been a lot of heat, and I was just staying out of sight. The cops had been hollering after me. I had went over to my friend's a couple months before. I stood over there and told my guy, "Don't move that truck. The cops is too hot."

But they wanted the system, the radio, the hubcaps, everything. They were getting ready to junk the thing, so they wanted the good stuff. "Don't do it man," I said. "They watching you all." But they didn't listen.

So we went over there and, BAM! Just like I said, the cops came out of nowhere. Guns out, helicopters, hollering for backup, put us on the wall, smacked us around a little. This and that. I was wearing my colors, so automatically I'm pulled in. Well, what did they expect?

They picked up seven of us. And I threw the keys on the floor. Woo, woo, woo. So they took us in for questioning and I said we didn't do nothing. They put me in a lineup. Nothing. So they let me go about one in the morning. I went to my friend's, came home for awhile, and then went to my uncle's.

After awhile I decided to come home to get some clothes and things. This was a couple weeks later. Woo, woo, woo. I'm walking down the block and this cop goes by, a detective. I see his car stop partway down. So I cut in this alley and cross back to my street. Wham. There he is. And he stops me. Asks me this and that. Woo, woo, woo. Blah, blah, blah.

So he says they think I had some illegal fireworks, and my dad's on the steps, and the detective says, "We'll take him down to check on these fireworks. We'll bring him back." And my mom is hollering from the window, saying "Ahhh, Ahhhh." And I'm saying, "It's OK, Ma. Don't worry. It ain't nothing serious." But she's crying and screaming, "My son, my son, they're arresting my son." And all the Mexicans hanging out and shouting from the windows. It was a big scene. It was embarrassing.

So then they put me in the car and drove me around. Showed me a picture and said, "Is this you?" I said, "Why?" They said, "Are you Jesus Garcia?" I said, "Yes." They said, "Is this you?" I said, "No, that ain't me." So this Mexican detective smacks me and says, "How can you say this ain't you, you dumb son of a bitch? This is *you*." So he kept hitting me and I kept on, and finally I said, "OK, man, it's me."

So they took me to the police station and I was there about three days. They come in saying, "You know what you're being charged with?" I said I don't know what you're talking about, and they say, "You being charged with first-degree murder with intent." I say, "What?! What!? I don't know what you're talking about." They say, "That drive-by a month and a half ago," and they smacked me in the head. I say, "No way."

So they bring some papers in there and they say, "Here, you sign this saying you know nothing about it, and we'll let you go home, but you got to stay home and don't go by your uncle's." I say, "Fine. Where do I sign?"

So I put my initials there. You know, Bill, I don't know how to read or write, but they never asked me could I read. They never gave me a phone call, but they did say, "You need to talk to a lawyer." So I just initialed it because they said to.

They said, "You'll be going home in a minute." I thought, cool, it's over with, I'm going home.

Then they said, "You been picked out in a lineup for first-degree murder with intent, a driveby in front of a school." And they said, "You charged with the murder of Manny Ortiz"—he was a Two-Six—"shooting him twice in the head with an automatic weapon, and with shooting Oscar Jimenez in the leg"—Woo, woo, woo. They went on like that. So I said, "I don't know what you all are talking about."

They brought me to the Audy Home. Nobody picked me out of no lineup. In fact, Oscar says I didn't do it. He says the guy who did it had a Playboy bunny tattooed on his arm upside down—I ain't got no Playboy bunny—and a teardrop on his face. No bunny, no teardrop. The guy was taller, plus no fingerprints in the car match mine, plus no gun. So what do they have? A statement.

Plus my ex-girlfriend says I told her I did it for my cousin Rudy— rest-in-peace—who had got shot in the head by some Two-Sixes. But to me that ain't enough to convict. A statement and an ex-girlfriend. Not enough. Oscar's still on the bricks, but the guy who shot Rudy— rest-in-peace—is in here. His name's Li'l Tony. I got into a fight with him when I first got here. See—he bit my hand. He had disrespected my guy, Baby T. He threw down a crown and he says to Baby T, "Rudy, rot in hell. Ha, ha, ha." So I said I'm going to have to beat you up.

He was passing in the hall, but I didn't see him and WHAM! he punched me in the eye. Woo, woo, woo. We boxing and I knock him down, pick him up, and knock him down again. Then the attendants all on me, and holding me, and I get one hand free and I punch him, he catches my hand with his teeth, and rips it right here. So I'm hitting him with my free hand, BAM, BAM, and then I get free and chase him all the way to the elevator and stomp him.

I got locked up, but I told the attendant and the supervisor and the social worker that he killed my cousin, and he disrespected my guy, Baby T, and he said, "Rudy, rot in hell," which disrespects my family. That's going to hurt me. I actually loved my cousin. And we don't pass by laughing saying, "Rocco rots," "Jimmy rots," "Enrique rots."

OK, out in the world we do that, but not in here. I mean that picture of Li'l Bear, that's in the world. But locked up in here, we've got no choice. We're in the same place and we've got to live together.

I got a lot of cousins in here. Jaime, he's like a cousin. And I got my boy Loco, I got Space, and I got Baby T, my shorty Joe. So I got about six. A bunch of my guys.

I get along OK with the other organizations here. I get along with the blacks—we straight. I ain't got nothing against them. I never had no problem. Nobody does that gang-banging stuff in here. Well . . . except Li'l Tony and so mostly we OK here.

I got a P.D.—he's pretty good. He says when we go to trial we show them they got nothing—no teardrop, no Playboy bunny, no gun, no matching fingerprints in the car, no eyewitness. Plus if the guy shows up who got shot in the leg and says it ain't me shot him, well . . . I should be OK.

All they got is the statement. But, see, they had me in there, hitting me, and my mom and dad wasn't there, and my lawyer wasn't present, and they disrespected me.

And plus they got this girl saying, "He told me . . . blah, blah, blah." That's just hearsay.

I think she felt mad because I didn't go up and see her a couple days, and she heard I was seeing Lita. She would page me and I didn't get back with her, so she probably thought I was cheating, you know.

This is my first arrest. I been station-adjusted twice, once for stealing a pit bull when I was a shorty, once for fighting where I got hit with a baseball bat. But this is my first time to Audy. I was arrested in Mexico once for breaking into a house and stealing some stuff, got two years probation.

I was out in my khaki suit—white tee-shirt all creased up, khaki pants and shirt, gold hood. My shoes are a certain way, and my belt hangs so, and I got a bandanna with King colors. So that don't really invite trouble with everyone. People respect that. But the cops, they say, "Oh, here's trouble," and they bother us. They always start it. To them the colors are trouble.

During school vacation everyone cruising down Twenty-sixth in their cars, just kicking. Drinking, having fun. So I'm walking with my brother from my house, got my bandanna on, black Dickies, Converse, and the crown on up. The cops just stop us and rough us up. I didn't have a gun—I'd put it up—but there'd been a shootout that day in a bowling alley, and a couple of Two-Sixes got shot down. So they stopped us, looked at the bandanna, and said, "What organization?"

I said, "Don't you supposed to know? If you seen me here and you know them colors?"

He smacked me and said, "Don't be smart with me. What you is?"

I go, "I'm a Latin King."

He says, "How old you is?" I say, "I'm seventeen." See I got a fake ID. And he says, "This shorty here, how old he is?"

I say, "Fourteen."

He says, "Man, you walking along with your colors on, and your shorty here. Don't you know that the S.D.s or the Two-Sixes or any-body going to come pass by and see these colors and they going to shoot? They don't care. Don't you want to protect your shorty here? How about if they kill your little brother? Don't you think?"

I told my little brother not to come with me. I told him stay home. So it's on my brother. But the cop says, "No, you out here in your colors." I told my brother to go home.

I snapping on my brother. I don't mind him being a Latin King, but I don't want him gang-banging. I worry about him getting shot. I want him to be careful. . . .

There's this guy that sells guns to us. His dad's got a gun store in Wisconsin somewhere or Indiana somewhere and he comes up to Chicago on business. He got a licence, so when he's up here to pick up the shit, before he takes it quickly to his dad, he brings his green truck around to the block and sells them off the truck. Cheap. And it's easy and safe.

You got to have a gun these days, because you don't know who's going to shoot you. It's not a choice. Everyone has one and you just got to have them.

Now since I been growing up, I didn't always have one. And I'm the type of person, I don't like to have a gun. I never carried one, every time I went somewhere. But I have them stashed here and there—got to—so I can get one if I have to. And sometimes you just have to. So on my street, in my hood, with my boys, I can get my guns quick. Passing by—woo, woo, woo—I can get it. Just to carry a gun, no, I don't do that.

We carry guns mainly for protection. We want to have a clean neighborhood, no drugs, no gang stuff. We sell weed, but we try to avoid bringing heroin or coke or crack into our community. These other organizations come into our territory, disrespect us, mess up the walls, graffiti everywhere, selling drugs. So we got to chase them out. We don't bring stuff in to mess up our people. We love our neighborhood. And if we don't chase these gang-bangers out, then the word goes around that we can't protect ourselves, and, man, that makes us look rotten, like we ain't taking care of our business, and you can get hit for that. The word gets out and—woo, woo, woo—I want that organization closed down.

The reason we got guns is if these other studs come to the neighborhood and mess with our stuff, we chase them out. So we try to avoid guys riding through here disrespecting us, which leads to bigger things. We try to say, "Just mind your own business and respect us and leave us alone." But if they come shooting at us—woo, woo, woo—well, we tell them we don't want no trouble, but if they want trouble, they going to get trouble. . . .

The worst thing in here is the loss of freedom. No attendant ever had to put his hand on me except for the fights I had. Other than that, we straight. I never had problems. If I have a fight—woo, woo, woo—when it's over, I just take my punishment. I'm the type of person gets along with people. Why I want to snap and do something stupid like break some glass out and get more days? I just do my time in the hole and move on. Only problem I got is I can't look at the world and do the things I want, you know. . . .

Mr. B is the type of person who understands how you feel being locked up. I mean, we already locked up, so why treat us wrong? Why disrespect us? Mr. B understands.

They know we come from a bad neighborhood. They know we've had it rough. A lot of us had no kind of life yet. So, OK, we locked up.

Why disrespect us? We catching case after case because we came from a rotten place, OK. This and that. So treat a guy wrong, that makes him hit him with a chair or something, because we don't care no more. What more can you do to me? Why not show me just a little respect?

So, Mr. B, he helps us out. He respects us. He try to be more than a teacher. He tries to be like a model to us. He say, "This is what I want . . . this is what I expect . . . this is how you got to be."

That's all you hear upstairs: "You lucky, man. You got Mr. B. You lifting weights and being treated with respect." He's cool man. . . .

I don't know much about County. I don't hear much. But there's more gangs there, black guys fighting each other a lot.

I'll have to see for myself. And to me, I want to go. I'm tired here, ready for a change. I'll learn more over there. See being locked up with older guys can be bad, because there's more trouble, but it can be good, too, because you learn more from them. You learn more stuff. They talk to you, help you grow up, tell you you ain't a kid no more, you got to carry yourself like a man.

They'll probably describe to you what it's like to be locked up, and help you see it's no joke. And they'll tell you, "I ain't seen the sun in a long time," and, "I ain't lied down with a girl in a long time." This and that. Blah, blah, blah.

So they tell you not to go through this. Go by the rules. They tell you listen to your moms, go to school, try to make something of yourself. They'll tell you, "You can hang with the guys, just try to stay out of trouble."

If I beat this and get out on the bricks, I'll stay out of trouble. I'll holler at my guys, "Hey, I got to go chill by my uncle's in Florida," and I'll tell my chief, "Hey, I'm leaving for a minute, I'll be back, but I got to go to Florida first."

Maybe I'll stay with my auntie for a couple months first. But I'll stay out of the neighborhood because if the cops see me, they'll pull me in. That's just the way cops are. They'll put a blunt on the floor and say, "I saw you drop that out your pocket." So I'm going to make them think I'm gone. I know cops. They'll burn me, man, they'll burn me.

Being in a gang don't give me much. But if I got a problem they'll help. Like say I go somewhere and get beat up. Who I'm going to have to defend me if I don't have an organization? How I'm going to survive? I can't be getting my mom and dad to come over and shoot somebody or beat them up. That's bogus. So, I got my boys. That's it. I don't like getting my family in trouble, so I got my gang.

See when I was seven, I knew this guy, Dray, and he'd treat my little brother, take him to the store, buy him things. He treated my brother like his own son. And he was a Latin King. So one day we're just hanging on the corner and talking to Dray and his boys, older guys, and this car passes by, someone throws down gang signs. He got mad, and they shouting back and forth: "Hey what's your business, man"; "I told you what I am"; "Go about your business, man." Blah, blah, blah.

And they pulled a gun and, BAM, shot him in the head. My little brother's best friend. My brother started crying and crying. My little brother was only about five then—he's fourteen now and still on the bricks—and too little to join. So I said, "Man, God bless him" and just joined the gang. I was seven.

My dad didn't want me to. He worked in a furniture factory then, but he messed up his leg on a machine and so he had to leave. He's in a warehouse now. But he said, "Don't do it." I said, "Don't worry, Pa, I'll be OK."

I love my Mom and Dad. They come every visiting day. Even if they got to take care of their problems, talk to my lawyers, pay bills, whatever, they always come see me first. I love my Mom and Dad.

It's getting closer and closer to me going to County. Man, I worry about my mom. She's going to start crying and crying. And in court, too, she'll be sobbing.

She's got an album of my pictures at home, and she tells me she looks at me and, man, she saying, "Look how cute he is," "Look how smart and sweet," "Look how we was raising him up." She raised me up the way she wanted me to be, and I give it to her. But I joined the gang because I didn't have no choice, because of my little brother. And that hurts her.

Maybe if she'd—woo, woo, woo—well it might have been different. But maybe not.

She wanted me to stay in school, to be something in my life.

If I do learn how to read and write, man, I'll do a lot of things. I pray to God I can learn it. A lot of people just look at me and say, "Man, you a smart boy. You got a great future." If I learn how to read and write, I'll be smart.

Man, if I learn how to read and write I'll change my life. I'll go to college, I'll get a good job. So I'm hoping I can learn it.

I don't remember my daughter's name, because it's a hard name, beautiful, but some Spanish Indian name. Her mother is named Natalie, but I always got to ask my mom for my little daughter's name. I want to be there for my daughter. I ain't never seen her, only pictures. My daughter, she's beautiful.

She got a lot of hair. She walks. And my mom says on the telephone from Mexico she just says, "Mama, Papa, Mama, Papa," and then she screams a lot. They say she's got a bad temper, just like me. She gets mad at anything.

I'm friendly and I try to control myself, but I do have a temper. I can explode.

I don't want to see my daughter through that glass at County. I told my Mom, "Don't bring her." That will make me mad and I'm likely to do something—escape or something.

It wouldn't be so hard to escape from here. Every minute of every day we think about it. Ito and me had it all planned. We watched every movement, everything that went on. We know how the system was. Especially on our way to court. We had one attendant tell us, "You get me fifty g's, and I'll take you out." Me and Ito thought about it. It's easy.

But we figured that if we escaped, then they'd think we did this other stuff. So when they caught us they'd say, "You proved you did this other stuff by escaping." So we decided to stay, do our time, get out, and you got nothing with the government no more.

When we got in the gang we were just shortys. The way we were violated was three of us had to fight each other. And you had to have heart. And I fought hard, about five minutes, and they said, "You're in." They showed me the handshake, the oath—woo, woo, woo—told me what the five points mean—woo, woo. That's it.

You get put on parole by the organization for about thirty days. And they testing you to make sure you can keep secrets. And every time you see the opposition you got to chase them out the hood. Show them you ain't with that. And I was a bad shorty. I kicked a lot of ass. I'd take those big liquor bottles and whack the opposition with them. Or throw them at their heads. Remembering it makes me laugh when I'm upstairs.

My uncle Rino—rest-in-peace—died right before I was arrested. I was up there yesterday thinking of my uncle, and my cousin, and that other kid.

———

Driving home at midnight I have the radio tuned to an all-news station. It's the annoying graveyard shift, lots of silly features, filler, the police blotter. Suddenly I'm riveted: "A West-Side man was found guilty of murder today by a jury in Criminal Court. Jesus Garcia was convicted of killing thirteen-year-old Manuel Ortiz, who was struck during a driveby shooting in 1994. Another man, Oscar Jimenez, was shot in the leg during the incident."

Woo, woo, woo.

8. Girl Talk

listen,
when I found there was no safety
in my father's house
I knew there was none anywhere,
you are right about this,
how I nurtured my work
not my self, how I left the girl
wallowing in her own shame
and took on the flesh of my mother.
but listen,
the girl is rising in me,
not willing to be left to
the silent fingers in the dark,
and you are right,
she is asking for more than
most men are able to give,
but she means to have what she
has earned,
sweet sighs, safe houses,
hands she can trust.

Lucille Clifton
"to my friend, Jerina"

"HERE COME THE BITCHES," Jefferson says quietly to no one in particular. Tobs doesn't want to hear the girls referred to as "bitches,"
and everyone has learned to accommodate if not to really comprehend
his sensitivity on this point. "Hey, cutie," Jefferson mumbles softly.
"Hey, old girl, what's your name?" The girls march on, eyes front, a few
sneaking looks, suppressing grins, peeking back over their shoulders.

Tyrone, Jefferson, and Jamie are crowded at the little window in the
door to Tobs's classroom, peeping at the other students marching to
their classes. "Yo," says Tyrone smiling, his pants slung low, halfway
down his ass, his big gut hanging out of his tee-shirt and over his box-
ers. "That girl keeps looking back at me. See her? Nice ass."

Jefferson, a big boy whose baby fat is melting away dramatically day
by day, laughs and says, "Sure that girl looking at you, Ty. She looking
and thinking, 'What's that?'"

Jamie takes the baton: "She saying, 'What? You got a mascot in that camp?'"

Tyrone is neither quick nor verbal, and he is no match. "Yes," he says, mainly to himself. "She looking at me, alright. Not you." By the time the girl disappears around the corner, the air has gone from him.

This is a tough place for a girl. The issues and feelings everyone confronts here—loneliness and the crowd, fear and confusion, vulnerability and shame—become amplified for young women because of a striking fact: today the inmate "count" stands at 843; of these, 804 are boys and 39 are girls. In this sea of boys, girls are an island of spectacular badness to themselves, interest and aching desire to many of their fellow inmates. Marching to the gym during the chaos of a fire drill, when the classes become disorganized and entangled, a young boy in dreadlocks, finding himself in the narrow stairway squeezed next to a couple of bigger girls, says cheerfully, "I got something here for you to suck on." Clarissa smiles and looks bashful as she pulls herself behind Diana, large and loud and full of energy, who shouts back, "I'd suck on a dead dog before I'd touch your nasty thing."

DeLois typically walks the halls with a bright smile and a word for everyone she passes, inmates and attendants and faculty alike. "I like to flirt," she says. "Guys like me. I'm beautiful, so when guys look at me I want to give them something to look at." DeLois is charged with murder in a gang driveby, and when she describes the action, it is with an unselfconscious B-movie vitality: the shivery suspense as she and her crew enter forbidden space searching for prey, the thrill of cruising back alleys and yards high as a kite, the cat-and-mouse, capture-the-flag excitement.

Miranda never smiles, holds herself close and tight. She's charged with felony-murder, involved in a home invasion at fifteen with her twenty-four-year-old boyfriend who shot and killed a man when he stumbled into the action. "I don't want to know these thuggy boys," she says. "I got a man on the outside. If anybody here touches me, well , " Her eyes narrow in threat.

The bare outline of Miranda's situation is revealing. She is involved in an adultlike relationship and charged with an adultlike crime. But she is still a minor, and there is a *prima facia* case of statutory rape involved, since her boyfriend is an adult. Over half the teen pregnancies in this country are the result of statutory rape—the girls are sexually active with men. New standards and attitudes, however, mean that statutory rape is rarely prosecuted. The most common defense against a charge of statutory rape is "the promiscuity defense"—demonstrating that the girl has had other sexual partners. "At its core," Michelle Oberman argues, "the promiscuity defense reflects a belief that, by virtue of multiple sexual partners, girls become less vulnerable to coercion, and in essence, gain the capacity to consent to sex. As one court put it, the defense exists because there is no longer any compelling need for protective measures for the sexually experienced child." In reality, Oberman demonstrates, prior sexual history is likely to signal a history of vulnerability, not worldliness. She points out that if it were true that "girls are powerless until they lose their virginity, at which point, they become fully empowered," transformed into capable, self-aware people whose consent is fully authentic, then "it might be better to encourage girls to lose their virginity by ten, so that they might better protect themselves from the hazards of adolescent sex."

Some of the girls in Audy Home are here for gang-activity, some for theft, some for running away. Several have children of their own. Most are awkward and unsure of themselves.

Like in any other school there are rivalries, courtships, breakups. But the coerced restraint and the fantastic numbers—the thirty-something to one odds—exaggerate an already complicated dance. The girls are powerless, overwhelmed, objectified. The boys are locked into an overdrawn caricature of male/female relationships invigorating a host of backward, medieval attitudes and activities.

"You couldn't design it any worse," says Frank Tobin. "The exaggerated interest in their bodies gets reinforced, the already narrow outlets for expressing dignity and beauty get clogged and shut off. The natural experimentation of adolescence meets an imposed, almost total deprivation, and the result is usually catastrophic and appalling."

Steven Schlossman notes that at the turn of the century 80% of the school reform population was boys, 20% girls, 100% poor. "Flogging . . .

cold-water baths, nausea-inducing drugs, severely restricted diets, and head-shaving," common disciplinary measures for girls in 1900, are gone as official policy. Once boys were charged mainly with theft and robbery, girls with "sex delinquency"—early exploration, out-of-wedlock pregnancies, including those resulting from abuse, practices thought to promote venereal disease and the birth of inferior children. Boys are still perceived as a threat to society because of violent or criminal behavior, girls because of sexual behavior.

Almost 25% of girls nationwide who enter the justice system do so for running away from home or violating curfew, as compared to 8% of boys. In Juvenile Court girls are treated as more vulnerable and needy than boys, and girls are seen as deviant if they do just exactly what boys do. A boy's sexual activity and history is only noted if his crime involves sex, while a girl's sexual history is often a permanent part of her record, even if her offense was, say, theft or running away.

Between 1987 and 1991 there was a 10% increase nationwide in the number of girls in juvenile courts, according to the National Center for Juvenile Justice. In 1994, 678,500 girls were arrested—25% of juvenile arrests. Many of these were status offenses—truancy, running away, being ungovernable—the traditional route into juvenile justice for girls. Yet arrests of young women for violent crimes is also increasing: during the 1980s the rate of increase for all violent crimes was 16.5% for girls compared to 4.5% for boys. While the increase is serious, the numbers remain small. In Cook County over half the girls detained are held for less than thirty days. While 60% are held as juveniles, an astronomical 40% are automatic transfers (ATs) to adult criminal court, typically for participating in criminal activity with boyfriends or male companions. From 1985 to 1989 the F.B.I. reported a national increase of 18.9% in the number of adolescent females arrested for murder and nonnegligent manslaughter. Girls were more likely to be charged with killing a family member (44%) than were boys (13.8%). They are also more likely to be processed informally and, when confined, to be held in a private facility.

While it is estimated that one in four girls in the United States is abused before the age of eighteen, that number doubles for juvenile delinquents. In other words, girls who have been abused are more likely to become delinquent; they are also far more likely to become pregnant than their nonabused peers. Abuse is a major reason girls run away, which often results in their first encounter with the law. Girls are twice as likely as boys to be locked up for violating a court order—incarcerated for a status offense such as violating curfew or running away while under court supervision—a practice known as "bootstrapping."

"Today we are starting a unit on Human Sexuality," Frank begins in his quiet, nasal voice.

"Yes!" says Jefferson quickly. "Yes, yes, yes! Tobs, can we make this a hands-on activity?"

"Calm down, Jefferson," Frank says good-naturedly. "Hands-on is not your issue. You're already hands-on. I want you to try to be brains-on, minds-on. You might learn something yet."

Jefferson looks around for an approving smile, then finally settles down, picks up his pencil, and opens his notebook. Frank passes out copies of a simple topology of life that begins with one-cell organisms, moves on to ferns and flowers, birds and mammals. At the top, a rendition of Leonardo's proportional man. Frank walks them rapidly through the hierarchy, talking about different forms of life and the attributes of each. "I wouldn't say a soybean experiences sexual urges, would you?" he asks. "But a dog, definitely."

He can be funny, serious, scientific, literary. He can be intensely personal one minute and scientifically objective the next. He is absolutely explicit. The class hangs on his words, eager in a way I wouldn't have predicted. "There's always a keen interest in this," Frank tells me later. "Under all the strutting, they want to understand what's happening to them and what sex is really all about. They come in thinking they know everything because they know how to get a hard-on. They slowly realize that they don't know shit."

"What do you think," he asks the class finally, "makes human sexuality different from the sexuality of other animals?" What a question! Jefferson screws his face into a bewildered smile. "Man," he says. "that's weird. That's sick."

"Why?"

"It just feels funny thinking about it. I mean, we're not dogs or monkeys, Tobs."

"Right," says Frank. "So what's different?"

Jefferson is flustered. Several other young men are openly confounded. "I mean, it must be different, right?" says Jamie. He then goes for the laugh: "Maybe because we can stay hard longer."

"Naw," says Tyrone. "I seen a dog screwing once and he just wouldn't stop. He was hard all day, like you."

"Maybe there is no difference," Jamie offers another option. "Just, like, everything mates with his own kind, but we're all alike beyond that."

The muddle continues with a wide range of propositions: only human beings look good (but not all of them); only human beings menstruate (except for some other mammals); only human beings are monogamous (but not all of them).

When Jefferson says, "Human beings fall in love," Frank seizes the moment: "Say that again, Jefferson." Jefferson repeats himself, and Frank takes over. "I think that's significant: human beings fall in love. What does it mean to fall in love?"

"You know, a special feeling," says Jamie. "Like real happy and deep."

"What else?"

"Like sometimes sad. Sometimes you ache for old girl."

"OK," says Frank, "but not just any old girl. A particular girl, a particular person. Not a thing. And there you begin to see an enormous difference between us and other animals. Freedom and the ability to make free, thoughtful choices—the power to choose—makes us the only life-form with the capacity to love. Because love requires free choice and an affirmative stance—you have to be able to say yes in order to love. That's a big one."

Frank talks about the dignity and sacredness of human life. They are silent. "Even here, locked up, even in prison you are unique, you possess human worth and potential and lovableness, you have a deep capacity for freedom and for love." He offers a dozen examples of how they might redefine circumstances in terms of options and, then, choices: to read or not to read, to read this book or that one, to follow the crowd or to be your own man, to fight or to resist. "Life doesn't just happen to you when you're free. You make your own life by living it."

"I want them to develop a profound respect for themselves," he tells me. "I want them to see something beautiful and dignified inside, so that they might see the beauty and dignity in others."

The Human Sexuality discussion goes on for weeks. Frank brings in diagrams, drawings, medical photos. Several students are dumbfounded. "What's that?" asks Lazarus.

"That's a clitoris," says Frank. "You don't have one. It's a source of intense pleasure for women. It's a source of female orgasm."

Female orgasm? What's *that*?

"My girl finishes when I do," says Jefferson.

"Think again," Frank responds. "If you love another person, and if you are aware of her feelings, her needs, her desires and pleasures, you pay attention differently."

Masturbation consumes two whole class sessions. "I don't jerk off at all," says Fredo. "I'm planning to be back on the bitches, and I know if you jerk off too much you can't get it up when it counts."

"No way," says Jamie. "You can always get it up. Somedays, if I'm down, I'll jerk off twelve, thirteen times. Just jerk off until I'm unconscious."

Everyone laughs.

"You're overcompensating," says Frank, "like overeating or something. As you learn to respect yourself, you'll get a little more balance."

Many students come to class with a strong sense that respect is based on power—especially the power to hurt. Frank explicitly refuses to force them to bend to his will; he believes in dialogue, persuasion, and he argues openly about the basis of respect: "Respect for other people should be unconditional. I respect you because you're a person. Our humanness makes us lovable, respectable, equal with others in fundamental ways. I respect you as equal to me, a fellow human being. I want you to respect me as equal, respect others, respect women particularly as equals."

"No way, Tobs," says Jefferson exasperated. He's been thinking hard for several days, but now he's had enough. "Girls are not equal. How come we're bigger and stronger? We're meant to be on top."

"My wife and I are equal as persons." Frank replies. "I respect her humanity, her intelligence, her heart, and her soul."

Frank tells me later that he sees the talk about sex, which comes so easily, as another arena to struggle over the meaning of respect and self-respect. "For the kids the symbols of respect are degraded and bastardized," he says. "They don't all have a lot of ways to portray dignity and beauty. Many lack visions of possibility, many are sadly deprived of pleasure in life. So what is left is hollow. I fight to build it up, to fill it out. I urge the guys to try it my way."

———

Cheryl Graves, a talented juvenile justice lawyer, coordinates a project in Audy Home called Girl Talk. "I just couldn't stand seeing all the worst things in their lives reinforced," she says. "I wanted to create a space where these young women could reflect on what's happened to them, get some straight information about health and their bodies, about sexuality, abuse, the criminal justice system, and then be more thoughtful about next steps." Girl Talk meets weekly for an hour and a half after school and draws on the wisdom and resources of the Children and Family Justice Center, the Music Theatre Workshop, Women in the Director's Chair, and the Chicago Women's Health Center.

All the young women in lockup attend Girl Talk, and several long-term residents draw real energy from it. It is almost always a good time. There are snacks and music videos, a protected space to talk about sex, health, guys, dreams, violence, a break from the monotony of the dead time on the units, a chance to form relationships with women like Cheryl, African-American, hip, compassionate. When the Girl Talk staff, led by Cheryl, come into the chapel where the meetings are held, the young women, crowded and waiting, stand and cheer. Animated greetings and lots of hugs fill the room with a powerful spirit. Diana, who loves Girl Talk and takes up a lot of space in every discussion, tells my colleague Therese Quinn, "Girl Talk's not mandatory—nothing's mandatory here—but, just like church, if you don't do it they'll put you in the hole." Diana is charged with murder. She and her mom and stepdad intended to rob a guy they knew; when things got out of hand, the guy "got killed in the scuffle."

In one Girl Talk session the young women answer a survey about ideas for future Girl Talks. Andrea, very still, almost frail, with big, very blue eyes, and brown hair, sits with Therese Quinn sobbing silently. She has only checked "Violence Against Women" on the survey. Therese will tell me later, "when I put my arm around her and asked her why she was crying, she said she didn't know where she would be on Thursday, when the judge would tell her where she was going to be living next. She couldn't go home. She might be sent to a shelter or foster care. She said she was at Audy Home because she was an accessory to a burglary, which wouldn't have warranted a stay here except that she couldn't go back to her home. She is sixteen."

Jennifer, a slightly tough working-class blond cheerleader, hanging with the black girls and a member of the Girl Gangster Disciples, asks Minerva how to spell "huero" (pronounced WE-do, and spelled huero or guero). Minerva says it's h-u-e-r-o. It's a friendly nickname that means "white girl," roughly (literally empty, rotten, spoiled, or blond). Jennifer writes "huero" on the survey where it asks for race or ethnicity. Therese asks how the different groups get along at Audy Home and Jennifer says, "We all pretty much do—we pretty straight." When Amanda says she hates the term "white," Jennifer asks, "What's wrong with it? Isn't that what you are? Do you like Caucasian better? I hate that." Then Jennifer asks Therese what she thinks, and she suggests "European-American." Jennifer says, "Yeah, I like European. That's better."

Girl Talk is an occasion to think, reflect, wonder, plan. During each session there is time to talk in small groups, time to write, time to read. After several months, Girl Talk produces a small book called "Girls Talkin . . . Poetry." It is thirteen pages long with a bright green cover, copied and widely distributed to classes in the school. The poems are sometimes bawdy, sometimes sweet, sometimes sad, sometimes silly. One young author writes:

My window is far away
just like that justice day
I want to go home
I hate being in my room alone.

Another calls her poem "Boys Can't Talk Girl Talk":

Boys can't talk girls talk
because you talk about things
boys shouldn't know
or have no right to know
but maybe they need to know?
or do they?

Boys can't talk girls talk
because women and men are different
but men need to know some things
about women in order to have a
relationship or do they?

Boys can't talk girls talk
because boys would take all of
the attention away from the girls and
would demand it themselves,
is it their security or our insecurity no more
what ever it is
boys can't talk girls talk.

───────

An alleged date rape after a party at our kids' high school became a huge focus of fear and anxiety, conversation, accusation, and contention. The adults, typically, knew almost nothing, but the kids were all abuzz. Would she tell her parents? Would she file charges? Would the event and the aftershock become openly acknowledged?

I overheard Zayd, Malik, and Chesa talking about it and, as usual, butted in. When they seemed evasive and somewhat light-hearted about what I took to be a most serious act, I began to question them sharply: "Do you understand what a profound violation, what a disgusting and vile crime is being alleged?" "Don't you see how badly she was hurt and how unjust and immoral it was?"

"Yo, pops," Malik demands, "we didn't do anything, OK? You're acting like we did it. We're talking about something that happened out there. What the hell?"

When I was calmer we talked more clearly about guilt and responsibility, assent and acceptance, desire and respect, boys and girls. The date rape helped us clarify several areas of agreement:

- Sex can be enormously pleasurable and powerful when it is mutual, respectful, authentic.

- When an older guy and a younger girl have sex, there's a concern about power and intimidation. (The girl in this instance was a freshman, the guy a senior.)

- If the guy uses alcohol and drugs to grease the wheels of cooperation, there's a real problem. (The guy in this case got her drunk.)

- If there is one girl and more than one guy, it's force for sure. (The guy arrived at the girl's house at midnight with his best friend, and the three of them drank heavily until the guy coaxed the girl into a basement bedroom practically within reach of the TV the three were watching.)

- If a girl says "no" at any point, everything stops there. (There's dispute about whether she ever said "no.")

It is also worth noting two issues about which we struggled but never really found complete agreement. First was the notion of deception and emotional fraud. I argued that mutuality required honesty and openness, an authentic dialogue, a serious attempt at understanding and empathy. Zayd responded that all relationships had an element of deceit built in—I give a girl a rose and I'm thinking things I'm not ready to share—and that you could never fully eliminate duplicity, in part because you could never be entirely sure of your own motives. I said something patronizing, like, "Well, you're seventeen so I'll give you a pass, but there's something better to grow into."

The second disagreement was articulated—for the millionth time—by my wife. She argued that sex for teenage boys and teenage girls in our culture is fundamentally different, and that the difference matters.

Boys are often looking for pleasure, plain and simple, and they rather thoughtlessly allow desire to dominate relationships. Desire is good; experimentation is normal. With some thought and care and imagination guys could resist this stupidity, but usually do not. Girls on the other hand are not motivated primarily by sexual desire in relationships; in the crisis of adolescence, they are searching for closeness, acceptance, popularity, love. They trade sex for attention, but the deal is fraudulent and the exchange unequal, sometimes disastrous. Our three boys listened, if somewhat blankly.

The girl never did tell her parents. Charges were never filed.

On another day in Frank's class the conversation turns to the physical expression, the external symbols of human relationships. "A handshake, a hug, eye contact, a verbal greeting—these are all representations of relationships," says Frank. "When you go to court, you look the judge in the eye and say 'Good morning, Your Honor' in a clear voice, and that will represent respect."

"But I don't respect that man," says Fredo.

"Fine, give him that hard look and mumble at him, and you'll be expressing something different," Frank says. "But he'll still get the last word."

The class returns to sex and intimacy. Frank argues again that relationships are essential to being human, and that respect is key in relationships. The physical expression of a relationship hinges on and is influenced by underlying values. "For the physical relationship to really soar, to become really joyous, you need to have profound respect and unconditional regard surrounding it and propelling it forward." The deeper the relationship, the more significant the representation. Sexual intercourse can be the ultimate intimate expression—the joining of two people. "It's profound, deep, mysterious, and marvelous if it is two people joining together," says Frank. "By the same token, it's a shallow lie, and it's dehumanizing to you and to her to have intercourse with someone you don't really even know."

"Tobs," Jefferson asks the next day at the start of discussion, "you ever had oral sex with your wife?"

I expect an outburst of laughter, and I wonder how Tobs will react. He is no prude, I know, and no question has yet embarrassed him or thrown him off. Nothing shocks him. Furthermore, Jefferson seems, at least this once, authentically curious.

"Well, Jefferson," he says, "oral sex can be a beautiful thing, like kissing, touching, or intercourse. Nothing to be ashamed of or to regret if it's an act of love. As for me and my wife, the sexual way we express our love for one another is intimate and private. We don't share that beyond the two of us alone."

When Frank talks about preparation for intercourse, and includes in his list of intimacies not just petting, kissing, and speaking about love, but also taking care of the kids, changing the diapers, and doing the dishes, Ty starts giggling. He tries to say something but stammers and laughs hysterically. It becomes contagious. Jamie tries to butt in but looks at Ty and his breath explodes from him. Soon no one can speak, everyone is convulsed in uncontrolled giggle fits. When it dies down a bit, eyes meet and it begins again. So much for Human Sexuality today.

9. Andrew

> Hold fast to dreams
> For if dreams die
> Life is a broken-winged bird
> That cannot fly.
>
> Hold fast to dreams
> For when dreams go
> Life is a barren field
> Frozen with snow.
>
> Langston Hughes
> "Dreams"

WINTER BREAK, the ten-day Christmas vacation, is not a welcome break for these students. It is both a marker of time passing—this is Ito's second Christmas locked up and he's looking toward perhaps twenty or more Christmases in chains, a time that stretches beyond the imaginable—and a bitter reminder of a better life barred to them. "My mom and sister visited on Christmas," says Ito quietly, looking down, his face a balance of pain, astonishment, and shame. "They cried so much I felt like—oh, man—I felt like jumping out the window." Not a real possibility, but escape or suicide, Ito was desperate to depart, to pass away.

Mr. B has brought copies of several newspaper articles, and after things settle down he distributes them to the class. "Here's some items you might have missed over the break," he says. "I want to go over a couple of them with you, and you can read the others at your leisure." The sheaf of articles represents one man's idiosyncratic reading of the *Sun-Times* and the *Tribune*: sports, headline news, features, amusing "dog bites man" fillers.

"I want you to take out the blue copy," says Mr. B, indicating an article from the *Tribune* with a bold headline: "Prison pushed for 2 youthful killers." The students find their copies and begin to study them. "Andrew," says Mr. B, "please begin reading." Once again reading will be round-robin, each student having a turn, everyone struggling, lurching, moving forward together. Andrew reads, barely audible, head down, face pulled together, tense in concentration:

> State officials argued Tuesday that two boys (ages 10 and 11) who dropped 5-year-old Eric Morse to his death from a 14th floor window in 1994 should be placed in a state youth prison because they have been violent and disruptive during their year-long confinement in the Cook County Juvenile Temporary Detention Center.

The reading continues for several paragraphs. It is Antoine's turn:

> But Herschella Conyers, an attorney for the older boy, said fights are common in the Audy Home detention center, which serves as a holding facility for juveniles awaiting trial or serving short sentences.
>
> "Any child who has been at the detention center for any length of time has probably caused a disturbance," Conyers said.
>
> The two boys' behavior while in custody has become a critical issue for state officials trying to convince Juvenile Court Judge Carol A. Kelly that the youths are too dangerous to be in a residential treatment facility and must be placed in a state youth prison.

And during Mario's turn:

> The two boys found delinquent, or guilty, of killing Eric Morse by dropping him from a Chicago Housing Authority building in October 1994, are the first defendants to be considered under a new law that allows children as young as 10 years old to be sent to a youth prison.
>
> Before this year, children in Illinois younger than 13 couldn't be placed in a state prison. The law was changed in response to the case of Eric Morse and that of Robert Sandifer, an 11-year-old boy murdered last year allegedly by his own gang.
>
> Kelly must balance the need to protect society against the potential for rehabilitation in a case that has attracted national attention and become a test of how to handle preteen killers.

When the reading is finished, Mario says that it's bogus to sentence them based on their behavior in Audy Home. That's separate, he says.

Antoine says he wishes one of them would start a fight with him because he'd kick their ass for what they did. But Mr. B steers toward the question of the boys' behavior in detention: "We all do things that we know are wrong," he says. "We all behave well at times, and not so well at other times. But I want you to think about this: your disciplinary record at Audy Home could make a difference somewhere down the line. You can't see into the future to know what will or will not make a difference. So it is in your interest to stop, think, and reflect before you act." The class is silent for a long moment. Andrew sighs a tired "Yeah," exhaling slowly.

The class moves on to another piece, this one an editorial from the *Sun-Times* called "New State Laws—The Good and the Bad." Mr. B says, "The editorial is the place where the people who own the newspaper write down their opinions. So this is the opinion of the owners of the *Sun-Times*, and we'll read it to see what their opinions are, and how those compare or contrast with your opinions. Think about whether you agree with their opinions, and if you differ, think about why."

LeMarque begins reading: "When the New Year dawns tomorrow, more than 100 new laws in Illinois will take effect for the first time. Some are good, some are bad—and others are just plain strange."

The editorial lists five new laws it calls "good laws" that "serve people": nonpartisan elections for Chicago's mayor, clerk, and treasurer, for example, and funds to clean up underground gas storage tanks. When Andrew reads about a law to stiffen fines for people who endanger themselves at railroad crossings the class rocks with laughter.

Mario says, "If I got my stereo going good—yeah, oh yeah—and I don't hear the horn, well I don't make it. Splat! Do I care about a five hundred dollar fine? It's unnecessary; just silly."

Merce adds, "Only a fat kid would get hit on a train track. I'm too swift to get hit. I'm like a cat."

Others join the chorus, posing, posturing playfully escalating the verbal swagger until it seems they are a group of superheroes, invincible, invulnerable. We are soaring, strong, smarter than the rest. Our bodies—rippling and tight—can do anything. We are alive, and inside the surging, roiling experience of our own unique existence, it is possible for a few moments to feel entirely free. The walls fall down.

Other laws lead to sharp debate:

A law to create harsher fines for people who illegally use handicapped parking spaces.

Andrew: "That's stupid, man. They waste a lot of space and there are too many of them."

Mario: "My grandmother needs that space. She's old and can't walk so well. I think people should stay out of those places for people like my grandmother."

A law making stealing headstones from a cemetery a felony.

Andrew: "That's dumb. It's bad to do, but it ain't a felony-type crime."

Mario: "Why? You thinking about doing it?"

A law providing for community notification when a sex offender moves into a community.

Antoine: "That's out of order. Bogus. If the individual did his time, how is he going to start to build his life outside?"

Jeff: "I don't care, because I ain't never going to rape nobody."

A law that says that breastfeeding a baby in public is no longer considered obscene.

Jesus: "Babies should be fed wherever they're hungry. Why they trippin'?"

Rasheed: "I ain't the baby. I ain't sucking on no breast. I don't care."

A law that stipulates a possible three-year prison term for stealing from a vending machine.

A chorus of negative reactions: Bogus! Bogus! Bogus!

Mario: "I done that a lot. Three years? No way."

Andrew: "We used to steal from the pop machine in church. Just for a little change."

Mario: "Alright, wait. Wait. I changed my mind. If your sorry self was jacking up your church, I'm for this law. Three years for Andrew."

Everyone laughs, slaps hands, and goes on.

———

Andrew is quietly rapping while he works:

> Five o'clock in the morning,
> Where you going to be?

Outside on the corner.
It's not a white man's finger on the trigger,
Carjacks, drivebys, calling each other nigger,
Why should I be right and suffer?
I'd rather do wrong, making that loot,
Being that hustler.

"Man, I love that rap," says Andrew. "Man, shit . . ."

"Mr. B," says Andrew from the wall a few seconds later.

"Yes?"

"Your favorite word is 'wall.' That's all I hear from you anymore:
Wall, wall, wall."

"I wish you'd stop using your favorite word—which I won't repeat—
so that I could stop saying 'wall'."

Andrew keeps a daily journal which he shares with me periodically.

> Good morning to myself well I just got my hair cut. I thought my
> waves was in but there not but I'll get em. The weekend was alright
> didn't too much go on one of my hommies left to the county today.
> I didn't get down in time to go to gym.

> Well this morning ain't too much going on. I was in the back lifting
> some weights and this afternoon I'll be going to gym in about 20
> minutes so let me do some work.

> Good morning we came down kind of late this morning cause the
> carts came up late but we down now and yes we is working. Mr. B put
> us straight to work so let me finish so I can turn it in before 11:20.

> Well I'm about to go to tutoring this morning. I'll be back.

———

Andrew explains life on the units. "Boring, mainly," he says. "Nothing
to do, just sit and sit and sit. Then some trouble might jump off, maybe
play some cards, and then sit some more. Go to gym. Shower. Boring."

When they leave school at 2:30, the students return with their attendants to the units upstairs. They assemble in a circle and turn their
pockets inside out to show they've brought nothing from school.
"Some attendants don't really care," says Andrew, "but some are always
trippin'."

To begin, there is "quiet hour"—time to study, do homework, read, or just be quiet at the tables. At 4:00 cards come out and the TV goes on. At 5:00 dinner is brought up on carts. After dinner Andrew's unit goes with another unit to the gym—forty guys playing ball, getting a sweat. At 6:30, showers—four at a time for ten minutes. Then cards and TV. At 8:30, everyone is locked in his room. At 9:00, lights out and about twenty kids from overflow are brought in to sleep on cots in the commons area.

"But me," says Andrew, "I listen to my radio for awhile or talk to Meathead next door. I get to sleep about midnight, but sometimes we wait until the attendants black out—they ain't supposed to, but you see them sleeping in their chairs—and we might smoke a blunt if somebody's got one."

> Good morning everybody I said when I came in but I'm about to go to tutoring. I'll be back.
>
> Well good morning to myself and to my teacher Mr. B. We had a little walk through on jobs. People came in from all types of jobs. Now we watching a movie on jobs and we going upstairs in a few.
>
> Well my weekend was alright. I avoided a fight Sunday cause it wasn't worth it but other than that everything is alright.
>
> Well I been to gym but the day ain't over yet let me get to work.

———

"Alright guys," says Andrew, holding up his hand for quiet. He is at the front of a classroom just down the hall from Mr. B's, speaking to a group of shortys—maybe twenty or twenty-five of them—about a project he and four other students, including Merce, are working on. "We're playwrights," he begins, "and we're working on a play about the Audy Home called 'Temporary Lockdown'. We want to tell you about the play and get your suggestions about it."

The five playwrights are under the direction of Meade Palidofsky, founder and artistic director of the Music/Theatre Workshop. Meade, an actress and writer herself, has been working with troubled youth in Chicago for years. She combines street toughness with a genuine regard for kids in trouble, a keen idea of how to use youngsters' own experiences as a vehicle to self expression, self-discovery, and learning. "Temporary Lockdown" describes the kids' experiences in Audy Home and is aimed primarily at the younger kids—the shortys—who are held in custody for brief periods of time, but have over a 60% recidivism rate within weeks of release.

"We spent a session discussing what a day at the Audy was like," says Meade, "what the routine was like and what might interrupt that routine—court dates, family visits, or confinement for fighting with other youth. Since this was to be a group writing project by new writers, I created a structure for the piece and gave each student a through line: 'Let's say this is your very first day on section. Remember how it was when you did all this for the first time.'; 'Let's say today is one of those days when you can't stop dreaming about what it's like on the outside. Let it affect everything you do that day.'; 'Today is your day in court. What's that routine like? What are your hopes and fears as the day passes?'"

Andrew, Merce, and the others encourage the shortys to think about how to write a rap poem. Merce asks, "What rhymes with 'way'?" The shortys start off slowly—day, may, say—but soon everyone is shouting out words faster than Andrew can write them on the board: ashtray, delay, milky way, ray, gray, slay. One little boy, his desk pushed off in a corner all by itself, has paid scant attention. He has occupied himself by tearing paper and scattering it around his area. Every so often he shrieks incomprehensibly, rolls his eyes, and spits. He looks unkempt, quite crazy. As the rhyming activity begins to peak it seems to draw his attention. Finally he says quietly, "play."

"Temporary Lockdown" is wonderful on the page, but gripping and much more powerful when the energy of the writers/actors feeds itself and becomes an authentic, spontaneous, wholly accurate expression of the life they are living:

> Living in Audy is strange,
> You try to fix up your life
> But you're surrounded by gangs.
> Society is getting too strong.

And if you don't put up a fight,
You won't live long.

I know it's hard cause it happened to me,
I first started on the bricks,
When I was pulling g's,
The money was rolling,
The fenders jocking,
And if it was two freaks,
Yeah, I'm rocking!

The stuff was just ruthless.
I had to compete.
I did wrong,
And ended up deep.
Locked up in the Audy
on Temporary Lockdown . . .

Get your life straight,
Try your best not to hate.
If there's a problem,
Try your best to have a debate.
Take off the frown—
You look like a killer clown—
Cause if you don't
You'll be in Temporary Lockdown.

———

In both Mr. B's and Frank's classrooms the day moves to a rhythm that is both planned and spontaneous, intentional and improvisational. The air fills with relaxed amusement this morning the moment Antoine appears in the doorway. He is the first student down from the units and he's a sweet, agreeable kid who speaks with a hushed voice much of the time. "Oh, man," he says suddenly, coming to an abrupt halt at the threshold as Mr. B heaves into sight. Antoine casts his eyes down as he smacks his forehead with his hand. "Oh, man, Mr. B," he repeats slowly and quietly, his face consumed now by an embarrassed smile.

"You forgot it, Antoine?" Mr. B smiles back, teasing, his voice rising in mock astonishment. "Antoine, I can't believe it. After all we went through?"

"Mr. B," Antoine pleads, framing his appeal in a submissive, ingratiating innocence. "I had the papers and the book all piled up, ready to go. It was right *there*. Then Jones asked me to pick up some scrap of nothing, and next thing, I'm here." The dog ate my homework.

"So you want to begin your wall time now, or after the others get down?"

"Aw, Mr. B, man. Mr. B." Antoine drags himself across the room in long arching steps, turns and leans his frame far back against the wall, legs and arms akimbo. He drops his head on his chest, half smiling now, and his body slumps, draped upon the cross. "I can't believe it, either, Mr. B."

Mario appears in the doorway. He glances at Antoine, suddenly amused. "Man, what you doing on the wall already?" he calls. "Took you two seconds to get in trouble?"

"Oh, man," Antoine whispers, smiles, and shakes his head slowly. He offers no explanation.

"Well," says Mario, looking at Mr. B with a smile and a wink, and shaking his fist in the air dramatically, "the struggle continues. Power to the people." Incongruous, theatrical—pure Mario.

Merce appears. Then Freddie, Ito, Andrew. The room is filling up, but most students, after greeting Mr. B, linger at the door and watch the languid parade.

"Close the door, gentlemen," Mr. B says after a few minutes. "You have fifteen minutes before we begin work." The door is slowly, reluctantly pushed shut, the crowd craning for one last look. Merce loiters and, peeping through the small window, says to no one in particular, "There's about twelve girls in that class." He taps loudly on the glass to get their attention. "Five minutes," says Mr. B, and Merce, looking like the cat caught with his paw in the fish bowl, slides over to join Antoine on the wall.

Jeff won't be here today. He's locked up for fighting according to LeMarque. And Zo got stuck upstairs. He argued with an attendant about what he was allowed to bring to class.

"It's one of the most difficult and destructive problems in this school," Mr. B tells me later. "There simply is no sensible communication system between teachers and attendants." This is a common problem in all schools: The link between teachers and parents, school and home, caregivers and protectors. It is a link that is, according to Mr. B, "vital but absent."

"Say a kid has been feeling sick," Mr. B continues, "or was acting depressed or aggressive at breakfast, or was threatened, or a hundred and one other possibilities—the only way I'll hear about it is if the kids themselves tell me."

Mr. B hears about it—whatever it is—more often than most other teachers.

"Mr. B, I can't get through to my moms, and I feel like I'm going to go off." "Mr. B, I couldn't eat this morning." "Mr. B, I'm tired."

He offers sympathy, advice, and straight answers. He genuinely likes his students; they feel it and respond. "Only thing that keeps me sane in this place is Mr. B," Andrew told me one morning. "Mr. B's like my pops," says Jeff. "Him and Tobs are both popses to me."

> Didn't too much go on upstairs so it ain't too much to talk about.
>
> Well this morning a fight broke out so it's good I was in the kitchen but everything is alright.
>
> Well my weekend was alright except for yesterday we didn't have any school.
>
> I just came back from tutoring about 17 minutes ago and I completed an assignment. I hope the day go alright while visiting at 7:30. Peace
>
> I just went to gym and got a good sweat off and hope the rest of the day be all good.
>
> So far my day kind of messed up, my girlfriend dumped me we working all morning but I ain't mad at you.

———

Each student cuts pictures and words from magazines to paste on a file folder and make a personalized container for his written work.

Antoine's is a collage of messages: Positive, READY or NOT, HARD LIVING, Perfect, One day He Soared, ESCAPE!

Rasheed's is decorated with a full-page picture of a young woman in a swimsuit on which he has superimposed the words "SHY," and "You get what you pay for."

Andrew's folder has a bold headline—PLAYER of the YEAR—at the top, and two subheads: WILD and LIKE A ROCK.

> Well we just came back from spring break it was alright. It's kind of nice to be back to work.
>
> This morning we got two people wolfing early. That's about all so far.
>
> I just got back from tutoring we had a nice conversation but now I'm back in class going to work I'll holler.
>
> I can't wait but I'm trying. See you.

"Mr. B," says Andrew. "It says on my card to do chapter four in history. But Mr. B, I *did* chapter four."

"The difference between you doing it and me having it could be substantial," says Mr. B.

"Substantial? What you mean?" asks Andrew, searching his folder. "Here it is, Mr. B," he says triumphant, holding aloft a stack of paper.

"Substantial means big or large or having a lot of substance. But in this case the difference was not substantial. This time we were both right."

"Man," says Andrew, eyes drooping, body slumping, voice sighing theatrically. "Man, Mr. B, I got to be up and ready at seven o'clock every day. That's unhealthy, getting up so early. No wonder I'm tired."

"Seven?" responds Mr. B with mock surprise. "I'm up every day at five. For me seven is just a hopeful dream."

"Right," says Andrew seriously. "But I got to get up at seven, no choice involved, and I don't even have a job."

Mr. B explodes in laughter and Andrew smiles up at him.

Andrew has never been to summer camp or traveled on an airplane or a boat. He's never been in Little League or played in an organized sports program, taken music lessons or special classes in photography or art, participated in a community service project. Andrew has never attended a school where he was allowed to bring the books home.

> Good morning I'm able to write a little bit but not enough but I'll holler later.

> Well this morning I'll be going to a party in another class It should be over about 10:30. So I'll holler. See ya!

> Well this morning me and Bill had a talk about my journal and I didn't go to tutoring.

> This morning I came down late cause I had to see the doctor for my hand but everything is alright.

> This morning it ain't no tutoring but the morning is going good so far but we going upstairs now.

———

Andrew beats out the rhythm and raps loud:

> Life is a test and a quest to universe
> And through my research I felt joy and I hurt
> First shall be last and the last shall be first
> The basic instructions before leaving earth.

Nothing to talk about.

Nothing to talk about.

10. Adolescence

As LeMarque eases into the classroom this morning, he looks—quite suddenly—big. "Morning, Mr. B."

"Morning, LeMarque."

As always, LeMarque goes to a shelf where Mr. B keeps a selection of men's shirts—striped, plaid, bright, button-down—and slips one on over his institutional tee-shirt. "Just pretending he's on the bricks," Antoine teases, "wearing that civilian shirt," but it's LeMarque's routine, and it never varies. This time, however, he fills the shirt as never before.

LeMarque had been the baby of the class when he started a few months ago, filled with childish wonder and innocence, blessed with a quick sense of humor and a sweet boyish smile. He had been the runt of the litter—wispy, thin as a nail. And now he is obviously filling out, chest and arms bulging, neck thickening, voice deepening. His metamorphosis reminds me again that these are boys becoming men. It is easy to forget, for these boys are charged with manly offenses, and most of them bring deceptive, oversized bodies with them to class.

"The contrast each kid presents can be hard to hold on to," says Mr. B, "but it is somehow essential to keep both in mind if I'm going to teach them effectively." Being and becoming.

In our culture "adolescence" is considered problematic at best. Teenagers are trouble. If you don't believe it, consult anyone who's raised one. Talk to a friend. Check with your own parents. Ask the kids themselves; they are painfully aware of the taken-for-granted view, and they will often worry and wonder about what's going on. I remember hundreds of times when acquaintances and even perfect strangers told us teenage horror stories, or, admiring our kids at nine or ten, teased us about what lurked around the corner when the dreaded teen years arrived.

The stereotype from popular culture is the sweet, young child who never did anything wrong suddenly transformed into a snarling beast with out-of-control hormones.

I Was a Teenage Werewolf. We can all agree that the transition from childhood to adulthood is not all sweetness and light. But what are adolescents like? What are their main needs and tasks? What would constitute a successful passage through these years? What kinds of environments or opportunities for experience would be likely to help? There are alternatives to the B-movie plot. We can to some degree answer our own questions and write our own scripts.

———

The onset of puberty is a biological fact: girls menstruate and then produce fertile eggs; boys ejaculate and then produce mature sperm. The tremendous drama of these events is significant enough to the individuals experiencing them. But the rapid and dramatic physical changes are just the tip of the iceberg. Adolescents also enter a new stage of cognitive development: they begin to think seriously about their own thinking and the thinking of others; they become capable of sustained abstract reasoning. They are intensely curious and often idealistic, willing to work hard on projects that interest and engage them. Willing to commit to a cause. Add to this all the symbolic meaning, all the social portent and subtle connotations of puberty, and you have neither interlude nor intermission. Rather, you have the immense journey of adolescence, a journey of peril and possibility, what Louise Kaplan describes as "social threat and . . . social rejuvenation." Adolescence is a time of upheaval, rebellion, liberty, revolution. No wonder adults look skeptically, condescendingly, doubtfully at these "hostile invaders of adult territory." No wonder we mythologize them as "monsters, saints, and heroes, and in the process trivialize them as well."

Louise Kaplan offers "a narrative of how a once powerless and morally submissive child becomes caregiver and lawgiver to the next generation." She draws parallels between our modern rites of passage—initiations, bar and bat mitzvahs, confirmations, cotillions, senior proms, graduations—and more ancient rituals and ceremonies, and argues that "in all times and all places . . . the time span between childhood and adulthood, however fleeting or prolonged, has been associated with the acquisition of virtue as it is differently defined in each society." The acquisition of virtue—that catches my eye. Because in our society and our culture and, Kaplan demonstrates, in others as well, a child may be good or well mannered or well behaved, but only an adult is recognized as having the capacity to be virtuous.

In the best of circumstances the tasks and strivings of adolescence are tumultuous—not necessarily destructive but filled with struggle. Adolescents "wish above all to achieve some realistic power over the real world in which they live while at the same time remaining true to their values and ideals," and, "though they themselves might be as surprised as their parents and teachers to hear it said, adolescents—these poignantly thin-skinned and vulnerable, passionate and impulsive, starkly sexual and monstrously self-absorbed creatures—are, in fact, avid seekers of moral authenticity." In many ways, our impulse toward ethical perfectibility is a legacy from our own adolescence.

I think of the kids I know in Audy Home and their hope to have some control of a world that seems to have abandoned them. Jesus and his gang control their little few-block territory, they have their group colors and uniform. Jesus insistently demands "respect": "Treat me right, man. Don't disrespect me." Ito says, "See me for who I am, man." He fears he is being looked at but never seen, his voice never heard. He wants to be noticed; he wants to be significant; he wants to make a mark. And Mario wants to get out of the Death March: "Don't throw me on the garbage pile, man."

Boys and girls share the crisis of adolescence, of course, but experience it differently in important ways. As Michelle Oberman points out, girls feel the profound physical changes of adolescence not as empowering, but as signaling a loss of control. They become objects of male desire, and as they begin to see themselves through the eyes of others, valuing or devaluing themselves through that lens, "self-esteem, body image, academic confidence, and the willingness to speak out decline precipitously." Girls become more vulnerable in many ways, including sexually, and the real dangers associated with sexual activity "tend to fall unequally on girls."

With the loss of adult protection, adolescence can become more than a passing crisis. I think of Jeff virtually raising himself, Freddie being profoundly estranged from his mother, or Alex out of the house and on the street at twelve. The pseudomaturity of these teenagers actually increases their vulnerability, their precariousness. The purposelessness and rolelessness creates a heightened sense of despair and an increased risk of disaster. Add to this the devastating effects of poverty, violence, and drugs, and the passage of adolescence becomes absolutely treacherous.

"I think I'll be going into confinement soon, Mr. B," says LeMarque lightly. He has already done nine days—two stints for smoking, one for fighting.

"Now, LeMarque, why do you say something like that?"

"Well, it's been a while—two weeks—and it just seems like time."

"LeMarque," Mr. B says with an amused and affected sternness. "Resist! Whatever rules you're planning to break upstairs—and I'll bet it's smoking, because you know you really *are* a tobacco addict—don't! I miss you when you get locked up."

"Naw, Mr. B," he responds smiling broadly. "I ain't planning to break the rules. I just think my time is coming."

His fatalism is characteristic. Fights occur. Cigarettes turn up. Guys get hurt. I'm often reminded of an incisive cartoon by Matt Groening: a child sits in the center of a room holding a hammer, surrounded by broken dishes; the shadow of an adult looms in the doorway and the child says guiltily, "Mistakes were made." This was, of course, the Watergate theme song.

"The whole time in confinement," LeMarque says now, "I did a trick with my comb and paper that Jordan taught me." Jordan is one of the attendants upstairs who has a reputation for fairness and kindness.

"What's that?" asks Mario, suddenly curious.

"Watch this."

LeMarque lays a scrap of paper on his desk, takes his plastic afro-pick out of his pocket and dramatically combs through his hair half a dozen times. "Now watch," he says exuberantly.

He moves the comb slowly toward the paper, watching intently, his tongue twisted in concentration. Just before the comb touches the paper, it jumps up and sticks to the comb.

"See!" explodes LeMarque happily. "See that, man! Check it out. That's electricity."

LeMarque's enthusiasm is mirrored by Mario's complete disinterest. "Whatever," he sighs with a bemused look, shaking his head. "LeMarque's just a big baby," he says later. "Just a little kid disguised like a gangster."

The next day LeMarque is absent, in confinement for smoking. When he returns, as he slips into another civilian shirt, he says, "You were right, Mr. B. Mr. B you turned out to be right. Some cigarettes turned up and—wham!—confinement."

"I didn't say that," Mr. B responds, laughing softly. "I didn't say cigarettes would turn up. I said you were planning to smoke. There's a large difference between those two statements. You *did* something, LeMarque, to get into trouble. It wasn't done to you."

"Whatever, Mr. B. Did you miss me?"

"I did. I did. I told you that I always miss you when you're not here. You add a special sparkle to this class. And, furthermore, you're behind in your work. So when we get to work this morning, in about ten minutes, I want you to really concentrate on working hard."

"OK, Mr. B," LeMarque says. "I will."

After circling the room, LeMarque asks, "Can I see your paper, Mr. B?"

"Of course."

LeMarque picks up the *Sun-Times* and begins to read intently.

"Mr. B," Freddie calls from his desk in the back of the class, holding a thick packet of accumulated math work sheets and wearing a look of prideful contentment. "Look at this work, Mr. B."

"Man," says Merce, "I can beat that. Can I have some paper Mr. B?"

"Sure, Merce. But you don't need paper to do the work. You need the *desire* to do the work."

"I do the work. Come on Mr. B, I work." Merce feigns surprise and hurt.

"You do the work, but just not enough of the work."

Zo joins in, holding up a sheaf of papers. "See this stack, Merce? Now that's work."

"Yes," agrees Merce. "But you've been here longer and I'm catching up."

"It looks like you've stagnated," Mr. B chides.

"Naw. I'm smoking now. I'm catching up."

"OK. Let's get to work, gentlemen."

"Mr. B," Freddie muses. "I'm going to save all this work and send it home to my moms. She'll like this stuff."

"I'm sure she'll be proud of you," says Mr. B.

LeMarque returns the *Sun-Times* to its customary place on the floor under Mr. B's desk, and, walking to his desk, mutters, "Everything in the paper is Gangster Disciples, Gangster Disciples. It's bogus. There's no Blackstone Rangers, no Outlaw Disciples. It's just us. And guys telling on everybody. Man, that's really bogus. But Larry's going to deal with this. Yes, he is. Yes, he is."

The Gangster Disciples have been in the news for weeks. Larry Hoover, the big boss, has been in prison for twenty years but has reputedly run the organization effectively from there—making policy, meting out punishment, bribing officials, determining rewards—with the help of a few top assistants and an ironclad, deadly disciple. Now one of the leaders has turned state's evidence, and a solid line of dominoes is toppling.

"Testifying against our boys is bogus," Andrew says in agreement as LeMarque passes his desk.

"Larry will get them," LeMarque says confidently. "No doubt about it."

———

LeMarque sits at his desk doing math problems. He talks constantly: "Why I'm doing that?" "OK, that's right." "Naw, that don't look right."

On and on, a steady dialogue with himself, his voice teetering precariously between the high pitch of several months ago and the deeper tones he's diving toward and will certainly reach once and for all in the next couple of months. He seems to love the sound of it, the vibration, the hum, the manly scratching, the unsteady modulating, this way and that. It is remarkably like our son Malik's voice. There is something precious about this moment—like Malik's, LeMarque's voice reveals the little boy even as it announces the emerging man. And in each case, there is something adorable in his sense of satisfied surprise just hearing himself. He draws out certain words, as in a song: "Hey, Mr. B. How'mmmmmm I supposed to finish this sheet?"

When he breaks into a rap song, another regular occurrence, it seems organic, logical: "I just want to feel the beat, take the meat, and taste the sweet . . ." He pauses, looks at me smiling, and says, "I'm going to get on the Jeff Johnson Show and sing that. I'll get rich and famous and then they'll have to let me out of here."

———

Mario pointed to my chest and asked, "What's that?" "What?" I said looking down and seeing nothing.

"Ha! I sent you off."

"Sent me off where?"

"Just sent you off, man. Don't you know what 'sent off' means?" The dictionary definition of his slangy phrase would be something like: To trick someone into doing something meaningless.

Mario and I play the "Five Questions Game." I think of five questions I don't think he can answer—Who wrote *The Tempest?* Whose face launched a thousand ships?—and he thinks of five questions that he and the other students can answer, but that he doesn't think Mr. B or I could answer. Once we begin, everyone wants into the game, and there are conferences all over the classroom where questions are formulated guaranteed to stump the old guys.

We begin to talk about the dynamics of knowledge and the nature of knowing, and we wonder about why some knowledge has greater value in society. Finally, borrowing an idea from Deborah Stern, a teacher-friend, the students write their first intelligence test:

THE HEADS-UP TEST

Many so-called intelligence tests are biased because they are based on information that people have not been exposed to. They don't really measure intelligence, but just whether a person has access to the same information as the test-makers. To show you what we mean, here is a test which you will only pass if you've been exposed to our information.

THIS TEST WAS WRITTEN BY MARIO, JEFF, MERCE, ANTOINE, FREDDIE, ZO, ANDREW, LEMARQUE, ITO, AND JESUS.

1. What does "heads-up" mean?

2. What does "low-key" mean?

3. What is an onion?

4. What is an "eight ball"?

5. What's a sword?

6. What does, "don't pour any salt on me" mean?

7. What's a trick?

8. What are drapes?

9. What are antennas?

10. What are trees?

11. What does "getting my money" mean?

12. What does "take your mask off" mean?

13. What are bolders?

14. What does "send-off" mean?

15. What does "yea-yo" mean?

16. What is "playing the role"?

17. What does "treat the rudies" mean?

18. What does "I'm spliffed out" mean?

19. What does it mean to be on cloud nine?

20. What does "let's go on a mission" mean?

21. What does "lay it down" mean?

22. What's a dub sack?

23. What's a nick bag?

24. What is lampin?

25. What is tweekin?

26. What does it mean to go to my crib and chill?

———

Mr. B is out today, and Mr. Donovan is the substitute. He is an experienced teacher in his forties, African-American, strong, and kind. He is also the cadre sub for the school, so all the kids know him, and he has the unenviable task today of providing some stability and coherence to a group of needy kids whose anchor is missing.

"We got a sub, motherfucker," says Freddie as he enters. "God *damn.*"

"Calm down," says Mr. Donovan. "Just for today. Now, calm down."

Jeff arrives. "Fuckin'-A," he says. "Where the fuck is Mr. B, nigger?"

"Now you stop cursing, or I'll send you up," responds Mr. Donovan, attempting to draw the line.

"Fuck you, nigger. I want to go up."

Jeff is out the door, stopped by an attendant and on his way back to the unit in seconds.

As the class fills up, the chorus of "motherfucker," "nigger," and "bullshit" feeds off itself and reaches a fever pitch. Mr. Donovan struggles helplessly for control, sending Jeff and then Freddie upstairs—their crimes are distinct in that they directly curse or threaten Mr. Donovan, while everyone else is just "motherfucking" in general. Class is chaotic beyond anything I've seen before, menacing, unhealthy, sad.

Andrew opens the door and looks down the hall. Mr. Donovan rushes over to close it. He touches Andrew's arm and Andrew draws back in a fighter's crouch. Mario clicks on the radio at full volume and Mr. Donovan rushes to the back room full of reprimand and counterthreat. "Don't turn that on," he shouts.

"Don't mean do, and do mean don't," responds Mario laughing. Everyone starts talking at once.

"I got to take my medication, man," says Antoine, furious. "If you don't let me go to Mrs. Anderson I'm likely to go off."

"I'm bored, man."

"See, man, none of this would be happening if Mr. B was here."

When Mr. B returns the next day everything is back to normal. Students drift in, greet Mr. B, and get to work. When everyone is at his desk Mr. B makes a short speech.

"The report I got from Mr. Donovan is that you were uncooperative yesterday," he begins.

"Oh, man."

"No way."

"Mr. Donovan was uncooperative."

"He was trippin'."

"Gentlemen," he begins again, "I'm sorry I had to be out. I missed being here, and I know you prefer it when I am here. But part of growing up, of becoming a mature person, is learning to adjust to new situations. You need to learn to get along even when things aren't going your way, and you need to learn to get along with all kinds of people, even people who aren't your favorites. You cannot be successful if you can't make adjustments."

"Maybe Donovan's angry because he can't adjust to us," offers Andrew.

"You're in charge of yourself," says Mr. B. "You can control you if you choose to. That's all."

WHAAA! WHAAA!

A blaring alarm signals a fire drill—my third—and the hall fills quickly with kids. Teachers march their classes toward the narrow stairway leading to the gym, attendants herd from behind. Groups merge and mix, laugh and exchange messages or threats. LeMarque finds his rappy on the stairs. "I talked to my lawyer. I said we met up early and went to the store and then to my house. Stick with that and we're out of here."

The line halts for a moment and someone reaches around two guys and flicks Freddie's ear. Freddie turns quickly and lands a powerful punch on the side of the head of the innocent guy right behind him. The innocent guy is staggered but lashes back and they tumble down the stairs taking blows to the accompanying cheers of scores of students. Mr. B and two attendants wade in, grabbing Freddie and the other kid, pinning them each to the wall, then hustling them up and out to be locked on their units.

Every kid in school is now in the gym, marching four or five abreast around the perimeter of the room—as the attendants in the center watch with lazy eyes—and then back up the stairs to class. Some safety goal may have been achieved, but there is always at least one fight, always the whiff of danger, always an alarming meeting of chaos and indifference.

———

After work today Mr. B dispenses chewing gum. Antoine, on punishment for cursing, comes off the wall to get a piece. Mr. B inadvertently hands him an empty wrapper and Antoine extends his arms and affects an expression of mock injury. "Mr. B, you're wrong," he howls, and everyone cracks up.

"Mario," says Mr. B after a few moments. "Can I talk to you?"

"Right, Mr. B," says Mario.

"Bring your chair," he adds, indicating a longer conversation.

Mario has been in Audy Home for eighteen months—he's the senior student in Mr. B's class—and next week he is scheduled to leave. He has agreed to a plea bargain that pleases him—time served plus one year for a charge of armed carjacking. "It doesn't really *please* me," he tells Mr. B, "because I hate saying I did something I didn't do. And I know everyone in here says 'I didn't do it', and so it sounds like I'm just saying what everyone else is saying, but the difference is that in my case it's the truth. I didn't do it. I don't know anything about other guys' cases."

So why did he plead guilty and why does he feel, if not pleased, at least relieved?

"I watched Harold get twenty-five years; Lazarus, thirty; Kareem, twenty-two. . . . I felt like I was in a death march and I wanted out. I kept looking at my life wasting here, the time I could do, thinking about how old I'd be when I'd get out—hell, I'm just sixteen!—and one more year looked good. I'll be docked for a year, seventeen and out. Then I can live again."

Mr. B begins by thanking Mario for being a model student, then reviews some of his work with him. He reminds him that the last few days here can be the toughest—a combination of high anxiety inside your own head, jealousy and testing from others. Mr. B urges Mario to stay calm and straight, to help the other guys by showing them how someone can approach the transition with purpose and maturity, and to come to him if he needs anything—advice, a sympathetic ear, anything at all.

"Thanks, Mr. B."

Mario has goals: he hopes to get his GED while in Little Joliet, attend junior college in Chicago and work with his uncle in construction after he's released. "It might be tough to do once I'm out," Mario concedes. "But my mom says that I have a strong mind. She's right about that because I think deeply, too deeply sometimes, and I can get my mind all agitated."

Mario is close to his mother, to his two sisters, and to his baby brother. "My momma is my rock; she visits me every week or I couldn't take it here." His momma drives a truck for UPS. "She says I need to be real and to do my own things. She says to do what I do for myself, and not for someone else."

Mario is affiliated with a gang, but, he says, he doesn't gang-bang or participate actively in the life of the gang. "Everybody's affiliated," he says. "You have to be. But I mostly stay to myself and do my own things." He's been arrested twice for stealing cars—"I messed up"—but both arrests were station adjusted. This arrest is different—a gun was used, a violent confrontation initiated—and so he is locked up. "It ain't going to happen again," he says firmly.

I ask Mario how fast he could get a gun on the bricks if I gave him two hundred dollars. Without a hint of irony he replies, "How many you want?" Two hundred dollars could buy a small arsenal, he tells me. "If you gave a shorty forty dollars, he'd have a .22 revolver in your hand in forty-five minutes." Jesus had said he could get two used nine millimeter handguns in an hour with two hundred dollars. He was figuring a profit for himself in that estimate. Woo, woo, woo.

Jane Addams, not long after the turn of the century, described an incident in which two thirteen-year-olds were arguing and one got a gun and killed the other: "This tale could be duplicated almost every morning; what might be merely a boyish scrap is turned into a tragedy because some boy has a revolver." Jesus had told me guns are important for everyone, for protection, for pride. With a gun you might rescue yourself from nothingness, your sense of despair might be purged. With a gun, no matter how small and terrified and marginal you feel, you can become part of an elite.

February 6. The hard ground is frozen through, the wintry waves upswept—all white and frosty—transposed in midcrash from furious motion to arctic glass. A fading, fragile sun offers no heat and precious little light to our dark smudge of a city nestled between Lake Michigan and the vast, flat plains stretching westward.

We are huddled—fewer than thirty of us—in an open space on the corner of State and Thirty-fifth in front of Stateway Gardens, a public housing community. A group of us are here the first Sunday of each month, our numbers diminished and a little disheartened in midwinter. We are black and white, young and old, friends and strangers—an eclectic and colorful collection. A large banner behind us proclaims: "Vigil Against Violence." It is dusk, and each of us holds a small white candle with a jerry-rigged paper hood to protect its dancing light against the wind.

Sokoni Karanja, a community organizer and activist, addresses the gathering: "We are here in opposition and in affirmation," he says. "We oppose the violence, the guns, the drugs, visited upon this community. We affirm life, and, as survivors, we commit our lives to the path of peace and justice."

Jamie Kalven, another organizer and well-known Chicago citizen, has a powerful explanation of the vigil's larger purposes:

> The power and promise of the vigil initiative reside, at this stage, not in our numbers but in the quality of attention the wakeful ness—we are helping each other to cultivate. This wakefulness is the opposite of the blindness—the condition of *not seeing*—that violence both demands and inflicts.

Violence erases. It removes from the world. It renders invisible. We collaborate in the reign of violence when we respond, as human beings tend to, by pushing the things we most fear the farthest from our sight. And we collaborate with violence when we deny what we know, because to acknowledge it would be to open ourselves to the demand that we act to change the world.

We seek by means of the vigil process to make absence present, to make silence audible . . .

The violence that haunts our communities is an expression of powerlessness. Freedom is choice; it is alternatives; it is options. Violence is a narrowing of options to a single disastrous course . . .

Among the powerful, there is much talk these days about violence. There is not, however, a comparable eagerness to talk about power. We condemn individual acts of violence. At the same time, we call to account the public and private institutions that contribute to the conditions of powerlessness out of which these violent acts arise.

Gathering on these occasions to read the names of those killed on the South Side since we last came together, we create a special sort of space. It is a space where we make ourselves available to the problem, where we open ourselves to the scale of the catastrophe. We do this together, because it is too daunting a task to do alone. In the space we create absence becomes present. It is a space for shared wakefulness. A space for listening deeply to silence.

We will now read the names.

Several of us are asked by Reverend Susan Johnson, a local pastor, to read a few names—those killed since our last monthly vigil, those killed only on the South Side of our city. The line of readers—each with five or six names on a card—stretches to the banner and beyond. The local alderman will read, the chief of police, teachers, doctors, principals, parents, children. The list is too long; the names are victims, of course, but in the bloodbath of drugs and gangs and guns, some were also perpetrators. It doesn't matter. Jamie's words ring in my ears as I read the names of five young people: Dewona Book, Sherman Hubbard, Andrew Liggett, Michael O. Sheldon, Dion Low.

A second banner lists the cumulative names of the murdered, including the names I just read, and as I finish and move back to the crowd I notice a tall young man—starter jacket, black knit hat pulled low on his head—reaching out to touch a specific name. He is weeping. I realize that Sokoni and Jamie and Susan have created through these vigils something remarkably powerful—a way for people to make meaning out of meaninglessness, to bring some order to chaos, to name ourselves in opposition, and in the moment of that naming to open a field of possibility. Like the AIDS quilt or the Vietnam memorial wall, the vigil personalizes loss, animates grief, encourages action even as it recognizes the inadequacy of that action. The vigil provides a way to live in the city—or in the modern world—as something more than an alienated, passive accidental tourist or a barricaded, paranoid prisoner. It invites us to embrace the world even as we fight to build a society that could be, but is not yet.

———

"I won't miss this place," Mario says flatly. "But I will miss Mr. B. He's the best teacher I ever had."

Why?

"See, Mr. B could be anywhere," he says. "He's smart, he's strong, and he could work at a lot of things. But he comes here to be with us because he's got a big heart and he actually likes us."

He has praise for others at Audy, too. "Mrs. Anderson, too, man. Mrs. Anderson could be downtown being president of something, but she cares about us. And Miss Lisa . . . Miss Lisa is real. She gives me lots of juice, lots to think about. She's a great lady. And, you, too, man. You don't have to come here, so you OK."

And then he circles back to Mr. B: "Everybody knows Mr. B is a great teacher. We've got weights, doughnuts, movies, pizza parties. He challenges us to be better. He lets us go see Mrs. Anderson or Mr. Williams when we need to."

Mr. B hosts a party for each of his departing students on his final day in class, usually featuring pizza, but occasionally hero sandwiches or tacos. The party is one way to mark the passing parade—the Death March in Mario's words—as something other than given, scripted, predictable. It is a way of saying, "Mario was here; he was our classmate and friend; we will miss him; we wish him well." The party is generally fun—eating pizza is near the top of the felt deprivations for these teenage boys—but never festive. Change is hard, and detention teaches youngsters to temper their commitments, to check their emotions, to avoid intimacy, to live inside themselves. In an odd irony, the culture of distrust and loneliness inside the joint strengthens formal organizational affiliations that boys bring with them. Gangs flourish.

"What should I bring for your last day, Mario?" Mr. B asks.

Mario locks his eyes onto Mr. B's and shakes his head "no." "I'm straight, Mr. B," he says quietly.

"I'd like to have a little party for you, Mario."

"Naw, thanks, Mr. B." Mario looks like he's going to cry. "I'm straight. Just another day."

"Well," says Mr. B, "that's OK, Mario. You know I'll miss you."

"Thanks, Mr. B."

Later Mario tells me that everybody wants to have a party for him— Miss Lisa, Mr. Williams, Mrs. Anderson—but that the only party he really wants is the celebration of his final release from custody. "I want to party with my momma and my sister and my girlfriend. When I get out we'll have balloons. Until then, I'll wait."

11. Freddie

THE POOL PLAYERS.
SEVEN AT THE GOLDEN SHOVEL.

We real cool. We
Left school. We

Lurk late. We
Strike straight. We

Sing sin. We
Thin gin. We

Jazz June. We
Die soon.

Gwendolyn Brooks
"We Real Cool"

"MR. B, CAN I MOVE MY DESK?" It's Freddie, stirring, posturing, slightly provoking.

"Where to?"

"Over there behind LeMarque."

"There's no room there, Freddie."

"Man, I'm saying. Come on man. Don't hurt me, man. I'm kicking, man. What about it?"

"You can move over there, to the empty desk in the front of the room."

"No, man. I need to do my work over there."

"You haven't been doing much work lately, so you think moving will help?"

Freddie is smiling and jiving, and not really expecting to be taken seriously, but he keeps the banter going, acting put upon, sheepish, and menacing in turn. "Oh man, like I got to be next to LeMarque, man."

"Don't put him here, Mr. B," LeMarque teases back. "He'll be pestering me. I got work to do."

"Quit talking to me, son," says Freddie, smiling with ferocious eyes. "You hear me, Joe? Don't talk so much."

Friday afternoon means doughnuts. "Never a reward, but just part of my routine—a gentle reminder that I care for them," says Mr. B as he hauls out two huge boxes and places them on his desk. "What kind you want, Antoine?" he asks softly.

"Could you hook me up with strawberry, Mr. B? Thanks, Mr. B." There is a sweet politeness in the exchange.

Mr. B dispenses a first round—chocolate-covered, sugar-coated, jelly-filled—and everyone stands around munching contentedly, joking easily, their faces happily dusted with sugar, glazed with frosting.

"Man," Mario begins, "I've been in here too long."

A chorus of responses:

"You ain't been in but a second."

"Now *I've* been in some serious time."

"Yeah, me too. Me too."

"I forgot what grass looks like. I forgot the smell of my mom's chicken."

"Naw. You're just a big kid. You don't know what real time is."

Mario again: "Somebody told me pop costs seventy-five cents from a machine. I thought it was thirty cents. I couldn't believe it. I been in here too long," he repeats, shaking his head.

"Yeah," agrees LeMarque, "I'll be out there on the bricks, walking along by myself and I'll be looking for an attendant. What I'm doing walking all by myself? Where the people asking where I think I'm going? Where's the attendant?"

Everyone laughs. Freddie slaps LeMarque's hand in appreciation and then builds on the moment: "I was out last year after being in here three months, and for days I'd jump out the bed at six. In my mind I'd hear, POP! POP! POP! Hmmmm . . ., and I'd jump." The general merriment explodes with Freddie's perfect simulation of lights coming on in the units—a heavy metal clap followed by the sharp electric purr of current vibrating through wire. "Man," he concludes, "this place messing with my mind."

"Mr. B," says Antoine, "can I get another?"

"Of course. What kind would you like this time?" Antoine picks custard and Mr. B reaches into the box with a paper napkin to pull one out. Everyone comes by for seconds and then thirds. After filling up,

Andrew says, "Drawer," and reaches to Mr. B's left to pull out some plastic wrap. He passes it around; several students tear off a piece to preserve their little bundles of contraband which they will smuggle upstairs to eat later.

"Mr. B," says LeMarque, "Mr. B, how you do this?" He is trying to tear a piece of plastic off the roll using the little sharp-toothed edge, making a mess of it. "I ain't never done this before."

"Here," responds Mr. B, showing him how to place his hands. "Hold this steady and press down on the edge like this; keep pulling this way." LeMarque holds a perfect piece of wrap in front of his face, a look of surprise and glee. "Thanks, Mr. B."

Freddie teases LeMarque for being a big baby, and LeMarque mimics pulling a gun from his belt and shooting Freddie—BAM! BAM!—in the head. His bright boyish face is suddenly terrifying in its seriousness, its coldness.

Andrew has a stack of four doughnuts wrapped, neat and tight, but in the next hour and a half, the package will be reduced by three. Andrew is always hungry.

The classroom is often relaxed, but Friday afternoon is remarkably more casual—students sit on their desks and chat together, wander freely into the backroom, and keep the radio playing to the limit of what Mr. B can stand. "My classroom feels to me like controlled chaos much of the time," says Mr. B, "but on Fridays, I'm not so sure. Just chaos, I guess."

The students know by heart the words to the popular songs that cycle through the preferred station—106 JAMS!—and when a favorite comes on, Antoine stands and sways, Mario pretends to be at a microphone, and they all sing in chorus: "As I walk in the valley of the shadow of death / Take a look at my life and realize there's nothing left / Cuz I've been blasting and laughing so long / That even my momma thinks my mind is gone . . . Spending most of our lives / Living in a gangster paradise."

When Coolio sings everyone joins in again: "Momma, I'm in love with a gangster / Momma, I'm in love with a gangster / Momma, I'm in love with a gangster / And I know he's a killer / But I love that nigger."

Most students have been in the weight room for about ten minutes when Merce bursts back into the main room laughing and fanning his nose with his hand. "Man, Mr. B," he exclaims with exaggerated disgust, "Freddie farted! I need some of that air freshener." Mr. B nods and Merce reaches into a desk drawer, takes out a can, and heads for the back room. A moment later he returns, spraying out the doorway and laughing. Freddie follows and Merce, teasing, starts spraying at him with relish.

"All right, Merce," says Mr. B, "put the air freshener back."

"OK, Mr. B, but Freddie's nasty."

"Shut up, man," says Freddie laughing. "A man's got to pass gas or explode."

———

"Man, I hate chapel," says Merce as he enters the classroom Monday morning. His unit is scheduled for a recreational period in the old chapel after school today—an activity that has nothing to do with religious worship—and Merce finds it boring and unnecessary. "Why we got to go down there in a crowd and just mill around? I'd rather stay upstairs."

"Get to work, gentlemen," says Mr. B, without addressing Merce's complaint. "We'll have free time later. I want you to start this morning with your regular work."

The students settle in variously, but eventually everyone is purposefully pulling along. The morning seems subdued. Mr. B, always low-key, is silent, and, curiously, the door to the back room is closed and locked.

At ten o'clock Mr. B asks the students to put their work away. "Before we take a break, gentlemen, I want to talk to you about a couple of items." Mr. B sounds serious, and today his tone is somber. Everyone stops working immediately and looks up.

"I'm sure you noticed that the back room is locked," he begins. "I don't like to keep it locked, because I want you to be able to use it. But on Friday, you broke my trust, and you disappointed me deeply. We're going to have to rebuild some of that trust before I will reopen that room."

He pauses and there is a dramatic silence. Andrew stirs self-consciously in his seat, Mario looks intently at Mr. B, and several boys lower their heads.

"I don't know who had a cigarette back there on Friday, and I don't want to know. I don't expect you to tell me, because I wouldn't want anyone to tell me. That's not my point." Again, he pauses.

"My point is about trust and about living together with trust and commitment: you know that I don't like being punitive. I don't want you spending time on the wall; I don't want to send you upstairs ever. You know, too, that I want you to set some goals for yourself and to work toward meeting them. I want you to be able to use the weights, to relax, and to listen to the radio when that's appropriate. I have high hopes and expectations for each and every one of you. But without trust we can't do much."

"Mr. B?"

"Yes, Rasheed."

"I don't even smoke. So what can I do?"

"You're not listening, Rasheed. It's not the one or two who smoked on Friday that concerns me. It's larger than that. What I want all of you to think about is how we can keep the back room open as a place for you to relax and lift weights, and how I can be assured that you will live within reasonable rules. I want to know I can trust you. I want to rely on you personally, not on rules and punishments."

He stops and there is a long, long silence. When he begins again, he develops a related concern: "In the next two weeks we could get several new students. I prefer starting one student at a time, so he can learn the routines and expectations and figure out what we do here. With several new guys I'm going to need each of you to help me help them get on the right track here." Pause.

Finally Andrew enters a tentative suggestion: "Maybe we could spend time before we go upstairs each day straightening things up and organizing the weights. . . ."

"OK," Mr. B responds, "that sounds reasonable, don't you think?"

An eager chorus of assent and nodding heads.

"And, maybe," says Merce, who has been in confinement on three separate occasions for smoking on his living unit, "if we see someone smoking or doing something else against the rules, we should just re-mind them, like, 'Hey, man, you're going to ruin it for everyone!'"

"Alright," says Mr. B. "That might be good, because you would be responsible for each other that way. And that's what we need to do so much in life. Be responsible. Help one another. So it's a start."

Freddie's prodigious Friday fart had been a smokescreen, and Mr. B is now clearing the air.

———

Merce begins this morning's oral reading:

> People ask Judge Richard E. Neville, who raised a stir by urging that drugs be legalized, "How are you going to protect my children?"
>
> "My response has been, 'Do you feel protected today under the current policy and all the money we're spending?'" the Criminal Court judge said. Neville made his controversial proposal late last month as a means to stem the nation's swelling wave of violence. This week, after dozens of phone calls, 55 to 60 letters and several TV and radio talk shows and interviews, he took a vacation.
>
> "Most of the comments have been very, very encouraging," Neville said. . . . "A few have been in opposition, but far more have been in favor of opening the dialogue . . ."
>
> Negative response did prompt one change, however. The judge now prefers the term "decriminalization" over legalization.

"All right, Merce," Mr. B stops the reading. "Thank you. What's happening here? What is this about?"

"Dude wants to legalize drugs."

"Speak English, Merce. Who is Dude?"

"This judge, Judge Richard E. Neville. He wants to legalize drugs. He crazy."

"Careful. Are you sure he wants to *legalize* drugs?" There is a pause as the students reread the few paragraphs. "What does decriminalize mean?" asks Mr. B, coaching. "What word do you see in the middle of decriminalize?"

"Criminal!" shouts LeMarque. "So he saying decriminalize, or make it not criminal. Same thing, Mr. B: legalize, decriminalize. Same thing."

"Well," says Mr. B deliberately. "You say it's the same thing, LeMarque, but he's making a distinction. Why?"

"Politics," says Merce quickly. "He trying to stay on both sides."

"OK, maybe. Let's read on."

"Wait," says Freddie. "This piece up here, 'How are you going to protect my children?' Who saying that?"

"That's a general question people pose to this judge. Here he is saying, 'Decriminalize drugs', and so a lot of people apparently are asking, 'How are you going to protect my children?', you know, once you do that."

"That's right," agrees Freddie. "Someone's got to tell children right from wrong. Like now kids get adults to buy them beer and wine. Well, what's to stop kids from saying, 'Here, man, go in there and get me a blunt'?"

"But should liquor be outlawed?" asks Mr. B. "I mean it once was, and Prohibition led to street gangs, murders, all of that. Should liquor or cigarettes be outlawed?" Maybe. But most students can't imagine that any more than they can imagine other drugs being made legal.

"But if you outlaw sweats," says LeMarque, "then some people get sick and stressed out and go to smacky ready rock. Right now they're killing us slowly."

Merce asks, "Is this judge really doing this?"

"No, he's just putting it out there for discussion. It's a proposal."

"It's crazy," repeats Merce.

"It won't change anything," adds Freddie. "People still be dealing because there will be people who can't get the legal stuff. Someone will deal to them."

"Let's read some more," Mr. B gently insists. "Freddie, your turn."

> The former prosecutor and defense attorney sparked the debate February 29 when he addressed a Chicago service club luncheon. The vast profits of the illegal drug industry spawn gang and individual violence, he said.
>
> Neville challenged politicians to weigh the cost and effectiveness of the war on drugs against making marijuana, cocaine and heroin legal, regulating their pricing and sales and reallocating funds for more drug awareness education. . . .

Interestingly, not one lawyer criticized his proposal, Neville said. The legal profession would stand to be one of the biggest losers if drugs were decriminalized, given the torrent of cases that flood the courts. Night drug court in Cook County has become "just a revolving door," accounting for nearly half the court system's criminal caseload, said criminal defense lawyer Jack P. Rimland.

"Why would the legal profession be among the big losers?" asks Mr. B.

"Because they getting rich on drug cases," says LeMarque. "They defend hundreds of guys and make a fortune."

"Right," agrees Freddie. "And you know how the police have to arrest a certain number of people or lose their jobs. Well, without drugs, what will the police do for a living?"

"So drugs are good for the economy, Freddie?" asks Mr. B with mock astonishment.

"Yeah, man, in a way. Sure. Keeps things going. Without it, police won't be raiding people's houses, so they either go out of business, or find a way to put murder weapons or something on people. They got to make their set number of arrests. When I caught my case, it was just the cop making his number. Like one day when I was just a shorty my mother was drinking a beer and a policeman told her to pour it out. He was way too little to be saying that to my mother. No way I was going to let him put handcuffs on her. But she poured it out, so he had to arrest someone else to make his number."

Antoine has followed along in his quiet way, but now asks, incredulous, "You mean, I could walk around with the stuff in my pockets?"

"Yep," says Freddie. "Most police just wink at blunts now. Some make you eat it and watch you get sick, but mostly they let it go. So blunts already decriminalized. And then, too, most drug cases thrown out anyway. So what's the difference? One thing is I be feeling foolish going into the drugstore saying, 'Excuse me, ma'am, which is the "ready rock" aisle?' That's going to be embarrassing." Everyone laughs at the impossible image.

Freddie entertains and provokes, is a superb conversationalist, and is eager to offer a monologue for as long as Mr. B will stand it. Which is no longer.

"Alright Freddie," he cuts in, "let Antoine finish this reading."

> Bill Nolan of the Fraternal Order of Police did not wilt in telling
> Neville the error of his thinking. "If legalization occurred, you'd
> have the United States of America become nothing but a bunch of
> potheads," said the president of the Chicago local that represents
> police officers.
>
> Comparisons Neville has made to drug laws and Prohibition "are
> apples and oranges," Noland said. Most people can have a social
> drink or two, but drug use leads to addiction "that gets worse and
> worse and worse."

"He's right," says Freddie. "Absolutely right. See, you then going to
have little kids doing it, everyone doing it. Like now only the hypes is
crazy. Then, if it's legal, anyone be crazy."

LeMarque says, "If they do this, and sell it in the stores, it's going to
be expensive. The government going to find a way to get over, to make
something on this one way or another. So, like, how they going to get
it into the country?"

"Right," Freddie says. "The hypes going to rush the transport.
Niggers going to be out there *taking*. Strong armed robbery."

Merce says, "Well, this judge going to be put out of office. The parents
are against him, the police are against him. What chance does he have?"

"Well . . ." it's Freddie again. "The hypes are going to vote for him.
They'll come to his house singing, 'Free at Last!'"

The conversation carries on into the break and the back room.
Freddie is still on it: "They should stop making drugs and tell those
Colombians to go home."

Andrew teases: "Oh, yeah. What would you do without your little
drugs to sell?"

Freddie smiles his broad but always slightly menacing smile, his
sharp teeth barely visible: "I'd find something."

Freddie is fifteen years old with a long and troubling record: possession of drugs, possession of a firearm, assault, possession with intent to
distribute, assault, selling drugs on public housing property—his A.T.
case. "I ain't got no *bad* case," he insists. "No statement or nothing. So
I'll kick it."

"I been in Audy four times, but I caught bogus cases," he says. "Like I shot a girl with a BB gun, but I was just playing, you know what I'm saying? Just shooting, shooting, shooting for fun. So this girl comes to Court and tells the judge and I said, 'Come on. You know I was just playing.'" He laughs. "Outside I told her she better not come to Court again, so she stopped coming and that one was dropped."

He's caught other cases: "I was just chillin and I caught this other case." Freddie hit a rival gang member in the forehead with a hammer, but that kid, too, failed to come to court. "See I'm innocent because I got all these S.O.L.s," he says, referring to dropped charges; if a case is "stricken on leave" technically there is leave to reinstate, but practically the case is over. "I'm innocent, man."

The A.T. case involved an incident at Robert Taylor Homes, Freddie's public housing home. "I saw them coming, but what could I do? I had five hundred dollars in my pocket and one hundred and fifty rocks. I'm running up the stairs—all the way to the thirteenth floor—and I'm knocking on doors, begging. I couldn't throw it away—just too much money involved—and the cops were everywhere. So I caught that case. You know what I'm saying?"

"Besides," he adds, "I'm just trying to make a little money. But now I'm through with that."

———

The Juvenile Court judge said that he believed Freddie's mother could not control him, a claim that Freddie dismisses as "bogus." "OK," he concedes, "we have our differences, but we, you know, love each other."

Freddie's anger is not toward her, but toward his probation officer. "That nigger said my mom can't control me, and that I had threatened him. That's bogus because he said that in Court which turned the judge against me. I didn't threaten him, but if he treat me like that, I'll follow him home next time or get one of my guys to shoot him. And that's no threat."

"I'll be straight soon," he says later. "I didn't pay attention to school before, but now I am. I'm trying to learn, even though Mr. B, he doesn't like me much, never lets me go to special programs. But I'm trying to learn, you know what I mean? I'm taking Bible studies here, and when I'm out, I'm going back to church. I'm going over to the United Center, get me a little job, sweeping the floor or something. Then maybe they'll notice me, and I'll be the next Dennis Rodman. They'll be watching me and I'll be all crazy—only thing I won't do is dress like a lady. Other than that, I'm Rodman for real, know what I mean?"

———

Freddie gets right up in Andrew's face with his mean smile. "You been smoking too much dope, son," he says. "I know it because I sold it to you. I ain't lying. I ain't keeping no secrets."

He walks around the room during free time like a panther on the prowl. He pokes everyone he passes, pushing the edge of danger, just this side of violence. When Andrew challenges him, he moves forward, laughing, mocking, "I'm just playing man. Don't act retarded, son."

"Everybody trying to kick with me," he says. "All these people trying to kick it with me. Why you all trying to kick it with me? Why all eyes on me? Son, why you want to kick it with big Freddie? Listen, Joe, don't kick it with me. I'm not going anywhere. I'll be here. Don't kick it, dude."

———

"We need guns," says Andrew to me one morning, "mainly for self-protection. So I agree with letting people carry out in the open like they said on the news they can do in Florida."

"Yeah," says Freddie, "like you could get gun guards for everyone, just like the security guards wear. And that way, you know, you could avoid accidents." He smiles again. "Man, can't you see us all here in our classroom, firearms strapped on." It is too ridiculous, and LeMarque and Antoine fall out of their chairs laughing.

"Anything you can get on the outside you can get in here," says Freddie. "*Anything.* Except for a gun, but, hey, what are you going to do with a gun? I mean you can escape, but no one really is going to escape."

Freddie practices the Mike Tyson look—crouched power in a hooded sweatshirt with threatening eyes cutting out of the shadows. "I like to fight, man. I'm Tyson for real and I want to show them something."

You can never be sure when he's jiving, when he's serious. "I got a sense of humor—that's just me. I got to laugh at shit. But I'll fight Andrew for real and show him what I'm made of. The fight will be after midnight on the unit. The attendants will set it up and it'll be a big show." He can turn menacing in a blink.

———

Looking for scissors in Mr. B's desk Freddie comes across a small memorial card for Effie Peters in one of the drawers. "Who's this?" he asks, holding the card for Mr. B to see.

Effie Peters was a kind and caring teacher in the school who died a few years ago. The card has a picture of a large man next to the words, "Striking in size. Soft in demeanor. Caring and sharing in spirit."

"I keep that to remember him," says Mr. B, "because he was a friend and he was a good teacher, and because this was his classroom before he died. So his spirit is here."

Freddie nods slowly and returns the card to the desk.

———

Being "on punishment" always hurts, but the screws are tightened by degrees. Every kid has a breaking point. Andrew was busted for smoking a cigarette, or "square"—two days in his room, forty-eight hours without a break. No problem. When Freddie and Andrew got into a fistfight the next week, it was three days each, and they were bumped from their rooms near the common area where the TV is—just barely—visible, to rooms at the far end near the bathroom. When Freddie punched out a window because "It stink there," he was moved again behind steel doors. When he started kicking the door and hollering, the attendants stripped his room, throwing a mattress on the floor at night.

"Man," says Merce, commenting on Freddie's eighth day in lockup, "you got to give him that. He up there chillin' hard. I can't do that. He's in his house shoes, stretched out on the floor, laughing to himself, saying anything."

"Man," says Freddie smiling slyly as he returns to class, "Taylor was trippin' this time. But I got through it just staring at the walls. We straight now."

12. Punishment

> I've known rivers:
> I've known rivers ancient as the world and older than the flow of human blood
> in human veins.
> My soul has grown deep like the rivers.
>
> I bathed in the Euphrates when dawns were young.
> I built my hut near the Congo and it lulled me to sleep.
> I looked upon the Nile and raised the pyramids above it.
> I heard the singing of the Mississippi when Abe Lincoln went down to New
> Orleans, and I've seen its muddy bosom turn all golden in the sunset.
>
> I've known rivers:
> Ancient, dusky rivers.
>
> My soul has grown deep like the rivers.
>
> Langston Hughes
> "The Negro Speaks of Rivers"

MICHAEL FREEMAN, a friend from South Africa, is staying with us for several days. He is an official with the Anglican Church in charge of voter education and registration. He had worked closely with the African National Congress during the resistance and now works with the Mandela government. Michael is in Chicago to exchange information with community-based voter projects and to meet with foundation officers about strategies for funding his efforts.

"You know," he tells us early in his visit, "we face a desperate problem with youth crime. Under apartheid our youth were rounded up and incarcerated in huge numbers. Now, with no formal education, and bearing the scars of growing up in prison, these young people must somehow integrate into the new society. It is a critical, monumental struggle for us." He would like to visit the Audy Home.

We arrive in class a few minutes late, and the students are already plowing into today's group lesson, a short story called "The Return" by the Kenyan writer Ngugi wa Thiong'o. Arrested and detained without trial in 1978 following the production of one of his plays, Thiong'o is well known in Africa as a writer of integrity and courage whose central themes—the exploitation of Africans by Europeans and neocolonial-

ists, the clash between traditional and invading cultures, the importance of education for creating a new society—resonate for millions
across the continent. Michael Freeman, of course, knows his work, and
has read "The Return" several times. He is visibly pleased to find it
here, and to hear it being read in this stark and surprising context.

"The Return" is the story of Kamau, a man coming home to his village after five years in detention. He carries his meager belongings in a
bag. Antonio is struggling through his part: "The bundle held the bitterness and hardship of the years spent in detention camps."

When Kamau arrives at his home village he gets an oddly chilly welcome. He notices that the village is both familiar and strange. Some of
the landmarks are the same, he can find his way easily to his street and
to his home, but the people . . . the people have changed. He realizes
that, of course, things are different, and he remembers talking of home
with his fellow prisoners as if time had stopped: a newborn baby, a
pregnant wife, an adolescent brother. "All of them longed for one
day—" Antoine reads, "the day of their return home. Then life would
begin anew."

But five years! Naturally people have changed and grown. Babies
have been born, old people died. He would adjust.

It is Rasheed's turn to read, and there is a long pause as he stares at
the page. Rasheed is a good reader, and this should give him no trouble, but still he pauses. No one speaks. Finally he draws a breath and
reads slowly, ardently: " He had suffered many humiliations, and he
had not resisted. Was there any need? But his soul and all the vigor of
his manhood had rebelled and bled with rage and bitterness." Michael
Freeman, his eyes misty now, stares straight at Rasheed.

Kamau discovers that his wife, who he had imagined would be waiting for him, has run off with a friend. The man had been detained with
him and, upon release, had come home and told the villagers that
Kamau was dead. Outraged and overwhelmed, Kamau rushes to the
river—the living river, changing and constant both, where he had
bathed as a child—and tosses away the bundle of "little things that had
so strangely reminded him of her and that he had guarded all those
years."

Kamau realizes suddenly, to his surprise, that he is relieved to watch the bundle disappear. "Why should she have waited for me?" reads Rasheed, and his voice breaks. "Why should all the changes have waited for me?"

A protracted silence follows Rasheed's reading. Several students keep their heads down in their books. Antoine shakes his head slowly. "Man," he says in his whispery voice, to no one in particular. "Man, this is like when we get out. A lot of things are going to be new. That's weird." He continues, reading now, "Why should she have waited for me? Why should all the changes have waited for my return?" He shakes his head again. "I know how he feels. I want everything to stand still."

"Yeah," says Andrew, "but I'm realistic, too. Things change. People change. You've got to expect a difference. Look, I've got a girl out there, and I want her to wait for me. But five years? No, that's too much to expect. I'd want her to get on with her life."

"Well," replies Antoine. "If I had a female out there I wouldn't expect her to wait forever. But to wait some? Yes. I'd want her to wait a year at least, and I'd want her to stay in touch with me, like to be my friend."

"Five years," LeMarque says wistfully. "In five years people don't know you no more. You got to start over again. Five years ago I was a little shorty—eleven years old." He smiles his dazzling sweet smile. "And five years from now . . . I'll be twenty-one." He stops short, and the smile disappears abruptly. "I don't care," he says flatly.

"I do," Antoine says, "I care. If I get five years—and, God, I hope I don't get that—I wouldn't even go back to the neighborhood. I wouldn't stay in the city. I'd go to my sister's in Tennessee and get a job and leave all this behind."

"It sounds good," says Rasheed. "But it's hard to do. I'm going to go home and stay with my parents, and I'll just stay in the house, never go out."

"No way, man," replies Freddie. "You'll get sucked back into the life, into everything all over again. You'll be dead or back in here. Me, I'm trying a different environment, a new city or something, like Antoine. And I'm getting a job for sure. A job will keep me straight."

"What kind of job you going to get?" teases Merce. "You can't do nothing, nigger."

"I'm, serious, man," says Freddie. "I'm not kidding. I'm back in here because I went back to the old environment, got into the same old stuff."

"But what happens," asks Merce, "if you can't get a job? No one wants to hire you, say, you're a gang-banging ex-con and you're broke, you want a car. What then?"

Freddie answers, "Material things aren't important to me anymore. My life is important to me. God sent me up in here to spare my life. I'm paying attention to that."

"I like that," says Antoine fervently, "because I agree with Freddie. I'm not going to get in trouble again if I can beat this one thing. I'm not. I'll get a degree, I'll get a job. I'm not coming back."

LeMarque is skeptical: "I ain't going to lie, guys. When I get out I'll be good for a couple of weeks, but then I'll get in the scene. I'll see those dollars flowing, and I'll think, 'I want some of what everybody else has got.' Bam! I'll be hanging."

A couple of students laugh, and Merce shakes his head in disbelief. LeMarque's statement so clearly misses the spirit of the discussion, but it is honest and self-aware. It is an important counterpoint to fantasy and illusion.

———

Prisons, and the imprisonment of individuals as punishment for wrong-doing, are relatively recent human inventions, born of the triumph of rationalism and the impulse to reform. Before the nineteenth century common sanctions included public displays and ritual humiliations: whippings, brandings, hangings in the village square. Justice, such as it was, tended to be swift. People awaiting punishment were held together in jails, but the punishment was something other than being locked up. We remember colonial America: the scarlet letter and the public shunning, the banishment to the edge of town. We can visit old Williamsburg and see for ourselves the stocks where people were displayed, tortured, and shamed in front of the crowd.

Michel Foucault, the difficult but ultimately rewarding philosopher and historian, begins his germinal work on the birth of the prison, *Discipline and Punish*, with this:

> On 2 March 1757 Damiens the regicide was condemned 'to make the *amende honorable* before the main door of the Church of Paris', where he was to be 'taken and conveyed in a cart, wearing nothing but a shirt, holding a torch of burning wax weighing two pounds'; then, 'in the said cart, to the place de Greve, where, on a scaffold that will be erected there, the flesh will be torn from his breasts, arms, thighs and calves with red-hot pincers, his right hand, holding the knife with which he committed the said parricide, burnt with sulphur, and, on those places where the flesh will be torn away, poured molten lead, boiling oil, burning resin, wax and sulphur melted together and then his body drawn and quartered by four horses and his limbs and body consumed by fire, reduced to ashes and his ashes thrown to the winds.'

That's a one-sentence start to a several-page description of what happened to Damiens. It gets much worse. An eyewitness reports the difficulty of tearing flesh off a body with red-hot pincers, and how the horses failed to actually pull him apart, requiring the executioners to hack away with knives. The whole event takes a painfully long time, and when his limbless torso is tossed on the fire, he is still alive. The spectators apparently loved it and, according to one account, "were greatly edified."

Following this lengthy, disgusting description of the most gaudy kind of punishment, Foucault shifts abruptly to a more familiar form of discipline:

> The prisoners' day will begin at six in the morning in winter and five in summer. They will work for nine hours a day throughout the year. Two hours a day will be devoted to instruction. Work and day will end at nine o'clock in winter and at eight in summer. . . .
>
> At the first drum-roll, the prisoners must rise and dress in silence, as the supervisor opens the cell doors. At the second drum-roll, they must be dressed and make their beds. At the third, they must line up and proceed to the chapel for morning prayer. There is a five-minute interval between each drum-roll.

This is from Leon Faucher's rules "for the House of young prisoners in Paris," and it was written a mere eighty years after the incredible execution of Damiens. The list of rules goes on and on, assigning every task, itemizing each expected act, anticipating every moment. Here is "meal": "At ten o'clock the prisoners leave their work and go to the refectory; they wash their hands in their courtyards and assemble in divisions. After the dinner, there is recreation until twenty minutes to eleven."

And "school": "At twenty minutes to eleven, at the drum-roll, the prisoners form into ranks, and proceed in divisions to the school. The class lasts two hours and consists alternately of reading, writing, drawing and arithmetic."

Foucault discusses these two dramatically contrasting forms of punishment—the gory popular killing and the rigid regimentation of time:

> We have, then, a public execution and a time-table. They do not punish the same crimes or the same type of delinquent. But they each define a certain penal style. Less than a century separates them. It was a time when, in Europe and in the United States, the entire economy of punishment was redistributed. It was a time of great 'scandals' for traditional justice, a time of innumerable projects for reform. It saw a new theory of law and crime, a new moral or political justification of the right to punish; old laws were abolished, old customs died out. Modern codes were planned or drawn up.

To us, the second form of punishment is familiar and humane, while the first is horrific and strange. Certainly, imprisonment as punishment is based upon notions of moral and spiritual reform—improving, training, remaking individuals for their own good and for the good of society. And so we build the "penitentiary," a place to do penance, and the "correctional facility," and eventually the "reformatory" and "reform school." But for Foucault something else is at work: "The transition from the public execution, with its spectacular rituals, its art mingled with the ceremony of pain, to the penalties of persons buried in architectural masses and guarded by the secrecy of administrations, is not a transition to an undifferentiated, abstract, confused penalty; it is the transition from one art of punishing to another, no less skillful one. It is a technical mutation."

In other words, the change may not be the triumph of a humane and decent modern culture as we would like to believe, so much as it is a new, rationalized, and systematic use of power and authority. The elaborate display of death may, in fact, involve the exercise of less power than the total regulation and careful control of every aspect of a person's life.

Foucault describes a modern "science of discipline" whose aim is to control and engineer individual human behavior, fundamentally to create people who are obedient. The prison is in a sense just a pioneer, a pure form for the development of the "science of discipline." Discipline, then, becomes a central feature in the schools, hospitals, mental institutions, factories, and the military.

Steven Schlossman points to the development in the nineteenth century of an "entire class of custodial institutions" (prisons, mental hospitals, poorhouses, orphanages, reform schools) "in response to widespread fears—real and imagined—of social and family disintegration. The new institutions would isolate 'deviant' from law-abiding citizens to prevent 'contamination,' teach inmates the necessity of highly disciplined behavior in a rapidly evolving social order, and . . . create exemplars of order for the citizenry at large."

It is no wonder that new teachers today develop an unhealthy obsession with "classroom management," or that colleges of education "train" teachers to think that "control" is foundational in teaching, and that "discipline precedes learning." Like other institutions practicing the science of discipline, schools obey the laws of spatial distribution ("everyone in his place"), minute control of activity (walk in a straight line to the bathroom), repetition (drill and kill), detailed hierarchies (layer upon layer of supervision and control, everyone looking over their shoulders and upward), and normalizing judgments (grades, gold stars, the proliferation of pseudoscientific labels to describe the deviant—B.D., E.M.H., L.D., T.A.G.). Through a Foucaultian lens it is possible to see the central lessons of school as just these: obey and conform, follow orders, know your place in the hierarchy, and value others' judgments more than your own.

The "science of discipline" achieves its full expression in "a simple idea in architecture," Jeremy Bentham's *Panopticon*. A dramatic innovation in the nineteenth century, it is the typical design for prisons today: a central tower with wide windows around which stretches a building containing individual cells. Each inmate can be seen by a central observer but cannot see the observer nor any other inmate. "All that is needed, then, is to place a supervisor in a central tower and to shut up in each cell a madman, a patient, a condemned man, a worker or a schoolboy," writes Foucault. "He is seen, but he does not see; he is the object of information, never a subject in communication."

The prisoners' constant visibility to the authorities guarantees order, and the effect of the surveillance is permanent, whether anyone is watching or not. The inmates are "caught up in a power situation of which they are themselves the bearers." The functioning of power, then, becomes internal, automatic.

In 1842 Charles Dickens wrote of the modern prison in *American Notes*:

> In the outskirts, stands a great prison, called the Eastern Penitentiary; conducted on a plan peculiar to the state of Pennsylvania. The system here, is rigid, strict, and hopeless solitary confinement. I believe it, in its effects, to be cruel and wrong.
>
> In its intention, I am well convinced that it is kind, humane, and meant for reformation; but I am persuaded that those who devised this system of Prison Discipline, and those benevolent gentlemen who carry it into execution, do not know what it is that they are doing. I believe that very few men are capable of estimating the immense amount of torture and agony which this dreadful punishment, prolonged for years, inflicts upon the sufferers; and in guessing at it myself, and in reasoning from what I have seen written upon their faces, and what to my certain knowledge they feel within, I am only the more convinced that there is a depth of terrible endurance in it which none but the sufferers themselves can fathom, and which no man has a right to inflict upon his fellow-creature. I hold this slow and daily tampering with the mysteries of the brain, to be immeasurably worse than any torture of the body: and because its ghastly signs and tokens are not so palpable to the eye and sense of touch as scars upon the flesh; because its wounds are not upon the surface, and it extorts few cries that human ears can hear; therefore I the more denounce it, as a secret punishment which slumbering humanity is not roused up to stay.

Foucault, the historian, tracks the dramatic shift from the public spectacles of diverse and gruesome punishments to a single type of punishment for all crimes: imprisonment. This radical new idea has become the stuff of common sense; we can hardly imagine anything other. Yet the dogma supporting imprisonment, Foucault points out, runs hard against the facts. The rationale for the value of imprisonment includes the notion that discipline, supervision, work, and a careful system of punishment and rewards designed to shape behavior will remake individuals into productive members of society. In reality, detention causes recidivism. Prisons create delinquents and the organization of delinquents. The newly freed prisoner lives in conditions practically guaranteeing reimprisonment: under surveillance, unable to find work, condemned to an environment of crime.

The reformist justification—the idea of rehabilitation and improvement through imprisonment—has always loomed large in debates and discussions about prisons. But in their own terms the reforms are a farce: parole and probation are only possible if caseloads are manageable and parole officers are diligent; psychiatric help is not an option so long as there is one psychiatrist for every thousand inmates. And on and on. Every reform costs public money; the public, never eager to spend on criminals, is increasingly unwilling to spend anything on prisoners. The rehabilitation argument is dead, and the idea of deterrence is rapidly disappearing. Swelling rhetoric and good intentions notwithstanding, prisons remain custodial places designed to incapacitate a certain class of people.

There has been an explosion in the prison population in the past two decades. The incarceration rate in the United States was 455 per 100,000 in 1992—five times the incarceration rate of England, Germany, Sweden, and Japan. And four American states (California, New York, Texas, and Florida) have prison populations that would place each of them among the largest prison systems in the world. Still, prison expansion continues, and prisons are one of the few growth industries in several states. That prison doesn't work seems to be increasingly beside the point. Norval Morris, former dean and distinguished criminal law professor at the University of Chicago Law School, says,

"The irony is that the less effective the prisons are in reducing crime, the higher the demand for still more imprisonment." He calls this the Humpty Dumpty principle: "If all the king's horses and all the king's men couldn't put Humpty together again, then, by heavens, we need more horses and more men."

In their history of incarceration, Norval Morris and David J. Rothman ask: Why the prison? and, What of the prisoners?

There are competing and contradictory answers: "The conventional contemporary answer to 'Why the prison?' includes the desire to deter crime, to express society's urge for retribution, and to reform the deviant, but adds as well the desire to incapacitate dangerous criminals." Of prison's success at reformation they observe, "It is hard to train for freedom in a cage." Retribution: "Historically, punishment under the aegis of the law, and not that of the victim, prevents lasting and socially debilitating blood feuds . . . [but] whatever practices are followed in a society at any time, the majority of citizens perceive these practices as too lenient toward the criminal." Deterrence: "Likely, the prison deters some citizens and some prisoners from crime, but equally likely, it confirms other prisoners in their criminality."

Moreover none of this speaks to why *prison*, rather than other possible means of achieving stated goals. There are a wide range of ways to disable someone (banishment, capital punishment, and home detention come to mind, not necessarily in that order), so "why invest in cells and walls?" Morris and Rothman argue that our "expectations of the prison . . . are unreal and contradictory." We want decent and humane conditions for prisoners, and we want them to suffer the pain of punishment; we want to help prisoners improve themselves, and we want to punish them for their wrongdoing; we want to prepare them for life after prison, and we want to hurt them for the injury they have inflicted. "The rhetoric of imprisonment," Morris and Rothman point out, is in "stark contrast" with "the reality of the cage."

In part the difficulty lies in finding an appropriate and consistent approach to punishment in a free society. How much punishment is enough? What are the terms of control? What are the acceptable boundaries of shaping human behavior? When does retribution, discipline, or chastisement become excessively cruel or punitive? Most of us would agree that the chain gangs and brutality of Southern prisons in the 1930s, for example, are beyond what a progressive or democratic society should tolerate. What are the limits?

Morris and Rothman discuss prison labor as an example of contradictory attitudes and irresolution. We want prisoners to "do hard and punitive labor, be productive, and help meet the costs of their incarceration," but we don't want them to "compete unfairly with free labor or with entrepreneurship." Charles Dickens observed in *American Notes*:

> America, as a new and not over-populated country, has in all her prisons, the one great advantage, of being enabled to find useful and profitable work for the inmates; whereas, with us, the prejudice against prison labour is naturally very strong, and almost insurmountable, when honest men who have not offended against the laws are frequently doomed to seek employment in vain. Even in the United States, the principle of bringing convict labour and free labour into a competition which must obviously be to the disadvantage of the latter, has already found many opponents, whose number is not likely to diminish with access of years.

But neither do we want to work them to death in the tradition of the salt mines and the galleys, nor to "unfairly" abuse them or exploit their labor as in the pre–Civil War South. "The prisoner should work and yet he is denied work"—this "paradox" is·unresolved.

———

In a study entitled "Youth Violence, Guns, and the Illicit-Drug Industry," Alfred Blumstein reports a surprising fact: from 1972 to 1993 serious crime in the United States has remained "strikingly flat," with the rate of robbery at 200 to 250 per 100,000 population, and the murder rate at 8 to 10 per 100,000.

This is startling because the popular perception seems to be that crime in our society is always rising—an ever-worsening spiral of violence. The fear of becoming a victim of crime is our constant companion: the lore of everyday life is filled with the stories of friends or relatives or acquaintances and our own near misses or ·actual experiences, which animate all the more distant hearsay. Having had my apartment burglarized, having had my car stolen, having been held up at gunpoint—each experience up-close and personal—I have a visceral response to the local news. My identification with the victim of a crime and dread of the perpetrator are strong.

I remember being called to jury duty in New York's criminal court a decade ago. In the first cut for a murder trial a judge examined a potential panel of about a hundred citizens. His first question: "How many of you have ever been the victim of a crime?" Under ten hands went up. "Come on," he scolded, "this is Manhattan." We all laughed knowingly. "You or an immediate family member," he encouraged, "mugged, robbed, battery stolen, car window broken, home invaded, pocket picked . . ." As his list grew the number of hands went up steadily. When about ninety hands were in the air, he smiled and said, "That's more like it," and we laughed again. Then he asked who felt that the experience meant that they would be unable to hear a criminal case fairly, holding to the required presumption of innocence. We were down to four of the original ten, each of whom stood and told an intense story of gore and horror, each of whom was dismissed. I can't speak for the other ninety-six, but both my sense of vulnerability and my store of anecdotal evidence were seriously enhanced by the experience that morning.

Beyond the personal, crime is a standard media event and a heated political issue. Respondents in a recent *New York Times*/CBS poll identified violent crime as "the biggest problem facing the nation." Yet the big news in 1995—from a *Time* cover story to a *New York Times* series—was that violent crime was down substantially. In New York the murder rate was down a whopping 31% in six months.

Politicians from left to right claimed credit, of course, while academics, criminologists, and policy-makers theorized: all the criminals are finally locked up; potential bad guys are scared straight by three-strikes legislation, the massive prison building program, and the reinstitution of the death penalty everywhere; community-policing is a kinder, gentler, more effective approach to fighting crime.

Somehow the good news fails to spell relief. After all the good news is distant, academic-sounding, statistical. If we believed statistics we'd

never play the lottery. Statistics are black and white, while the anecdotes and the nightly news are all in technicolor.

Furthermore, there is an industry (actually several industries) whose
very survival depends on the bad news. Bruce Shapiro, in an incisive
analysis in *The Nation* called "How the War on Crime Imprisons
America," reports that an organization called the Council on Crime in
America, co-chaired by former drug-czar William Bennett and former
attorney general Griffin Bell, is touring the country with an alarming
message: the decrease in crime is illusory, a misguided and weak-willed
criminal justice system is putting dangerous criminals on the streets
who continue to prey on our communities; and—most important—"a
ticking time bomb" of young urban males is in our midst. As the number of teenagers peaks, the bomb will explode and "make the . . .
Bloods and Crips look tame by comparison."

The intellectual force behind the Council is, once again, John
DiIulio, Jr., who has written that "superpredators" are the biggest threat
facing civilization, and that "All that's left of the 'black community' in
some pockets of urban America is deviant, delinquent, and criminal
adults surrounded by severely abused and neglected children, virtually
all of whom were born out of wedlock." For DiIulio crime is a convenient racially coded word. The least thoughtful, most draconian solutions feed and are fed by racial prejudice, assumptions of racial
inferiority, and a smug sense of superiority.

DiIulio describes prison as "socially beneficial and cost-effective," a
"crime-restraint tool." He argues for expanding the already expansive
prison construction effort, and for putting "more violent and repeat
criminals, adult and juvenile, behind bars longer." There is little doubt
who he intends us to lock up.

DiIulio's solutions (in this report and elsewhere) are dramatic: re-
think prisons as crime prevention institutions, ignoring both the punishment and personal rehabilitation purposes; allow prison officials to
run their institutions however they see fit without fear of federal judges
intervening in questions of conditions; and create church-run and
state-funded orphanages so that abused children can be removed and
parental rights terminated quickly. Bruce Shapiro writes that these pro-

posals amount to "the wholesale writing off of a large segment of the population as irredeemably evil," and, "by implication . . . mass preventive incarceration of young black males." DiIulio and company do not discuss jobs and poverty, segregation and isolation, community and the strengthening of grass-roots democracy, the miserable performance and unintended consequences of the war on drugs, or the formidable problem of guns. His kind of thinking leads to the view that "demographics are destiny," says Shapiro, and eventually "the end of the presumption of innocence." From there the answer is easy: "authority of prison and authority of the state," something Shapiro understates as "a powerful and dangerous formula."

Alfred Blumstein's research points in a different direction as he untangles, examines, and remixes the crucial variables of age, guns, and drugs. Among other things, he has found that "homicide rates by youth eighteen and under have more than doubled. . . . The number of homicides juveniles committed with guns has more than doubled . . . and . . . the arrest rate of non-white juveniles on drug charges has more than doubled." These "three doublings" (which are complemented by no increase in drug arrests for white juveniles, no change in the number of murders committed without guns, and a decline in the homicide rate for older people) tell a terrible story. With the arrival of crack cocaine in our cities in the mid-eighties, dealers began recruiting numbers of juveniles as cheap labor in the drug trade, handguns become easily available, and young street dealers felt the need to be armed to protect product proceeds. Blumstein calculates 18,600 "excess murders" were committed by 15 to 22-year-olds from 1986 to 1992—murders exceeding the mean for each age from 1970 to 1985. And Shapiro, drawing on Bureau of Alcohol, Tobacco, and Firearms statistics, claims that gun manufacturing fell by nearly half between 1982 and 1986, "resulting in nearly 2 million fewer handguns in circulation." The industry more than rebounded in subsequent years: by 1993 "U.S. handgun manufacturing had doubled to an all time annual high of 2.8 million weapons."

How important are guns in the pattern of lethal violence? According to the Centers for Disease Control and Prevention, firearms were used in 72% of U.S. homicides in 1994. Franklin Zimring reports an important and revealing contrast: "The serious assault rate in the United State is about 30% greater than in England. The homicide rate is 530% greater." The difference? Mostly the easy availability and use of handguns.

The Second Amendment to the Constitution states that "the right of the people to keep and bear arms shall not be infringed." These words mark the entrance to the National Rifle Association's headquarters in Washington, D.C., but what is left out is critical. Preceding these well-known words is this phrase: "A well-regulated militia, being necessary to the security of a free state."

The Bill of Rights outlines in the clearest possible language what broad, individual rights every citizen possesses. Only here, in the Second Amendment, is the *purpose* of that right stipulated. And that stipulation has framed the case law surrounding gun ownership and weapons restrictions from the start. The Supreme Court argued in a 1939 case, for example, that Jack Miller violated the national Firearms Act when he transported a sawed-off shotgun across state lines. Since the "obvious purpose" of the Second Amendment was to "assure the continuation and render possible the effectiveness" of state militias, Miller would have had to prove that his sawed-off shotgun had "some reasonable relationship to the preservation or efficiency of a standing army." Militias were, after all, institutions of the state, like the National Guard.

Drugs and guns go hand-in-glove, and guns are "diffused" to other young people; that is, "as more guns appear in the community, the incentive for any single individual to arm himself increases." The armed drug-dealing teenagers are emulated by other teenagers in a concentric circle of doom.

Blumstein argues persuasively for more aggressive and creative approaches to confiscate guns from teenagers. He describes, for example, an experiment in Kansas City, Missouri in which "intensified enforcement in one patrol beat led to an increase of 65% in gun seizures and a decrease of 49% in gun crimes, with no comparable improvement in a comparison beat." Getting guns out of the hands of teenagers helps. Blumstein notes that billions of dollars are spent every year to try to stem the illegal drug market, whereas almost nothing is spent on the illegal gun market, though it might be a more effective approach "by using information from the youngster carrying the gun to work up the distribution chain, and by using the gun serial number to work down the distribution chain."

A study in the *New England Journal of Medicine* found that a gun in the home increases the risk of suicide fivefold; a second study found that the risk of a murder in the home went up 2.7 times. Still, manufacturers market aggressively to women in the pages of the *Ladies' Home Journal* and elsewhere, claiming that a handgun will protect you in your home: "Self-protection is more than your right," says a Colt .38 ad, "it's your responsibility." The photo is of a mother tucking her trusting child into bed.

Blumstein raises tentatively the question of legalizing drugs as a means of destroying or undermining the market. He is careful here to urge that we take a more intense look at the costs and benefits of current policies. But he leaves no doubt that simple, quick-fix solutions will come back to haunt us.

Bruce Shapiro makes the point strongly: "Eventually most of the 1.5 million-and-growing Americans incarcerated today are going to come out uneducated, unemployable, politically disenfranchised and angry." He quotes the police chief of New Haven on the same point: "If we continue to quick-fix by expanding our prisons, this drop is just the lull before the storm. You will within a few years have a significant segment of society who are *prison-influenced* and *prison-behaved*."

————

Mr. B speaks for the first time, summing up one lesson from "The Return": "We're all in different places in our lives, different spots and circumstances," he says. "We each have choices to make, and I like the way you're thinking about your own lives and what choices you'll have to face."

The energy driving the discussion flows through and over Mr. B's comment. Freddie pushes on: "OK, sure, you're going to have a hard time staying straight. But I have a strong mind, and I'm going to do it my way. Anyway, I'm leaving the organization—I'm in here because of fights over money between my buddies."

Antoine picks up the theme: "My buddies ain't my buddies. Hell, I'm in here for supposedly killing two guys inside my own organization. I got to get my life together, now, because I'm not getting another chance."

Rasheed replies, "If you're still in the organization, then they are your buddies, whether you like it or not."

"Really?" says Mr. B. "Whether you like it or not? See, gentlemen, I'm in several organizations myself. All voluntary. I choose to stay or to leave. And if I'm sick, I expect my church to help me out, for example, or if I can't work, I expect my fraternity to send money to my family. Is your organization good for you? Is it good to you?"

Several students look at him with poker faces, a couple smirk, but Freddie pipes right up. "My bond last time was $2500, and I sat for six months." And he is quickly back to his resolutions, devotions, and promises: "I ain't going to fight unless I absolutely have to. I'm trying to get out of here, out of the organization, and out of town. I don't want any set time."

"Well Freddie," says Mr. B, "those are worthwhile goals. One thing you should work on—all of you—is knowing that you will get angry, because we all get angry, but that you can learn to control that anger. I control my anger. You can, too." He continues, "When you're fifteen or sixteen it may seem that you're invulnerable, like Superman. You start to think, 'I can't get hurt. I can't die. I'm young, strong, and fast' . . ."

"Naw, Mr. B," Antoine interrupts, "after I got shot in the neck, I knew I could die." Antoine is tall, with long, gangly arms and the eyes of a veteran professional boxer—puffy, scarred, hollow. "But I do have nine lives," he smiles "because I'm still walking."

Andrew says, "Yeah, but that's his point, meathead. You sound like, 'Hey, shot in the neck, still walking, I'm a cat.' You're being stupid, just like he said."

"I didn't say anything about being stupid," Mr. B corrects. "I'm just urging you to consider things."

"But, Mr. B," says Antoine, "you know, when you come up like that, it's hard to get rid of."

"All I ever tried to do," says Freddie, "was to make some money. I never got shot, and I never shot anyone."

"I did," says Rasheed. "I got shot in the leg and it hurts like hell when it's cold."

Suddenly everyone is comparing wounds and scars and pains. Shoulders, stomachs, arms, bellies. Antoine got shot in the chest and the neck and it took two surgeries and eight months to get the bullets out. "I hear guys saying, 'I want to get shot once to get rid of the fear,' and I say, 'No you don't.'"

Andrew says he got shot in the butt, and everyone cracks up. "Don't show me the scar," begs Freddie.

"I'm me," says Antoine finally after the excitement dies down. "And I'm scared of dying. So why am I still out there doing it?" He shakes his head in disbelief and confusion.

Freddie says, "I'm not scared of dying, but I don't want to die."

Antoine answers, "I'm scared. Because you don't know what's going to happen when you die. Do you go to heaven or hell or just lie there in the casket?"

"What's the difference, man?" asks Freddie. "I saw my friend up on the operating table bleeding and screaming and shit, and I tell mother-fuckers—excuse me, people—"

"On the wall," says Mr. B.

Freddie heads for the wall with a parting shot, "Guns are killing us, man. That's all I got to say."

"Guns and drugs," adds Antoine.

"Zo," says Mr. B, "everyone's been so busy talking and we haven't heard from you. Do you want to speak on any of this?"

"I'm straight, Mr. B." Zo is large and soft, with squirrel cheeks, run-away pigtails, and tired eyes.

Andrew observes, "Some guys don't like to show their feelings, Mr. B."

"Oh, I know, Andrew," says Mr. B. "I'm sympathetic because I'm like that myself. Zo? Anything at all?"

"Freedom is good," says Zo. "Change isn't so good, but it happens. When I get out I'm getting some type of education, a job, and then I'll work on a family. Those are good changes. Changes in freedom."

"What do you think of the image of the river in this story?" asks Mr. B. "Is the river something like that?"

"Maybe it's like good changes or necessary changes," says Zo.

"The river is familiar, but it changes every day," says Mr. B.

"Like life itself," adds Andrew.

As we prepare to leave, Michael Freeman shakes every boy's hand. "It was a pleasure meeting you," he tells the class. "I hope some day you will visit me in the new South Africa, and you can taste the freedom you talked about here." He embraces Mr. B—"I admire what you are doing with these young men, Mr. B"—and we are off. As we make our way through security, Michael looks heavy with sadness. "So many black boys in cages. This feels like apartheid," he says shaking his head.

————

The next day Andrew reads aloud from the newspaper:

> [Prison chain gangs] would bring back the post-Civil War practice of shackling together prisoners to do hard labor, a practice that suggested images of slavery to some . . . Prison officials, including state Corrections Director Odie Washington, opposed the measure because it would duplicate the work now done by 2,000 unchained inmates.
>
> But State Senator David Syverson (R-Rockford), the bill's main sponsor, said the objections were outweighed by the possible deterrent effect. "We're not saying this is the panacea to solve all of our problems, but it's a tough-love measure," Syverson said. "Some people work well under humiliation."

"That's bogus, Mr. B," he says. "I don't work well under that."

13. Graduation Notes

for Mungu, Morani, Monica and
Andrew Crefeld seniors:

So much of growing up is an unbearable waiting. A constant longing
for another time. Another season.

I remember walking like you today down this path. In love with the
day. Flesh awkward. I sang at the edge of adolescence and the scent
of adulthood rushed me and I thought I would suffocate. But I
didn't. I am here. So are you. Finally. Tired of tiny noises your eyes
hum a large vibration.

I think all journeys are the same. My breath delighting in the single
dawn. Yours. Walking at the edge. Unafraid. Anxious for the
unseen dawns are mixing today like the underground rhythms
seeping from your pores.

At this moment your skins living your eighteen years suspend all noises.
Your days still half-opened, crackle like the fires to come. Outside. The
earth. Wind. Night. Unfold for you. Listen to their sounds. They have
sung me seasons that never abandoned me. A dance of summer rain.
A ceremony of thunder waking up the earth to human monuments.

Facing each other I smile at your faces. Know you as young heroes soon
to be decorated with years. Hope no wars dwarf you. Know your
dreams wild and sweet will sail from your waists to surround the
non-lovers. Dreamers. And you will rise up like newborn armies
refashioning lives. Louder than the sea you come from.

Sonia Sanchez
"Graduation Notes"

I watched our son Zayd pitch a shutout for his high school team one
spring afternoon on a field at the edge of Lake Michigan. He looked
strong on the mound, unstoppable. It was their final baseball game of
the season, and I assumed he would go off with his team to celebrate,
but he told me he wanted a ride home, adding, "When I saw you arrive, I felt like the cavalry was coming to the rescue."

It seems one of his teammates, Sam, a senior class officer and popular school leader, had organized a group of friends to "kick his ass."

Why?

Reluctantly, Zayd explained that Becca, another popular kid who
had gone steady with Sam for four years, had recently broken up with

him. When Becca and Zayd went out, Sam felt humiliated, betrayed. He was nursing the righteous taste for revenge.

"Do you want me to intervene? Is this something that's gotten out of control?"

No, no, no. He had told me too much already. It would be OK.

"I don't want anyone to get hurt," I said. "I don't want this to go beyond trash talk." Zayd assured me he could handle it.

The next night—a prelude to graduation—is "Senior Sleep Out," a school tradition in which the senior class stays overnight in a park near the school, to party and celebrate. Zayd, predictably, decides not to participate: he is alienated from the "in group," from the crowd activities, and, in his own words, has "zero school spirit."

In the middle of the night we are startled out of sleep by what sounds like a car accident—a solid thud, crashing glass, tires shrieking. I look out the window to see a small station wagon racing down the street away from us. It takes a moment to dawn on me, but I slowly realize that our car has been trashed. Sure enough, when I go outside I find a large cinder block on the front seat and shattered glass everywhere. I am furious.

I spend the next few hours awake, angry at Zayd for letting it get to this point, angry at Sam (or whoever he encouraged to do this), uncertain about whether I've interpreted things correctly, upset that whatever happened I'm going to have to spend time and energy fixing it. I imagine getting even, making Sam feel small and hurt, going to the school administration indignant that they had let this happen at Senior Sleep Out and demanding that Sam be suspended and not allowed to graduate. I want Sam's parents to feel awful, want him to realize how outrageous this is. I've always been kind to Sam, and now he's hurt me. I picture him squirming a bit as he begs my forgiveness.

Thankfully, all of this plays out in my incensed imagination alone, and by the time morning comes I have moved on to thinking about how Mr. B or Tobs would respond. I am now resolved on an entirely different course. I wake Zayd up and tell him the car has been smashed. He sits straight up, blinks back angry tears, punches his fist into an open hand, and spits out the name: "Sam!"

"I think so, too."

"I'll kick his ass."

No. Instead Zayd gets ready for school and I explain what I had thought through as possibly a more productive course of action. I am trying to be Mr. B. Together we lift the cinder block out of the front seat and clean up the car as best we can. Zayd drives me to the park where the seniors are starting a groggy early morning, and proceeds to a shop to get the car fixed.

When I walk into the park I immediately encounter Sam's best friend, Josh, and his look instantly betrays him: surprise (perhaps that the morning had come at all, that the night before was not in some special, protected timeless zone where everything was possible and consequences unheard of), defensiveness, embarrassment, a hint of fear.

"Hi, Josh. Where's Sam?" I say.

"Sam?" The look of guilt deepens.

Sam.

In a few minutes Sam, Josh, Jimmy, a third friend, and I are seated on a wall. Each kid is churning, rehearsing his pathetic alibi, looking ill at ease. In the near distance a small knot of other kids, working hard to look uninterested, has gathered to watch.

"Sam," I begin, "you know I love you." I hear the air go out of him, and the tough-guy defensive look gives way. I realize he might cry. Looking at the others I say, "And I care about each of you. I won't do anything to hurt you, and what I'm about to say is just between us. I don't want anyone in the school administration to know about this because then someone will definitely get hurt, and I don't have an interest in your parents knowing, although you can each decide about that for yourself."

I pause and return to Sam. "Sam, there's a lot that's going on that's none of my business. I don't know and I don't think I should know." I am practically quoting Mr. B. "I don't know the details of what caused the tension between you and Zayd, and I don't want to know. I don't know who trashed my car last night." Sam moves to interrupt, but I hold up my hand. "And I don't want to know. Do you hear me?" I repeat. "I don't want to know who did it. I don't want to get to the bottom of it."

The three seem shocked into silence. Jimmy's trying to affect the look of the wrongly accused, but it's a bit off because no one has been accused. Defenses are dropping, but not completely—they're waiting for the catch, the clever grown-up trap.

"I need your help," I continue. "I know you feel that Zayd wronged you, and maybe he did. I just don't know. But I do know that there's an escalating tension between you, and that it's getting out of hand. I want you to lower the tension before someone gets hurt. I think you have the power to do that, to lower the tension. Can you help me in that way?"

Sam's words rush from him, "Bill, I didn't break your window . . ."

"Wait, Sam," I interrupt. "I don't want to know who did what. I'm only asking if you can lower the tension."

"Yes, I can. I'm sorry it got out of hand. It was stupid to threaten Zayd the other day. Nothing more will happen."

"OK," I continue. "Now I think because of that tension someone threw a cinder block into my car last night. I don't want to know who did it, but I think the trash talk and the excitement and the group-think got the better of someone, and so our car was hit. So I want you, Sam, to take responsibility for paying for the repairs."

Jimmy leaps in: "We were here all night . . ."

Sam cuts him off. "Wait . . ."

"I'm saying you should take responsibility," I continue. "You can talk it over, collect money from everyone who participated or everyone who knew about it. Whatever you want to do. But I know you can get to the bottom of it and I can't, and then I want you to give me the money to fix the car."

A moment passes. "OK, I'll do it," Sam says, looking me straight in the eye. "But I want you to know that I didn't trash your car . . ."

"I don't want to know," I say again.

"But I *want* you to know. You're right about what got it all started, and I'll take responsibility." He pauses and adds forcefully, "I'm sorry . . . and thanks."

We shake hands, and I feel relieved and a little ecstatic.

What is the goal of punishing kids after all? Is it to show kids who's stronger? They have little doubt. Who's more clever? Who holds the power over them? Is it to send thunderbolts of righteousness into their midst, to smite them down? Are we trying to humiliate them? It wouldn't be difficult to do, but to what end? Do we want to retaliate? For what?

What I had hoped to do was to create the conditions where doing the right thing became a real option. Not a foregone conclusion, but a choice. I also wanted to avoid the predictable feeling of having won an empty victory—the sense of losing even as you win.

There is, of course, the danger that adults will fail to communicate a sense of right and wrong, peril and safety, good and bad when we act and interact with the children we raise. But another danger is that the punishment will be so strong that it obliterates or overwhelms the misdeed. What we remember, then, is the hurt, not the crime that putatively led to the hurt.

Children raised with dignity have a better chance of acting dignified; children growing up in peace and tolerance will more likely be tolerant themselves. Perhaps two simple guidelines can help us: respect the human dignity of each child; repudiate violence as a means of resolving disputes, solving problems, or giving lessons.

Is this good enough for my child? That's the standard we might approach when we think of justice for kids. The question cannot be about some abstract child, every child, the mob of children. That turns other people's children into things—objectifies them—and makes throwing them onto the garbage heap not merely possible, but quite likely. To ask, is it good enough for my child?—not, is it a perfect arrangement for my child?—is to begin to set limits of acceptability.

When Jane Addams asked, "How shall we respond to the dreams of youth?" John Dewey, in a similar spirit, answered, "What the best and wisest parent wants for his own child, that must the community want for all of its children. Any other ideal . . . is narrow and unlovely; acted upon it destroys our democracy." This is a way of personalizing the problem, of considering policy from the bottom up.

From the top down it looks different. It is much neater, far easier, and too often wrong. Chicago's Mayor Daley, for example, supports get-tough-on-crime proposals, as befits a man in his position. As state's attorney he was tough, aggressive, unyielding; only 3% of cases brought to him by the police were screened out of the courts (as opposed to 16% under his predecessor). He was particularly tough on youth crime, building a reputation as a stern father carrying an oversized stick. As mayor he has supported, among other things, seizing automobiles driven by young people stopped after curfew in order to "get the attention of their parents."

Mayor Daley's kids went to school with our kids—nice enough kids, but certainly no saints—and they got their dad's attention on several occasions. When one of them was picked up for curfew violation, the cop drove him home and saw him safely inside. When another had had too much to drink or smoke at a party that was spiraling out of control and hit another kid with a baseball bat, the weight of the legal system was lifted just enough so no further hurt would be inflicted. Frankly I find those responses entirely understandable, even admirable. What is unconscionable is if only the Daley kids get that special treatment, only the privileged deserve those second and third chances. If it's OK for young Daley, why not for Tyrone Henderson?

Or think of a little-known chapter in the life of the legendary Ella Fitzgerald. Orphaned as a teenager, abused by her stepfather, she drifted into petty crime: she ran numbers, begged, became a lookout for a whorehouse. She was sent to a juvenile detention center where she lived in a racially segregated cottage and was beaten, refused food, and put in isolation for long periods. Within a few years of being paroled to Chick Webb's band, she had become a soaring success. "We didn't know what we were looking at," reminisced her English teacher decades later. "We didn't know she would be the future Ella Fitzgerald." The last superintendent of the facility added, "How many Ellas are there? She turned out to be absolutely one of a kind. But all the other children were human beings, too. In a sense they are all Ellas."

I think, too, of another important and renowned Illinois politician, Adlai Stevenson, former Governor, former ambassador to the United Nations, Democratic candidate for the presidency in 1952 and 1956. At twelve, he killed a playmate with what he thought was an unloaded gun. It certainly influenced his life; it undoubtedly left permanent scars. But he was not a murderer or a thug, and the adults who cared for him, who loved him, helped him find ways to live through and beyond it. Why not Ito?

The rhetorical frenzy promoting "family values," an expected feature of every political campaign, is not only an outrageous display of self-righteousness and transparent hypocrisy (all those deserted wives and abandoned children in the politicians' closets), but an abdication of responsibility for the names never mentioned. Focusing exclusively on a romanticized responsibility of *these* parents for *their* children, the "family values" rhetoric ignores the potential responsibility adults together might assume for all children, for our own *and* for other people's children. To ignore your personal duty to a child you invited or thrust into this world is entirely unacceptable; but to feed or care for only your child while a mob of wayward kids knocks hungrily on the door is also indefensible. The moral challenge lies in both one's personal duty and community responsibility.

Struggling to be a decent parent, a kind and just parent, we try to call on our own lives—What was it like for me? What do I want for them? We wonder about our deepest values, and consider how to enact them, to embody them, in situations we understand only dimly. Our children, in the words of the prophet, are not our children. The young come through us but are not us; they are arrows pointed toward a future we will never see and can never know. And so we struggle to find ways to hold on and let go, to protect them when necessary and to unleash them when possible, to nurture them in order to send them forth.

The story of my childhood has me at center stage, with minor and major supporting characters making entrances and exits. My parents play parts that are sometimes sweet, often irrelevant, increasingly annoying. Of course they were important, but since it's my play, they're akin to stagehands; they built the set and adjust the lights but I'm the star.

I'm sure my parents' stories of me as a child are quite different. In my story of Zayd's or Malik's or Chesa's childhood, after all, I'm more than a bit player. But it's important for me to remember my own parents, for in Malik's story of his own life, *he* is at center stage and I'm the stagehand. It's important not only to know that there are various perspectives, but to acknowledge that in any community or school or family, I am one person, that many stories are being lived and enacted. From the start my children knew things, experienced things that I could neither know nor experience. That sense of moving beyond, of passing by, can be a source of joy, but also of pain and confusion.

———

Every teacher recognizes the ebb and flow of classroom life, the need to be able to teach somewhere in the space between the syllabus and an accident. Of course most policy-makers, legislators, and educational researchers concern themselves only with teaching as formula. They long for the essential in teaching and strive to map its contours and complexities once and for all, Rand-McNally-style.

Effective teachers, while they often bow before educational theory, in fact enact an entirely different idea in the classroom. There are, of course, large ideas and general rules living inside a teacher's mind, but they live alongside the concrete, specific details of every situation, particulars that must somehow be taken into account. In this view teaching is a negotiation between the teacher's agenda, society's demands, and the various dreams of youth. Teaching well requires judgement, choice and possibility. It is not entirely uncontrollable, but neither is it dominated by the teacher's calculation. It is not exactly a random shot, but it is always a gamble. Theoretical knowledge can be useful, but it is never enough, it is always incomplete. The imperative, then, is to find a way to ground teaching in the complex, day-to-day, street-level reality that presents itself in a classroom.

The argument about the nature of teaching is an ancient one and traces its roots to an argument about the nature of knowledge. Abstract theoretical knowledge finds its champion in Plato, who believed that reality was only an imperfect reflection of purely intellectual Forms or Ideas. Concrete skills and the tacit knowledge of excellent practice, on the other hand, is promoted by Aristotle. Aristotle argues that "every statement (*logos*) concerning matters of practice ought to be said in outline and not with precision. Statements should be demanded in a way appropriate to the matter at hand." An Aristotelian teacher might have lesson plans, but they would be written in disappearing ink.

To illustrate his argument about "the matter at hand" in the practice of law, for example, Aristotle argues that, "All law is universal, but about some things it is not possible to make a universal statement which shall be correct." The particular case demands responsiveness, flexibility, care, and practical thought. The specific matter is simply too idiosyncratic to neatly conform to general rules or abstract principles. "The error is not in the law," Aristotle continues, "nor in the legislator, but in the nature of the case, since the matter of the practical is essentially variable. When the law lays down a general rule, and a later case arises that is an exception to the rule, it is then appropriate, where the lawgiver's pronouncement was too unqualified and general, to decide as the legislator himself [or herself] would decide if he [or she] had been present on this occasion." Human beings are not mathematical constructs; real justice demands an accounting of the rich diversity embodied in lived lives. Aristotle concludes that, "The essential nature of equity is thus to correct the law in situations where it is defective on account of its generality."

Plato, of course, hates all that. He embraces law, endorses perfection, worships hierarchy. That is why in Raphael's famous fresco, "The School of Athens," Plato points his finger heavenward, while Aristotle points to the earth.

Tobs and Mr. B point down to the earth and look to the practical. Every student has a name and a face. Each has his own temperament, personality, history, strengths, capacities, weaknesses, and needs. Each brings a large bag of hopes, dreams, aspirations, skills, and abilities into the classroom. Mr. B needs to talk to each one, to begin to know him, to touch him in order to teach him. Tobs looks to the spiritual, the specific living soul inside each boy. They are practical men, wise and responsive Aristotelian teachers trying to act exactly as kind and just parents might act.

———

Ito is luminous and grinning broadly as he marches into South Chapel with his forty-odd fellow graduates. When he spots his mother in a somber dress and small black hat on a folding chair near the door, his smile softens and he waves. She waves back, a restrained gesture that wants to draw no attention, and smiles through tears that have fallen all morning in anticipation of this moment. Her inadequate white handkerchief is holding up as well as can be expected. She is proud, hurt, embarrassed, sad, angry, thrilled—everything mixed up beyond words, but visible now in her tormented and triumphant face, wet and smiling.

The graduates are identically dressed in black mortarboards and blue and gold graduates' robes with prison pants and sneakers peeking out below. They range in age from fourteen to seventeen, and each is receiving an eighth grade diploma. Each carries a white carnation with a straight pin through its stem. They file two by two to the center aisle, turn and march step by halting step to the reserved seats near the front while "Pomp and Circumstance" is hammered out slowly on an unsteady upright piano off to the side. When each student is standing in front of a chair facing the dignitaries on the stage, the piano, thankfully, ceases, and we are seated.

The audience is all color and emotion: mothers and fathers, sisters and brothers, teachers, attendants, volunteers. Babies are crying and eating, children fidgeting, parents and teachers in equal measure sobbing or beaming. There is pride and sadness in every corner, and an unmistakable wave of love and support sweeping from back to front, up and over the students.

The program begins with a greeting from Rayon Hedges, master of ceremonies. Rayon introduces Trip and Jason, who lead the Pledge of Allegiance and the singing of the National Anthem. Then Wray Harris sings a stirring "Lift Every Voice and Sing," once called the "Negro National Anthem," by James Weldon Johnson:

> Lift ev'ry voice and sing
> Till earth and heaven ring,
> Ring with the harmonies of Liberty;
> Let our rejoicing rise
> High as the list'ning skies,
> Let it resound loud as the rolling sea.
> Sing a song full of the faith that the dark past has taught us,
> Sing a song full of the hope that the present has brought us,
> Facing the rising sun of our new day begun
> Let us march on til victory is won . . .

Silk Johnson is the student commencement speaker: "I challenge myself and I challenge you to use time more wisely, obey your parents, stay in school, complete all assignments, and stay off of drugs and out of gangs."

The superintendent of schools speaks next, tells the graduates he is most proud of them, that they have done a remarkable job, that he hopes each will go on to high school and higher education in order to meet the complex challenges of the twenty-first century. He urges them to strive for greatness, to hold to little virtues like persistence and honesty, and to build "self-pride as your greatest, but hopefully not your only, tool as you establish an indestructible future."

Several special awards are given next: excellent citizenship, top grade point average, most improved student, and two prizes for students who achieved perfect scores on the mandatory Illinois Constitution Test.

As in all graduations, the presentation of diplomas is the key event and central moment here. The students line up to the left and wait nervously. To the right, a line of designated loved ones—mom or dad, family member, special teacher, someone chosen by the student to receive the carnation each student has been crushing or cradling in his or her hands for most of an hour. The "pinning ceremony" is an ingenuous solution to a problem that came up only yesterday—with the flowers ordered and ready, someone on the jail side realized that there were forty-some straight pins about to enter security. Rather than cancel the flowers the school suggested that the flowers be pinned on a guest at the time the diploma is granted.

Finally the principal reads out "Rayon Hedges" in a booming voice, and Rayon bursts to the center accompanied by extravagant applause. He gets a hug and a diploma, a handshake from the superintendent, and a long embrace from Miss Lisa, his teacher. Pinning the carnation on Lisa is almost too much for Rayon—he fumbles, he jabs himself a couple of times, but finally there it is, a little crooked, a white, slightly wilted thing, hanging precariously from Lisa's shoulder.

When Ito's name is called he strides to the center and holds his mother for a long moment. When he pins the carnation to her dress, she stands tall, gleaming, and for the first time today looks joyous.

Finally the audience applauds all the graduates, and the graduates turn to applaud the audience. Standing, the entire room recites an affirmation:

> Wherever I am,
> I shall always be myself,
> And no one else.
> I shall be me.
> If it's going to be,
> It's up to me.

Epilogue: Jeff's Letters

You tried
> when others rejected me.
You cared
> when others neglected me.
You listened
> when others ignored me.
You cheered
> when others bored me.
You cried
> when others hurt me.
You prayed
> when others jailed me.
You came
> when others failed me.

Alphonzo Travis
"Your Poem"

JEFF WROTE BACK as soon as he got my letter:

Dear Ayres:

Well I want to start this letter off by saying hello and I hope your OK. Well as for me I'm stuck in a room because they are over crowded. They are all mest up. The system. First I went to St. Charles for a week. I was in confinement for that week now I'm in Joliet in confinement I don't know for how long. These rooms are nothing like the Audy Home! It is very cold and this food sucks! And the gang banging is ruff! I saw a guy get beat down with a broom stick and stabed in his face so that should say it all. (When would they learn?) I'm gonna try to stay out of trouble so I can probably get on a honer dorm but I have to ignor alot of stuff! It's going to be hard because I got into this known gang. I mean it doesn't bother me at all that people disrespect but if I don't stand up for it this own gang would come after me! Not that I'm scared but it's like I'm fighting both sides! Well theres alot of stuff going on so I am trying real hard to keep my head on my sholders but a lot of people are gonna try to take me down, its going to be hard! Well if you can please tell Mr. B. I said hello and the classroom. Well I hope to here from you soon! I'll stop here until next time. P.S. About this fucked up paper, that's how fucked up this place is! Sorry!

Jeff.

Jeff's P.S. refers to the fact that his letter is written on the back of two pages torn from an orientation booklet for inmates. The first is the Table of Contents: Academic Programs, page 11; Access to Courts, pages 16-17; Meritorious Good Time, pages 18-19; Volunteer Services, page 18. And so on. The second is a medical bulletin to all inmates from Dr. Ronald M. Shansky:

> We have recently been reminded of the fact that inmates are tattooing each other or using needles to inject drugs into themselves. An inmate who died quite recently from a severe form of hepatitis was linked to some tattooing. Remember AIDS and Hepatitis are spread through tattooing and using needles to inject drugs. Both diseases can be fatal. Continuing to use needles in these ways will result in some of you dying a painful premature death. Protect yourself by telling the person who offers you a needle NO THANKS! You don't want to commit suicide.

I show Mr. B Jeff's letter, and he shakes his head slowly as he reads. "Poor Jeff," he says finally, "if there was ever a kid unprepared for what awaits him . . ." His voice trails off. "You know, it makes you think about what we're doing here," he says a few minutes later. "It makes you ponder what we're trying to accomplish, and how we know if we're successful."

We talk about the excruciating uncertainty of teaching in any situation, the difficulty of knowing with any confidence when this or that activity or lesson or intervention made a difference—teaching's idiosyncratic and maddeningly invisible nature—and how it is precisely this aspect of teaching that is painfully pronounced when teaching student-inmates in a detention center. And we return to Mr. B's larger question and ask what we are trying to accomplish with a kid like Jeff. What is a realistic goal? What should we as a society hope for?

"We can't do everything," says Mr. B, "so I do what I'm capable of doing: I provide a safe place and a steady routine. I build a relationship with each kid. Then, day in and day out, the regularity of it, the consistency and the certainty of it, give the kid something to hold on to, to count on, to be comfortable with. Then usually good things can happen to them—and God knows not enough good things have happened in the lives of these kids yet. Mostly they've come from chaos or pain or trouble—they're castoffs who fell right through the cracks. So what I've seen is with a consistent, reliable classroom I can show even the toughest kid a different way to live over time. That's my modest goal."

Frank Tobin echoes his friend's perspective: "In a year or a year and a half every kid I've taught has changed. I try to get them to relax a little, to drop that hard survival mode for a while, to reflect on their lives and their choices and their hopes. They can grow up a little then, mature a bit. Once the kid feels even a little bit lovable I've got an opening and I know I'll succeed. All I need is time and focus."

Frank says now that the "real truth" about these kids' lives is complicated. "They have a lot," he says, "and they need a lot. Mostly they need a steady experience of a different way of living." Frank argues that if the government took half of what it spends on prisons and invested that money in neighborhood youth programs that were small, intense, personalized, and consistent—something he calls "front-end programs"—kids could be overwhelmingly diverted from detention, from prison, and from crime. "But it's hard to convince people," he goes on, "because these kids have been so thoroughly demonized in the public's eye. If there's going to be a future, not just for this or that kid but for our whole society, we ought to be thinking in terms of redemption." Frank reminds me of Eugene V. Debs's famous dictum—"As long as one man is in prison, I am not free"—because of his emphasis on shared responsibility. Frank adds a spiritual dimension.

Alex Correa is set on redemption. "I have to believe that people can be better," he says. "I'm the proof. Don't get me wrong, I'm no saint, but if I didn't believe in redemption I'd still be living in a cage. No, I believe in change and recovery and getting it together to start over." Alex attributes his turn-around to meeting Tobs—"someone, finally, who believed in me as a person"—to hard work and discipline, to faith in God and "getting down on my knees and begging for forgiveness." Alex now runs a successful physical fitness business, and he increasingly speaks publicly about juvenile delinquency, crime and punishment, and the need to get guns and drugs—"adult-made products"—out of the hands of kids. "I talk about my life a lot these days, and I hope it holds some lessons for people, for policy makers as well as for kids in trouble. I was living a personal hell, and yet I can look back and say it might have been worth it if I can use my experience to help save others. I want to follow Jesus Christ. I want to make a difference for other kids." He is living redemption.

Alex reminds me of Jane Addams's reflections on the larger meaning of Juvenile Court years after its founding:

> The year 1899 was distinguished by the opening of *two courts, each the first of its kind in the world*. The first Juvenile Court was opened in the conviction that the existing court procedure was not fitted to a child's needs; and a court was established at The Hague in Holland, dedicated to the conciliation and arbitration of all difficulties arising between nations. These widely separated courts are not so unlike, if we take the point of view of mankind's long spiritual struggle to maintain and purify the reign of justice in the world, with the obligation laid upon each generation to find the means by which justice may be extended.

The reign of justice. As a society we want to know what works, we want to avoid risk, but we also want to inflict no more pain than is absolutely necessary. We want to be fair and decent and generous, but we don't want to be terrorized or wounded for our good intentions.

The current get-tough policies do not ensure our collective well-being. They are expedient for politicians—a Chicago alderman I know said he had never heard of anyone losing votes by advocating more rigorous sanctions on kids—but they are also expensive and, in general, do not work. What is needed is a rich and varied continuum of community-based options for kids in trouble.

The overwhelming majority of delinquent youth in detention are nonviolent offenders. These kids need alternatives to gangs and crime, programs that engage them and teach them and employ them and find a place for them, a positive role to play. Teenagers are by definition immature; they need to find a structure through which they can survive poor judgment and impulsiveness.

Even kids who have committed more serious crimes need programs that help them find an alternative to a criminal life. Several states are experimenting with "blended sentences"—trying kids who have committed serious crimes as adults and then, if they are found guilty, suspending their sentences and referring them to juvenile programs. Any violation results in a quick return to the adult system. In this way, the seriousness of a crime is made unmistakably clear, but a door is opened for possible redemption.

Ohio is experimenting with a different approach: the Department of Youth Services keeps 25% of its budget but divides the other 75% into eighty-eight separate accounts, one for every county in the state. Each county is assessed $75.00 a day for each child sent into the youth correction system. At the end of each month unused funds are sent to the county for their youth program. In the first four months of this experiment there was over a 50% drop in the number of juvenile offenders sent to state jails.

———

Another letter arrives from Jeff:

Dear Ayres;

What's up? Well I hope by the time you get this your OK! Well I got your letter and was wondering if I could get some kind of help cause I'm trying to learn something or write a book or something but I don't have any help here these school is all fucked up and we only go half a day so it's all fucked up if you could help me let me know! Well I hope you are OK. I'll end this letter here.

Sincerely,
Jeff.

Jeff reminds me that teaching is transformative work, animated by the fundamental message of the teacher: You can change your life. With considerable effort, that message might come to inform all our work with children, even children in crisis, even tough kids in terrible places. You can change your life.

Notes

Page 20. All quotes from "The Piano Lesson" by August Wilson are from *African American Literature* (Orlando, FL: Holt, Rinehart and Winston, 1992).

Page 26. Settlement house philosophy described in Jane Addams, *Twenty Years at Hull House* [1910] (New York: Macmillan, 1981), p. 98.

Page 29. Statistics on Juvenile Court cases are from the Juvenile Court Project, Northwestern University Legal Clinic fact sheet, 1992. Discussion of how juvenile offenses are handled in court draws on Steven Drizin, *Dissent of Steven A. Drizin from the Illinois Legislative Committee on Juvenile Justice's Report to the General Assembly and the Governor*, Northwestern University School of Law, Chicago, June 1996.

Page 30–31. Audy Home figures taken from: David Reed, Northwestern University School of Law; Ken Keller, Research Department of Juvenile Court, Illinois, unpublished private correspondence; Children and Family Justice Center, *Juvenile Trends over a Decade, Cook County Juvenile Court 1983–1993* (Chicago: Northwestern University Law School, 1994); and Steven Drizin, *Dissent of Steven A. Drizin from the Illinois Legislative Committee on Juvenile Justice's Report to the General Assembly and the Governor*, Northwestern University School of Law, Chicago, June 1996. Number of reports of child abuse in 1993 taken from C. Sweeney, "Portrait of the American Child, 1995," *New York Times Magazine*, 8 Oct. 1995, pp. 52–53. Discussion of legal process once a child is taken into custody and referred to Juvenile Court is taken from Justice for Youth Campaign, *Guide to the Juvenile Justice System*, 2d ed. (Chicago: The Chicago Bar Association, 1992).

Page 32. Statistics on transfers to adult court are taken from Steven Drizin, *Dissent of Steven Drizin from the Illinois Legislative Committee on Juvenile Justice's Report to the General Assembly and the Governor*, Northwestern University School of Law, Chicago, June 1996, pp. 9–12, and Justice for Youth Campaign, *Guide to the Juvenile Justice System*, 2d ed. (Chicago: The Chicago Bar Association, 1992), pp. 7–13.

Page 40. Quotations from Illinois Appellate Court and from George Herbert Mead in B. Krisberg and J. Austin, *Reinventing Juvenile Justice* (Newbury Park, CA: Sage Publications, 1993).

Page 41. Children's Defense Fund figures on abuse and poverty are from *Wasting America's Future: The Children's Defense Fund Report on the Costs of Child Poverty* (Boston: Beacon Press, 1994), pp. 35–36.

Page 42. Quotations and history of "child-saving" and early reform schools taken from Steven Schlossman, "Delinquent Children: The Juvenile Reform School." In Norval Morris and David Rothman, eds., *The Oxford History of the Prison: The Practice of Punishment in Western Society* (New York: Oxford University Press, 1996), pp. 363–89. Addams's observation about "children of foreigners" from *Twenty Years at Hull House* [1910] (New York: Macmillan, 1981), p. 181. National Academy of Sciences' conclusion reported in National Research Council Panel on High Risk Youth, *Losing Generations: Adolescents in High-Risk Settings* (Washington, D.C.: National Academy Press, 1993), p. 156.

Page 43. Addams on "the divine fire of youth" from *The Spirit of Youth and the City Streets* [1909] (Urbana: University of Illinois Press, 1972), p. xxviii. Pennsylvania Supreme Court quotation in Schlossman, "Delinquent Children." In Morris and Rothman, *The Oxford History of the Prison*, p. 366.

Page 68. "Father charged in 'hellish' abuse," *Chicago Tribune*, 6 Feb. 1996, p. 1.

Page 70. "Abuse reports a lie, 3 kids insist," *Chicago Tribune*, 7 Feb. 1996, p. 1. "Doctors not backing down," *Chicago Tribune*, 8 Feb. 1996, p. 1. "Couple accused of abuse released as case unravels," *Chicago Tribune*, 22 Feb. 1996, pp. 1, 20. Editorial, "The incredible shrinking abuse case," *Chicago Tribune*, 23 Feb. 1996, p. 18. \

Page 71–72. "Is there any real hope for young killers?" *Chicago Tribune*, 26 Jan. 1996, p. 1.

Page 73. "Grim reality check on youth crime," *Chicago Tribune*, 31 Jan. 1996, p. 14.

Page 74. *Newsweek, U.S. News and World Report*, and *Time* quotations in M. Males, "Wild in deceit: Why 'teen violence' is poverty violence in disguise," *EXTRA!* (March/April 1996): 7. "Shootings in city drop," *Chicago Sun-Times*, 10 June 1996, pp. 1, 2. Gallup Poll results cited in Males, "Wild in deceit," *EXTRA!* (March/April 1996): 7–9.

Page 75. Males, "Wild in Deceit," pp. 7, 8, 9.

Pages 75–76. Bob Greene, "When right and wrong are words without meaning," *Chicago Tribune*, 29 March 1996, p. 1. James Q. Wilson and John DiIulio quoted in F. Zimring, "Crying wolf over teen demons," *Los Angeles Times*, 19 Aug. 1996, p. B-5. Zimring discusses DiIulio's projections in "Crying wolf."

Page 77. Bernard Goetz's testimony quoted in A. Nossiter's article, "A gunman's tale of fear, hatred, and drugs," *New York Times*, 13 April 1996, p. 1.

Pages 79–80. "Jurors hear Wallace's words on son's death," *Chicago Tribune*, 20 April 1993, p. 1. "Wallace trial in son's death begins," *Chicago Tribune*, 19 June 1993, pp. 1, 2. "Living in squalor: A complex tale of urban survival," *Chicago Tribune*, 2 Feb. 1992, pp. 1, 6.

Page 83. Nelson Algren, *Chicago: City on the Make* (Chicago: University of Chicago Press, 1951, 1979), p. 14.

Page 86. Reginald McKnight, "The Kind of Light that Shines on Texas." In *African American Literature* (Orlando, FL: Holt, Rinehart and Winston, 1992), pp. 556–65.

Page 115–16. Michelle Oberman, "Turning Girls into Women: Re-evaluating Modern Statutory Rape Law," *The Journal of Criminal Law and Criminology*, 85 (1994): 15–79. Steven Schlossman, "Delinquent Children: The Juvenile Reform School." In Norval Morris and David Rothman, eds., *The Oxford History of the Prison: The Practice of Punishment in Western Society* (New York: Oxford University Press, 1996), pp. 363–89.

Pages 116–17. Statistics on girls in the juvenile justice system cited in The Office of Juvenile Justice and Delinquency Prevention, *Prevention and Parity: Girls in Juvenile Justice* (New York: Girls Incorporated, 1996).

Pages 126–27. "Prison pushed for two youthful killers," *Chicago Tribune*, 3 Jan. 1996, pp. 1, 2.

Pages 139–40. Louise Kaplan, *Adolescence: The Farewell to Childhood* (New York: Simon and Schuster, 1984), pp. 13, 35, 50.

Pages 140–41. Michelle Oberman, "Turning Girls into Women: Re-evaluating Modern Statutory Rape Law," *The Journal of Criminal Law and Criminology*, 85 (1994), 55–56; ibid, p. 63.

Page 150. Jane Addams, *The Spirit of Youth and the City Streets* [1909] (Urbana: University of Illinois Press, 1972), p. 61.

Pages 166–67. Ngugi wa Thiong'o, "The Return." In *African American Literature* (Orlando, FL: Holt, Rinehart and Winston, 1992), pp. 873–78.

Pages 170–72. Michel Foucault, *Discipline and Punish: The Birth of the Prison* [1975], trans. A. Sheridan (New York: Vintage Books, 1995), pp. 1, 6, 7.

Page 172. Schlossman, "Delinquent Children." In Morris and Rothman, *The Oxford History of the Prison*, p. 368.

Pages 173–74. Foucault, *Discipline and Punish*, p. 200. Charles Dickens, *American Notes and Pictures from Italy* [1842] (London: Oxford University Press, 1966), p. 99.

Pages 175–76. Morris and Rothman, *The Oxford History of the Prison*, pp. ix, x. Dickens, *American Notes*, pp. 50–51. Alfred Blumstein, "Youth Violence, Guns, and the Illicit-Drug Industry," *The Journal of Criminal Law and Criminology*, 86 (1995): 10–36.

Page 177. The *New York Times*/CBS poll results were reported in "Crime joins economic issues as leading worry, poll says," *New York Times*, 23 Jan. 1994, p. A1.

Page 178. Bruce Shapiro, "How the War on Crime Imprisons America," *The Nation*, 22 April 1996, pp. 14–21. DiIulio on the black community and on prison quoted in Shapiro, "War on Crime," pp. 17, 15.

Page 179. Shapiro, "War on Crime," p. 18. Blumstein, "Youth Violence," *The Journal of Criminal Law and Criminology*, 86 (1995): 29.

Pages 179–80. Bureau of Alcohol, Tobacco, and Firearms statistics cited in Shapiro, "War on Crime," p. 18.

Page 180. Estimate of the Centers for Disease Control and Prevention of the percentage of homicides commited with firearms reported in "Guns used in 72% of murders," *Chicago Sun-Times*, 7 June 1996, p. 22. Franklin Zimring, "Reflections on firearms and the criminal law," *Journal of Criminal Law and Criminology*, 86 (1995): 1–9.

Pages 180–81. Blumstein, "Youth violence," *Journal of Criminal Law and Criminology*, 86 (1995): 10. The studies on the risk of suicide and murder in homes with guns are A.L. Kellermann, et al.,"Suicide in the home in relation to gun ownership," *New England Journal of Medicine*, 327 (1992): 467–72, and J. Kassirer, "Guns in the household," *New England Journal of Medicine*, 329 (15) (1993): 117. Shapiro, "War on Crime," p. 19.

Page 190. Jane Addams, *The Spirit of Youth and the City Streets* [1909] (Urbana: University of Illinois Press, 1972), p. xxviii. John Dewey, *The School and Society* [1900] (Chicago: University of Chicago Press, 1990), p. 7. "The gap in Ella Fitzgerald's life," *New York Times*, 23 June 1996, p. 4.

Page 193. Aristotle quotations are from J.P.A.M. Kessels and F. A. Korthagen, "The Relationship between Theory and Practice: Back to the Classics," *Educational Researcher*, 25 (3) (1996): 17–22.

Page 200. Addams on Juvenile Court quoted in S. Hart, *The Pleasure Is Mine: An Autobiography* (Chicago: Valentine-Newman, 1947), p. 95.

Page 201. Ohio's experiment discussed in Steven Drizin, *Dissent of Steven A. Drizin from the Illinois Legislative Committee on Juvenile Justice's Report to the General Assembly and the Governor*, Northwestern University School of Law, Chicago, June 1996.

Credits